Degree
Mills

Degree Mills

The Billion-Dollar Industry
That Has Sold Over a Million Fake Diplomas

Allen Ezell and John Bear

Prometheus Books

59 John Glenn Drive
Amherst, New York 14228-2197

Published 2005 by Prometheus Books

Inquiries should be addressed to
Prometheus Books
59 John Glenn Drive
Amherst, New York 14228–2197
VOICE: 716–691–0133, ext. 207
FAX: 716–564–2711
WWW.PROMETHEUSBOOKS.COM

09 08 07 06 05   5 4 3 2 1

Library of Congress Cataloging-in-Publication Data

Ezell, Allen, 1941–
    Degree mills : the billion-dollar industry that has sold more than a million
fake college diplomas / Allen Ezell and John Bear.
        p. cm.
    Includes bibliographical references.
    ISBN 1-59102-238-X (pbk. : alk. paper)
    1. Diploma mills. I. Bear, John, 1938– II. Title.

LB2388.E94 2004
378.2—dc22

2004020142

Printed in the United States of America on acid-free paper

To all those who pursue the facts and truth about
academic credentials and institutions.

Always be vigilant and may your quest be successful.

And to our wives, Donna Ezell and Marina Bear,
for your support and your guidance and for patiently listening to
all those DipScam and degree-mill stories over the years.

Contents

Acknowledgments

FROM ALLEN EZELL

M y thanks go to all those FBI employees who participated in or supported DipScam, from investigation through prosecution, especially those at the Charlotte, North Carolina, office. Dip-Scam would not have been possible—or a success—without their dedicated efforts. To Jim, thanks for bringing my first case to me. Special thanks to Supervisor Raymond J. Bowley, Special Agent in Charge (SAC) Robert L. Pence, and AUSA's Jerry Parnell and Harold Bender, who were there at the inception of DipScam. To Assistant United States Attorney (AUSA) Debra J. Stuart for her persistence over the years in allowing the ball to continue rolling forward and her tenacity in the prosecution of these cases. Thanks also for her hundreds of hours work on our one trial, which for various reasons, we will always remember. And thanks to US Magistrate Barbara Delaney for the many hours that she spent with the DipScam defendants and their litigation. The assistance given by IRS-CID and US postal inspectors was invaluable to the success of DipScam.

To the Honorable Robert J. Potter, United States District Judge, Western District of North Carolina (known to the defense bar as "Maximum Bob"), it was an honor and pleasure to be in his court. I will always remember his comment to me, "If you do *your* job, I will do *mine*," and so he did.

The DipScam defendants and some of their antics have left us with many true stories that we will tell for years to come. Thanks also to Col. Hazel Benn (deceased), the American Association of Collegiate Registrars and Admissions Officers (AACRAO), and Carolyn Parham, Alabama AACRAO (and SACRAO) for welcoming me into their organization nationwide. Twenty years later, I continue to enjoy an excellent relationship with AACRAO.

Special thanks for a job well done to my daughter, Cindy, for her preparation of my many PowerPoint degree-mill presentations.

FROM BOTH AUTHORS

Grateful thanks to Gus Sainz for his major research efforts; to Professor George Gollin, who came to this field late but soared to the front with his copious research, writing, and dedication to making the problems known; and to Marina Bear, Heather Ammermuller, and Brad Belden for valiant copyediting and proofreading assistance.

Thanks to Jerry Click, Rich Douglas, Bill Gossett, and Kristi Hansen for reviewing the manuscript.

For their general support and helpful writing on degree mills, in print, on news forums, and in personal communications, thanks to George Brown, Bill Dayson, Maxine McCarty, Jim Frey, Dale Gough, Mike Lambert, Greg Ashe, Mary Adams, Steve Levicoff, Tom Nixon, John Wetsch, Mark Israel, John Weaver-Hudson, Chip White, Tom Head, and oh so many others.

We are grateful to all the state and federal people who have addressed the problems in the past and, we hope and trust, will continue to do so. We are pleased by the attention that Sen. Susan Collins of Maine and Rep. Tom Davis of Virginia have brought to the problem of degree mills in recent years. And we have said many times that if every state had a state attorney like Jeffrey Brunton of Hawaii and a regulator like Alan Contreras of Oregon, the degree problem would diminish promptly and dramatically.

Hundreds of people in the media deserve the thanks of the authors and of society in general for discovering and reporting on degree-mill operators and their schemes. Mike Wallace of *60 Minutes* was the first to do a major national report. J. W. August of ABC San Diego returned to the topic again and again in the early years to great effect, as has Greg Hunter, consumer editor of *Good Morning America*.

We appreciate the good work of our agent, Laurie Harper, and our editor at Prometheus, Steven L. Mitchell.

And, for reasons only he will know, we thank the man we know as J. J. Doe.

Introduction

For Nicolas Tanasescu, it's just another day at the office.[1]

He takes the trolley from his flat at the western edge of Bucharest, Romania, and gets off at Calea Victoriei. He walks half a block down a nondescript street in the business district of the Romanian capital city and turns left into a narrow passageway, Pasajul Victoriei. Number 48 is an old red-brick two-story building. Downstairs is a bar, "TZ's Cotton Club," and a modeling agency called Top Model. Nicolas climbs an unmarked wide staircase leading to the upper floor.

It is nearly 10 PM, and there is a steady stream of men and women climbing the stairs for their night's work. The office runs twenty-four hours a day, seven days a week, but the 10 PM to 6 AM shift is the busiest, with about fifty people—Romanians, South Africans, and a scattering of other nationalities—sitting at computer terminals in what they call the DL Room: an array of small drab cubicles.

Most are in their twenties and thirties. All of them speak excellent, if slightly accented, English. Like most of the others, Nicolas earns just over a dollar an hour. That's not a great wage even in this economically depressed country, but with unemployment around 10 percent, he is glad to have this job.

He fits a telephone headset and microphone apparatus to his head, adjusts the small computer screen, and settles in for his night's work: telephoning potential customers all over North America.

The office manager, who is also the owner of the business, strolls up and down the aisles, amiably nodding and smiling at his employees.

He is a short, plump, bald American who looks to be in his sixties and sports a white beard and always wears an American baseball cap. He is, in fact, a rabbi from Boston, Massachusetts, who divides his time between Romania and another branch of his business in Jerusalem, where the office closes for the orthodox holy day at sundown on Friday.

On an average day, he earns more than $150,000. A million dollars a week. Fifty million dollars a year. And he's been doing this for more than eight years.

His business is selling fake university degrees, by telephone, to people all over the United States and Canada. More than two hundred thousand degrees have been sold to date, including bachelor's, master's, MBAs, doctorates, law degrees, and medical degrees in every possible specialty, from neurosurgery to pediatrics.

What's going on here?

This is one of the most recent and most ambitious manifestations of a business that has been around since at least the fourteenth century: the selling of university degrees to people willing to pay the price and to take the risk.

Nicolas dials his first client, a businessman in Cleveland who has responded to an unsolicited e-mail, and leaves a message on an answering machine somewhere in New York City: "Hi, this is Nicolas. I'm a registrar with the University Degree Program. I apologize for my European accent. We just wanted to contact you to tell you that, because we have some spaces left in our program, we reduced our registration fee by more than $2,000. What I am going to tell you is very important, so if you don't understand everything I say, just let me know. If now is a good time for you, I'll explain our new program and answer any questions that you might have."

The odds are one in three that within the next fifteen minutes, Nicolas will make a $2,000 sale, perhaps more if the man in Cleveland decides to buy two or three degrees complete with transcripts and a degree-verification service.

Just another day at the office.

•   •   •

We estimate that Nicolas's employer has sold more than $400 million worth of fake degrees to Americans and Canadians. And he is employed by just one of many sellers of fake and worthless degrees, each of whom is earning many millions of dollars a year.

We know these numbers through a combination of methods: unhappy "deep throat" employees who supply the information, detective work of various kinds, and the most accurate means, the inspection of the evidence collected in those cases when federal search warrants are executed. (There has been no search at Nicolas's employer.)

For example, the California-based degree mill called Columbia State University, which pretended to be in Louisiana and sold its PhDs by return mail for $3,000 each, made bank deposits of well over $10 million during its last four years of operation.

And when the FBI executed a search warrant at LaSalle University in Louisiana (not to be confused with the real LaSalle in Pennsylvania), the FBI found evidence of $36.5 million in recent bank deposits and was able to seize $10.75 million that had not yet gone toward the lavish lifestyle of the university's founder.[2]

In 2001, we estimated worldwide sales of fake degrees at $200 million or more. Things have gotten much worse since then. We believe it is very safe to say that cumulative fake degree sales have exceeded a billion dollars over the past decade. At an average cost of $1,000 per degree, this suggests at least one million customers.[3]

Is this selling of degrees something new? Not at all. It has been identified as a major national problem for nearly one hundred years. Here's a brief overview of the history of the problem; these matters will be discussed in more detail in the next chapter.

In the 1920s, there were dozens of page-one degree-mill stories in the *New York Times* alone: "Diploma Mill Facts Laid before Senators," "Says 15,000 Have Bought Bogus Medical Diplomas," "Spiegel Held for Selling Fake Law Degrees," "3,000 Fake Diplomas Obtained in Chicago," and so on.[4] US Senate hearings on degree mills were held in 1924, but no action was taken.

This pattern—problem, concern, publicity, demand for action, and then nothing—was to repeat itself several times in the decades to come, roughly in twenty-year cycles.

In the 1940s, the National Education Association established a Committee on Fraudulent Schools and Colleges and launched a "crusade" against degree mills, publishing articles in their journal with titles such as "Degrees for Sale."

In 1950, Benjamin Fine, the distinguished education editor of the *New York Times*, stated that there are "more than 1,000 questionable or outright fraudulent schools and colleges in the United States."

In 1959, US Secretary of Health, Education and Welfare Arthur S. Flemming stated in a US Office of Education press release dated October 29, 1959, that "Degree mills have become such a blight on the American educational scene that I have come to the conclusion that the Department of Health, Education and Welfare has a responsibility about them."

A year later, Flemming wrote that

> I am not so optimistic as to believe that we have uncovered all degree mills since public attention was drawn to this situation five months ago. Therefore . . . we will continue to make known the existence of degree mills whenever we find them operative. It is in the public interest for us to create a national and international awareness of the inadequacy and utter worthlessness of degree mills.[5]

Twenty years later, Allen Ezell's DipScam task force in the FBI marked the first and only time that a government agency attacked the problem. But with Ezell's retirement in 1991, DipScam ended.

In the last major congressional look at the problem, in 1985 and 1986, Rep. Claude Pepper's Subcommittee on Fraud concluded that more than five hundred thousand Americans were currently using fake degrees.

In 1998, Ezell and John Bear addressed a group of federal personnel officers and federal background investigators, giving information on the growth and seriousness of the degree-mill problem. A good many people left that auditorium in Pittsburgh seemingly determined to *do something* about this national problem.

In the summer of 2003, Ezell and Bear were invited to Washington by the Office of Personnel Management as principal speakers in two four-hour workshops on degree mills.[6] Nearly five hundred HR and security officers left that hall seemingly determined to *do something* about the problem.

In early 2004, a diploma-mill summit was held in Washington, where representatives of the FBI, the FTC, the OPM, the Government Accountability Office, the Office of Personnel Management, the House of Representatives, and the Senate vowed to "protect the federal work-force" from the scourge of fake degrees.

In April 2004, the Office of Personnel Management held two more workshops on degree-mill issues for hundreds more HR and security officers. In May, the US Senate Committee on Governmental Affairs, chaired by Sen. Susan Collins of Maine, held two days of hearings titled "Bogus Degrees and Unmet Expectations: Are Taxpayer Dollars Subsidizing Diploma Mills?" In July, the Council on Higher Education Accreditation held a two-day workship, focusing both on degree mills and accreditation mills.

Is Washington really waking up to the problem? Or is this just another cyclical resurfacing of concern that will fade away just as it did in the twenties, the forties, the sixties, and the eighties? Have things gotten so out of hand—like Nazism in the thirties, civil rights abuses in the fifties, or drugs in the seventies—that this time it cannot be easily ignored?

As we both watched and participated in various events throughout 2004, we grew increasingly pessimistic. Perhaps the most telling thing about Senator Collins's hearings was that there was absolutely no presence of any law enforcement agency.

No speaker urged the participation of the FBI, the postal service, the Secret Service, or any other enforcement agency to help with the problem.

No one suggested asking the US Attorney's office to initiate a criminal investigation.

No one suggested impaneling a federal grand jury, which could subpoena the records of the less-than-wonderful schools that refused to furnish such information to the committee.

No one noted that the fake-degree service called Degrees-R-Us, from which Senator Collins purchased two degrees more than three years earlier, is still in business and still selling fake degrees.

Two senators present, both former attorneys general, joked that if they were still in office, they would know how to handle the degree mills.

Maybe good things will happen. Maybe there will be some significant changes. But change often requires outrage. A woman might spend years petitioning for a traffic light on a busy corner, but nothing happens until a child is killed by a speeding car. Attempts to launch a health-care program for the elderly were ineffective for half a century until enough people got sufficiently angry that Congress finally listened and Medicare came into existence.

Perhaps an even closer analogy can be found in the matter of child abuse. For the first half of the twentieth century, it was generally believed that child abuse was a rare and isolated phenomenon: an occasional and clearly aberrant instance here and there. And then some investigators—demographic detectives, in effect—began accumulating data: published accounts, police reports, and especially the incidents known to social service agencies, therapists, and charity groups but never "officially" reported. Only then did it become apparent that there was a huge nationwide problem in this area. It was not just an isolated angry or deranged mother beating her baby but hundreds of thousands, perhaps millions, of cases of children suffering, even dying, at the hands of their parents, other family members, and friends.

A comparable situation exists with regard to the use of fake degrees and fake credentials. It is not just the occasional user of such degrees discovered by an employer, the media, or a law enforcement agency. It is truly a national, indeed an international, epidemic in which hundreds of thousands, very likely millions, of people are using degrees they did not earn.

But unlike a medical epidemic, in which one can observe large numbers of people suffering from smallpox, measles, and so forth, these fake degree cases are uncovered one at a time, often far from the glare of publicity. And when there *is* publicity, it is generally local at best and quickly forgotten.

Infrequently, a fake-degree case gets national attention, as happened in 2003 with the newly hired and almost instantly fired Notre Dame football coach who didn't have the degree he had been claiming to have for years. Generally, when the media do address the issue—a *60 Minutes* degree-mill segment in 1978, a *20/20* segment, and three *Good Morning America* reports in the early 2000s—they seem to be in the category of just another nine- (or fewer) day wonder: Elian Gonzalez, dog-mauling deaths, people trapped in a mine, a pop star's latest antics, and, oh yes, here's a prominent politician, business leader, minister, or professor with a fake or useless degree.

In rare instances, the media have had a major impact, but only, it seems, if they pound away at the issue until it truly cannot be ignored. One of the rare instances of success was in 1983 at a time when many suppliers of fake degrees had moved from California to Arizona. The largest newspaper in the state, the *Arizona Republic*, assigned its two top investigative reporters, Rich Robertson and Jerry Seper, to the story, and what emerged was a devastating report, featured on page one for four consecutive days under the headline "Diploma Mills: A Festering Sore on the State of Arizona." To show readers, and the legislature, how easy it is, the paper even founded its own university and accrediting agency.

A crusading newspaper can have a dramatic effect. This four-day page one series in the Phoenix newspaper brought about public outrage followed by new legislation. Every one of the state's many degree mills either closed or moved elsewhere.

The four stories plus additional information and photographs were combined into a booklet available free to the public.

Now the issue could no longer be ignored in Arizona. Under mounting pressure from the public and the educational establishment, the Arizona legislature promptly took action, and within a matter of months, every one of Arizona's several dozen active phonies had either closed or, more commonly, moved on to Louisiana, Utah, Florida, Hawaii, and other states that at the time had no laws to prevent this sort of thing.

What will it take to make these matters a national concern and a national priority? Clearly it needs to be more than people like these with fake degrees:

- the founder of a popular sex therapy clinic in upstate New York who bought his PhD for $100
- the fake MD in North Carolina convicted of manslaughter when a child he took off insulin because "she did not need it" died
- the head of engineering for a major city's transit system

- the superintendent of schools for California's second-largest school system
- the coaches of two major university sports teams and the head of the US Olympic Committee, discovered within weeks of each other
- the fire chief for one of our largest cities
- generals in the Pentagon, scientists at NASA, and high-ranking officials in the Department of Defense, the Department of Homeland Security, and even in the White House Situation Room, all with fake degrees: all publicly noted, occasionally written about, and pretty much dismissed as isolated and presumably rare incidents.[7]

We don't have a single "magic bullet" solution, although we do have many recommendations, set forth in chapter 6. We only hope it will not require a major and dramatic incident to bring about the needed awareness and changes: a pilot with fake credentials who crashes his jumbo jet, a scientist with fake credentials who sets free a plague virus, or the havoc that could be wrought by one of the many "engineers" with fake doctorates in nuclear engineering safety.

WHAT, EXACTLY, IS A DEGREE MILL?

It is generally advisable to define the "beast" before going out to attempt to slay it. In the case of degree mills, this turns out to be an elusive task.

Let's begin with the most basic words: *degree* and *diploma*.

A *degree* is the title one earns from a legitimate school or simply buys from a fake one: Bachelor of Arts, Master of Science, Master of Business Administration, Doctor of Philosophy, Juris Doctor (law), Doctor of Medicine, and scores of other titles.

A *diploma* is the certificate—the piece of paper or parchment—that signifies that a degree has been awarded.

Schools award *degrees*. And then they present the graduate with a *diploma*, which is, in effect, an announcement, a proclamation of the degree that has been awarded.

Degree mills issue diplomas. Diploma mills award degrees. We can live with either word, but we have selected "degree mill" as our term of choice since it refers to the entity *awarding* the degree and not just to the decorative announcement framed and hung on the wall.

Different people define these words differently, depending on their intention. There is far from unanimous agreement on just what a degree mill is.

Almost no one would deny that a "university" operating from a mailbox service that grants the PhD in three days is a degree mill. But what about an institution that operates legally in a state with minimal regulation and requires three months and a thirty-page paper in order to earn its PhD? What about one that requires six months and sixty pages? How about twelve months and one hundred twenty pages? One person's degree mill may be another's innovative new-style university. Clearly more definition is needed than just time and work required.

Until now, only three books have been devoted entirely or largely to degree mills. Here's how each of them define the term.

In 1963, Robert Reid wrote that "degree mills are those institutions that call themselves colleges or universities which confer 'quick-way,' usually mail-order degrees on payment of a fee. These institutions turn out ... degrees without necessarily requiring the labor, thought, and attention usually expected of those who earn such degrees."[8]

In 1986, David W. Stewart and Henry A. Spille wrote, "Basically a diploma mill is a person or an organization selling degrees or awarding degrees without an appropriate academic base and without requiring a sufficient degree of postsecondary-level academic achievement."[9]

In 1990, Steve Levicoff, realistically acknowledging that no single definition can work in every situation, offered a list of sixty-two characteristics sometimes exhibited by degree mills, and he suggested that each reader would have to decide how many of these characteristics it would require before calling a school a degree mill.[10]

In Allen Ezell's presentations to academic and business groups, he often uses this definition adapted from several publications of the US Office of Education: "Degree mills are organizations that award degrees without requiring [their] students to meet educational standards for such degrees. They receive fees from their so-called students on the basis of fraudulent misrepresentation and/or make it possible for the recipients of its degrees to perpetrate a fraud on the public."

It would be wonderful to have an infallible and undisputed test of what is a mill and what isn't, but clearly there is no perfect definition that works for every person in every case. We offer in chapter 2 our list of ninety-two things that schools do to fool people. If a school has eighty or ninety of these characteristics, almost no one would deny it is a mill. But what about sixty-three? Or forty-two? Or seventeen? Some would say yes and some would say no or maybe. The important thing is to be clear about why you say something is, or is not, or probably is.[11]

In general, it seems to us, identification as a degree mill comes down to consideration of these five crucial issues:

  a. degree-granting authority,
  b. credit for prior learning and experience,
  c. amount of new work required,
  d. quality of new work required,
  e. who makes the decisions.

Let's look at each of these issues in a bit of detail.

a. Under what authority are the degrees granted? Who has given the school permission to grant degrees? How have they made that decision?

Authority to award degrees needs to come from an independent entity, almost always a government agency. Some mills claim to give themselves the authority through their corporate charter, but no legitimate school does this.

We are talking about well over three hundred government agencies, and that means more than three hundred different policies and procedures. There are the 191 members of the United Nations, a few dozen countries that haven't joined the UN, and dozens of territories, colonies, and protectorates. There are countries where some or all of the school decisions are made one step down from the national government: the fifty US states, of course, as well as the Canadian provinces and territories, the Swiss cantons, and others.

Some government agencies have a comprehensive and responsible method for determining who can grant degrees; others are little more than rubber stamps or have a simple and trivial process. And a great many are somewhere in between, thus subject to various interpretations, depending on who is doing the interpreting and for what purpose.

b. How much credit is given for prior learning, and how is that decision made?

It is an academically valid and well-accepted practice to give credit for learning experiences that took place prior to enrollment. A typical example is skill in a second language. If an American student takes four years of French in college, she will earn about twenty-four semester units and achieve a certain level of competency in the language. But what if she reached exactly the same level of competency on her own, whether through taking a Berlitz course, living in that country, or learning from her grandmother? Many schools will award credit, although not necessarily those twenty-four units, once the competency has been demonstrated on a meaningful written and oral examination.

Credit is responsibly given for a wide range of prior learning, ranging from an Army map-reading course, to an IBM in-house training program, to earning a multiengine pilot's license, to extensive independent study in Buddhist philosophy, to achieving a high score on the Graduate Record Examination in math.

While each school makes its own decision on how much credit to give, many rely on recommendations made by the American Council on Education's (ACE) College Credit Recommendation Service, described at www.acenet.edu/calec/corporate. ACE evaluates thousands of learning experiences and publishes its recommendations on how much credit to give for each experience in several large volumes each year.

While there can be a considerable range in the amount of credit given for the same experience, the bad and fake schools regularly abuse this process by making outrageous credit awards. For instance, a good score on the ninety-minute College Level Evaluation Program (CLEP) test in history is worth one or two semester units at many schools and as much as five or six at a few. But degree mills have been known to give forty or fifty semester units, or even the entire bachelor's (typically 120 units), master's, or doctorate degree, for one CLEP test.

Again, we have a continuum, with the least-generous legitimate school at one end and the degree mills at the other. If the amount of credit awarded for a Navy music course ranges from three units at School A to one hundred twenty units at School Z, where does one draw the line between "good school" and "bad school" and perhaps another line between "bad school" and "degree mill"? And, most significantly, *who* draws that line?

c. How much new work is required to earn the degree?

While there are three regionally accredited US schools that will consider awarding their bachelor's degree totally based on prior learning (if there is a great deal of it), the vast majority of schools require at least one year of new work, no matter what the student has done before.[12]

At the master's and doctoral level, giving credit for prior learning is minimal and rare. We know of no school with recognized accreditation that will award its master's degree for anything less than one academic year (eight or nine months) of new work. The doctorate requires at least two years of new work, but usually three to five.

It is a common approach for degree mills to look at an applicant's C.V. or resume and say, "Ah, yes, you've been selling life insurance for three years. That is the equivalent of an MBA," or "We have determined that your five years of teaching Sunday school can earn you a Doctor of Divinity degree."

Once again we have a continuum. At one end are the schools that require a great deal of new work after enrollment, and at the other end are the degree mills that offer any degree, including the master's or doctorate, entirely or almost entirely based on the resume.

Is a three-page paper and one short open-book quiz sufficient for a master's degree? A thirty-page paper and a one-hour unproctored exam? Ten thirty-page papers and five two-hour proctored exams? Where does one draw *this* line, and, again significantly, *who* draws it?

d. How does one judge the quality of the work done?

Even more complicated than evaluating the *quantity* of work done to earn any given degree is the *quality* of that work. A brilliant thirty-page thesis might be considered more worthy of a master's degree than an ordinary hundred-page one or a poorly done three-hundred-page one.

Once again we have a continuum from A to F (or 4.0 to 0.0) grades, and we have the complicated issue of who makes those grading decisions and on what basis.

The quality of work done has been used in courtroom trials and other public situations to help prove that a given school is a degree mill. A high school teacher with a dubious PhD sued his school district, which had refused to pay him at the doctoral scale as the union contract required. The district had acquired a copy of this man's seventeen-page doctoral "dissertation" directly from his alma mater, an unaccredited California university. The arbitration committee was clearly not impressed with this work, which the committee said was nothing more than a book report, and denied the claim.

That situation turned out well. But what if the three arbitrators had "voted" two to one? What if the lawyer for the defendant had found three professors who said that the work *was* adequate? What if the degree holder had hired an academic writing service (and there are plenty of them) to write a good dissertation for him, *after* his degree was challenged?

e. Who makes these decisions? How do they do so?

Gatekeepers and decision makers must decide where to draw all these crucial lines: how much credit for life experience, how much work to earn a degree, and what quality of work. Whenever possible, they will make use of external examiners: scholars from other schools and agencies, who will review the processes and determine that they are valid and equivalent to what their own institutions do.

All of this means that there is no short, simple, universally accepted definition of a degree mill. The complexity of the current educational situation precludes that. We can, however, say that a degree mill is an entity in which

- degree-granting authority does not come from a generally accepted government agency,
- procedures for granting credit for prior learning, and for determining the amount and quality of work done to earn the degree, do not meet generally accepted standards, and
- those who make the decisions on credit, and on quantity and quality of work, do not have the credentials, experience, or training typically associated with people performing these tasks.

The content of this book has been shaped by this definition and by these four additional factors:

1. *The continuum concept.* While we have our own clear ideas on where to draw lines on the continuum that runs from "degree mill" to "legitimate school without recognized accreditation," it is equally clear that many others have *their* clear ideas, and they are different from ours. A school whose degree can qualify you to take the bar or a state licensing exam in California can get you arrested on a criminal charge in Oregon. Every decision maker and gatekeeper draws his or her line in a different place.

2. *Our litigious society.* In this great democracy of ours, anyone can

sue anyone else, and except in the rarest instances of wildly frivolous actions, the courts accept these suits. In the mid-1990s, LaSalle University (Louisiana) sued John Bear for a seven-figure amount because he had identified the institution as a degree mill. The following year, the proprietor of LaSalle was indicted on eighteen counts of mail fraud, tax fraud, and other charges; pleaded guilty; and was sent to a federal prison. But before this happened, John Bear had to spend thousands of dollars to respond (successfully) to this action that he believed to be both frivolous and vengeful.

In the late 1970s, Allen Ezell, John Bear, and a whole bunch of others (including CBS, the FBI, and some state attorneys general) were sued for $500 million by an already-imprisoned degree-mill operator, claiming libel, slander, and a conspiracy to put him out of business. We were content to let CBS and the others speak for us, but a lot of attorney time was booked before the courts eventually threw that one out.

And a few years ago, the Canadian publisher of John Bear's book on online degrees was sued by an unrecognized Canadian school unhappy because it *wasn't* listed in the book.[13] Eventually, again after time and expense, the Canadian court declined to accept the case.

But we also want to point out, in passing, that things might have been different if media peril insurance ("libel insurance") were available and affordable, and/or if the US courts were (in this respect) more like those in some Commonwealth countries. When our colleague George Brown, an Australian, was sued in Australia by a "school" allegedly in England that he had called a degree mill, the plaintiff was required by the Australian court to put up a multi-thousand-dollar bond. When the "school" did not press the suit, presumably because it would have meant revealing the names of the owners and its location, the court canceled the suit and gave the bond money to Mr. Brown.

3. *The fact that information and opinions on degree mills are readily available.* Anyone who needs to decide whether a given school is a degree mill (based, of course, on where he or she decides to draw the line on that continuum) will find plenty of information available in places ranging from government sites (such as the one run by the state of Oregon, which identifies hundreds of illegal schools by name) to news forums, such as DegreeInfo.com, where responsible people call many institutions degree mills (often we agree with them, but choose not to use those words) to companies in the business of checking academic credentials and issuing opinions on the legality and legitimacy of schools.

We provide detailed information on how to check out a school, and determine what others have to say about it, in appendix G.

4. *Your authors are glad to talk to you and share their opinions.* Even before this book came out, both authors were spending quite a few hours each week sharing opinions on schools with government officials, state regulators, news media, registrars, human resource people, and a great many individuals who simply want to know, "Is this school OK?" We intend to continue to do this; again, details are in appendix G.

Add to these the recognition of the speed with which situations change as the Internet and other advanced technologies make it increasingly easy for degree mills to launch, move, and cover their tracks, and you can see why this is not a reference book with an annotated list of a thousand or more school names. It is, rather, a consumer awareness work. With the information in this book, any intelligent reader can, at the very least, recognize the red flags that signal a less-than-legitimate enterprise and can develop sufficiently sensitive degree-mill "radar" to know when questions need to be asked and of whom to ask them.

NOTES

1. His name has been changed for this otherwise-accurate account.

2. Following an indictment on eighteen counts of mail fraud, tax evasion, and money laundering, James Kirk, also known as Thomas McPherson, pleaded guilty to one count and was sentenced to five years in federal prison.

3. The cost of a fake degree can range from under $100 to more than $5,000, and prices are usually negotiable.

4. We are grateful to Dr. Robin Calote for sharing her alarmingly large collection of degree-mill articles from the 1920s.

5. Press release, US Office of Education, April 11, 1960.

6. Bear was invited back to do two more of these workshops the following year.

7. Many more of these "time bombs" are described in appendix F.

8. Robert H. Reid, "Degree Mills in the United States" (PhD diss., Columbia University, 1963).

9. David W. Stewart and Henry A. Spille, *Diploma Mills: Degrees of Fraud* (New York: American Council on Education, 1988). Both were then employed by the American Council on Education when this was published.

10. See Steve Levicoff, *Name It and Frame It* (Ambler, PA: Institute on Religion and Law, 1993), which looks primarily at Christian degree mills.

11. This is very similar to the process of fingerprint identification, in which each examiner has his or her own number of "points of identification" required to make a match. It is called a floating standard.

12. Accreditation is explained in some detail in appendix E. The three schools that award bachelor's degrees based on prior learning are Excelsior College in New York, Thomas Edison State College in New Jersey, and Charter Oak State College in Connecticut.

13. John Bear and Mariah Bear, *College Degrees by Mail and Internet* (Berkeley, CA: Ten Speed Press, 2001).

I

History of Degree Mills

The history of fake degrees and diplomas is logically divided into three eras: the period from ancient times up to the start of Dip-Scam in 1980; the DipScam era, including the Claude Pepper hearings (1980 to 1991); and the period since then.

THE FIRST ERA: 700 (OR EARLIER) THROUGH 1979

Perhaps the earliest use of what we would call diplomas is found in western Europe among the Merovingian and Carolingian people. As J. M. Wallace-Hadril writes, these "diplomas . . . were official instruments, couched in an elaborate form of words and authenticated in several ways, whereby kings made known their gifts and grants to communities or individuals, and did so in what seemed to them the safest and most permanent manner."[1]

And yet, the author explains, "[i]n spite . . . of all precautions, it was not very difficult for medieval scribes to forge diplomas well enough to deceive rivals. . . . So there are many bogus diplomas" from that era.

For all we know, there may be older fake diplomas in clay pots by the Dead Sea or daubed onto papyrus in the tombs of ancient Egypt, but at least we know that fake diplomas have been a problem for a minimum of thirteen hundred years.

The first academic degrees were awarded in Europe in the eleventh century at the University of Bologna and soon after at Oxford and the Sorbonne. It seems safe to suggest that fake diplomas followed closely on the heels of the real ones. By the fourteenth century, according to Barbara Tuchman, diplomas from Oxford or Cambridge served, in effect, as the "library cards," necessary to gain admission to the research facilities of the University of Paris.[2] As a result, there was quite an active traffic in the buying and selling of fake diplomas. It was also the case that it required as much as fifteen years of study beyond the master's degree to earn a doctorate, a fact that may have motivated some younger scholars to acquire the doctorate by other means.[3]

The earliest mention of a fake school established for the purpose of granting degrees, as contrasted with the forging of diplomas from real schools, is a tantalizing reference in an 1883 treatise.[4] The author, in the midst of complaining about "[t]he bogus degrees [that may] claim to have issued from some university which is nonexistent," says that the sale of degrees was commonplace at least since the year 1730. The tantalizing part is that he does not name any names, nor has any other scholar yet discovered which fakes he may have been referring to.

In his 1963 doctoral dissertation on degree mills, Robert Reid reports that the earliest date associated with a known fake is 1797, the year on the seal of the Colonial Academy.[5] However, as Reid correctly points out, it has always been common for degree mills to lie about how old they are.

Because of this proclivity for lying, we cannot know if the "honor" of being the first American degree mill goes to the Colonial Academy, to Milton University of Maryland (claimed to have been founded in 1847 and definitely incorporated as a university in 1909), or to Richmond College (claimed to have been chartered in Ohio in 1835 and definitely soliciting students in 1876).

Certainly by the 1880s, there were quite a few fake colleges and universities in operation and often in legal trouble. Reid cites American University in Philadelphia (charter revoked by the courts in 1880), Livingston University of America (charter repealed by West Virginia in 1881), and Western University (chartered in Illinois in 1897). The US Commissioner of Education at the time, John Eaton, referred each year in his annual reports (1876 through 1881) to the "scandal and disgrace" of degree mills in the United States.

During the early years of the twentieth century, fake medical schools proliferated, leading to the only US Senate hearings ever held

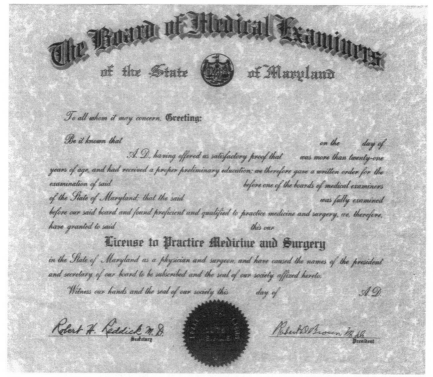

Along with their fake medical degrees, one degree mill provides a realistic-looking license to practice medicine in the state of Maryland.

on the matter of fake degrees. The report of the Subcommittee of the Committee on Education and Labor, chaired by Sen. Royal Copeland of New York, himself a medical doctor, suggested that there were "at least 25,000 fraudulent doctors, doctors who have fraudulent . . . medical diplomas, practicing in the United States."[6]

One curious (by twenty-first-century standards) recommendation of this subcommittee was in fact implemented, amending the postal laws to make it illegal to grant degrees for work done entirely by correspondence. Needless to say, this law was never enforced.

According to a German scholar fascinated by American degree fakes, the 1930s were the "golden age" of degree mills, fueled in part by the depression and the wish for inexpensive degrees.[7]

In 1950, the distinguished education editor of the *New York Times*, Benjamin Fine, wrote that there were "more than one thousand institutions operating unethically, of which "at least one hundred of these [are] diploma mills where one can buy . . . a high-sounding doctorate for less than $50."[8]

Fine's article upset so many people that the large and powerful National Education Association launched a well-publicized effort to identify and outlaw degree mills. But they were unable even to agree on what sorts of laws should be enacted, and their efforts faded away. By 1957, the dubious Association of Home Study Schools, which Reid says "represents many of these phony colleges and universities," were claiming that total enrollment in "their" schools was 750,000 students, paying an annual tuition of $75 million.[9]

Reid's excellent research and writing on degree mills, culminating with his 1963 doctoral dissertation at Columbia, was clearly designed and intended to stir things up among the regulators, the state legislatures, the media, and the public, but it was not to happen. John Bear wrote Reid a "fan letter" after discovering his work in the seventies and received a rather despondent reply. "Sometimes I think the Kennedy assassination, the Vietnam era, and the whole cold war thing diverted the attention of the decision makers in Washington and in the state capitals away from degree mills, but I can tell you, it has been extremely discouraging to see how little has been done over the past two decades. Perhaps the 1980s will bring about a turn for the better."[10]

THE SECOND ERA: PEPPER AND DIPSCAM

The 1980s did indeed go a long way to fulfilling Reid's hopes. Between the FBI's DipScam operation and Rep. Claude Pepper's hearings on degree fraud, the topic of fake degrees had more government attention and public awareness than at any time before or since.

The Pepper Hearings

In the course of far-reaching hearings relating to fraud against the elderly, Congressman Pepper's subcommittee on health and Rep. Don Bonker's subcommittee on consumer interests discovered early on, during 1985, that the problem of fake degrees and credentials extended far beyond the fake medical doctors, nurses, and other health-care practitioners. Indeed, one of their most popular witnesses was then-imprisoned degree salesman

Anthony Geruntino, who said that although he had sold thousands of fake degrees, he did not sell medical degrees, since that "would be unconscionable." (Geruntino's conscience did not stop him, however, from selling engineering degrees to people at Three Mile Island and Westinghouse Nuclear or degrees, including doctorates, in aerospace engineering to people at NASA's Johnson Space Center and Kennedy Space Center.)

The subcommittee staffs did good and comprehensive work in looking into both the fake schools and the people using fake degrees. To demonstrate the ease of operating in the fake-degree world, and with an unerring sense for getting publicity, they invested $1,800 of taxpayer money in buying a PhD in psychology for Mr. Pepper from Union University in Los Angeles, thereby making him "Doctor Pepper."[11] Then they established and ran advertisements for their own fake school, the Capitol Institute of Advanced Education.

Their numerical estimates are scary indeed: "[A]pplying the rate of bogus [health] credentials . . . to all other occupations, there would be as many as 2 million bogus practitioners in this country. . . .

"The American Council on Education estimates there are . . . about 400–500 diploma mills in operation around the country. . . .

"The National Council for Accreditation of Teacher Education estimated [that] fully one sixth of all [doctorates] in education were phony. If one generalizes from this estimate to all doctorates granted [in the past five years], this would translate to nearly 40,000 Americans holding bogus doctorate degrees alone."[12]

Pepper concluded with these recommendations:

1. "With the release of this report, I am calling upon the Federal agencies to investigate the qualifications of employees."
2. "I am asking that they provide the Subcommittees with a statement of the actions they have taken to verify the authenticity of those employees' academic credentials."
3. "I am also requesting that they take appropriate action where necessary to ensure that these sensitive posts are occupied by . . . genuinely qualified individuals."
4. There should be a "computerized national clearinghouse on fraudulent credentials," accessible to government agencies, businesses, and consumers.[13]

Pepper was a well-liked and powerful politician and a skilled power broker who genuinely was concerned about fake degrees, but on those four recommendations, he had almost no success.

DipScam

DipScam represents the longest-lasting and most effective effort by any government anywhere to deal with the degree-mill problem. Both for historical interest and as an indicator of the kinds of things that could still be done, we will look at DipScam in some detail: how it came into being and the cases it dealt with. The case histories are presented in Allen Ezell's own voice, based on interviews conducted by John Bear in 2001 and 2002.

Southeastern University

In a very real sense, it was Howard Cosell who was instrumental in the founding of DipScam. One evening, on *Monday Night Football*, Cosell was extolling the virtues of NFL player "Boobie" Clark, who, he reported, had just earned his degree from Southeastern University in Greenville, South Carolina.

As it happened, some FBI agents in Greenville saw this and said, in effect, "Hey, wait a minute. This is our town. We don't have any such university here."

Then a resident of Charlotte, where I was based, obtained a bachelor's, master's, and doctorate degree from Southeastern, complete with transcripts, and no work done.

I had never worked a phony college case, but I'd done a lot in white-collar crime. I took the information I had to an assistant US attorney, who saw harm to society, so he authorized me to begin a mail fraud and fraud-by-wire investigation. Since I was in North Carolina and the school was in South Carolina, we had the interstate nexus needed to make this a federal case.[14]

Our source introduced me by telephone to Dr. Alfred Jarrette of Southeastern University, and I negotiated for the purchase of a bachelor's, master's, and doctorate, all backdated. I did no work at all, sent him the money, and in due course received the diplomas and transcripts.[15] My calls were from one state to another, making this a federal crime of fraud by wire.

The FBI's DIPSCAM operation began after Allen Ezell was able to purchase this diploma from Southeastern University.

After the sale of more degrees to another FBI agent, we were invited to come to Greenville to be photographed in caps and gowns. Jarrette felt we could help him make money and offered us one-third of the revenues if we would raise money for his school.

Since Southeastern also claimed a religious connection, to show *that* was bogus, a third agent arranged to purchase a degree in theology for $5,000 to be picked up in person.

With the cooperation of North Carolina National Bank, now Bank of America, we ostensibly applied for jobs. The bank wrote to Jarrette to verify our degrees, and he wrote back a glowing letter confirming them. We wanted to show how far he was willing to go.

On the appointed day, we three agents went to Jarrette's home, but now as FBI agents with a search warrant, which we served at the door.

In our search, we found many Southeastern student records along with a loaded shotgun, which was legally his, so it was returned to him upon our departure.

Jarrette sat very quietly while we went about our work. He had been expecting to sell a $5,000 degree, and instead he got three feds with a warrant. In executing a search warrant, one person keeps a detailed record in duplicate, one copy for the owner of the goods, the other for the court.

We gave Jarrette his copy of the receipt and headed back to Charlotte, after reassuring him that this was not the end of the world. But for him it was. The next morning, we learned that Jarrette had gone to dinner with a friend, given away some of his possessions, and then committed suicide with a .38. (We don't know where this second gun came from.)

In analyzing the seized papers, we learned that Jarrette had sold 620 degrees, including 171 to federal, state, and county employees. *Parade* magazine later discovered even more graduates, including a fairly high official at the US Department of Education who had purchased his PhD in criminal justice for $1,800.

The seized materials also showed that Jarrette had traded degrees with a man named James Vardamon Kirk: two Southeastern degrees for Kirk, backdated to 1974 and 1975, in exchange for a law degree from Kirk's school, backdated to 1978.

This was the first we heard of Kirk, then of the University of San Gabriel Valley, later to found Southland University (California), and International University (Louisiana). We started paying attention to Kirk's activities, and he later went to prison for his fake LaSalle University.

L. Mitchell Weinberg, the Medical Schools in the Briefcase

In late 1981, we presented a list of possible fraudulent colleges and universities to the US Attorney's office. The list includes the fake Johann Kepler School of Medicine, run by a man named L. Mitchell Weinberg. We established parameters on how we would proceed, and DipScam came into being.

Once it had been named, it started getting special attention: publicity, press releases, an article in *US News*, and a spot on the *CBS Evening News*. This was all orchestrated not from Washington but by my special agent in charge (SAC) in Charlotte.

Initially, degree fraud was just a part of my normal white-collar crime work, which included bank fraud, embezzlement, bankruptcy

UNITED AMERICAN MEDICAL COLLEGE

UNIVERSITY MEDICAL CENTER
POST OFFICE BOX 248   OAKVILLE, ONTARIO
CANADA L6J-5A2

TRANSCRIPT OF PERMANENT RECORD

LAST NAME   OTHO ALLEN EZELL, JR.

IDENTIFICATION NO.	BIRTHDATE	SEX
7076	8/24/41	Male

PRIOR DEGREES

DEGREE	SCHOOL	DATE
Ph.D.	TAEC	7/21/76
M.S.	"	7/21/73
B.S.	"	7/21/71

CODES

P   Pass
F   Fail
CHI   Credit by Transfer
CBE   Credit by Evaluation
CEC   Credit by Examination

A total of 1840 (Resident) Hours are transferred on (UNITED AMERICAN MEDICAL COLLEGE) transcript from previous attained studies towards (Doctor of Medicine) Degree as follows:

PHASE I — Basic Science Subjects	CBT	
I. Anatomy — includes gross anatomy, embryology, and histology.	640	Hrs.
II. Physiology — includes physiology of blood and lymph, circulation, respiration, excretion, digestion, metabolism, endocrine, special senses and nervous system.	320	Hrs.
III. Chemistry — Inorganic, Organic, Biochemistry and Nutrition — includes physical chemistry, chemistry of foods, digestion and metabolism.	320	Hrs.
IV. Pathology — includes General and Special Pathology.	180	Hrs.
V. Bacteriology—includes Parasitology and Serology.	320	
VI. Hygiene and Sanitation and Public Health — includes sanitation and hygienic procedures and regulations and the prevention of disease.	60	Hrs.
TOTAL BASIC SCIENCE	1840	Hrs.

COMMENTS

Passed, qualifying Examination for the degree of DOCTOR OF MEDICINE.

M.D., Degree Awarded September 17, 1978.

All work Validated.

Honorable Dismissal Granted.

PHASE II — Clinical Subjects	
I. Physical, Clinical, Laboratory and Differential Diagnosis.	P
II. Gynecology, Obstetrics and Pediatrics.	P
III. Roentgenology.	P
IV. Geriatrics, Dermatology, Toxicology, Psychology, and Psychiatry.	P
V. Jurisprudence, Ethics, and Economics.	P
TOTAL CLINICAL	2080 Hrs.
Principles	880 Hrs.
Practice	1200 Hrs.
Required elective	80
TOTAL	4000 Hrs.

DEGREE(S) AWARDED

DOCTOR OF MEDICINE(M.D.)

E. M. Weinberg, M.D.

I certify that this is a true copy of the student's record that on original transcript without a signature and university seal.

Sept. 17, 1978

This is the transcript that accompanied the diploma granting Allen Ezell the Doctor of Medicine degree. The medical school was run from a New York hotel room.

fraud, and so on. But before too long, degree cases were occupying about 80 percent of my time, and other agents were brought in as well.

Weinberg claimed his medical school was in Zurich, Switzerland, but in reality he used various post office boxes in New York State and actually ran the school from his room at the Greystone Hotel in New York City. Wherever his briefcase was, there was the medical school.

In addition to medical degrees, Weinberg sold transcripts, wallet ID cards, memberships in his World International Medical Association (claimed to be in Panama), PhDs from the North American University of Canada, and certificates from the Arkansas Board of Natural Therapeutics and Northwest London University.

Weinberg also operated under the identity of Dieter Luelsdorf, effecting a fake German accent as an administrator of the Keppler School. When I came to realize that Weinberg and Luelsdorf were the same person —they had an identical stutter—I arranged to be on the phone with Dieter at the same moment another FBI agent went to Weinberg's room at the hotel. On the tape, you can hear Dieter talking to me in his fake German accent, then a knock at the door, and then Weinberg's normal voice explaining to the other FBI agent that there is no one else there.

Based on this and other information, we secured a search warrant and found diplomas, seals, and other evidence in his magic briefcase. Weinberg kept almost no records. While it was clear he had sold dozens of medical degrees at $1,900 each, most of his customers were unknown, probably even to him. One significant exception was a man running a clinic in Orange County, California, with his Kepler degree. His specialty was determining whether women were predisposed to getting cancer by doing cervical examinations.

Weinberg, who was also connected with "Bishop" George Lyon's fake United American Medical School, pleaded guilty and was given three years at the Federal Correctional Institution at Danbury, Connecticut.

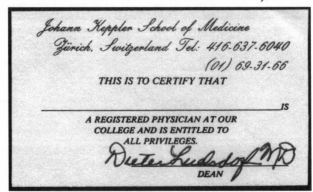

This fake medical school issued wallet identification cards so its graduates could secure hospital privileges and write prescriptions.

Bishop George Cook Lyon, Thomas A. Edison College, United American Medical College, Palm Beach Psychotherapy Training Center

We got onto George Cook Lyon and his various activities as an offshoot of Weinberg and his fake medical school. Weinberg had also offered the degrees of Lyon's United American Medical College.

Before we got involved, Lyon had been convicted of running a degree mill in Florida, had been fined $10,000, and had spent about six weeks in jail. On his release, he headed for Arkansas, and we got in touch with him there.

Another agent and I each purchased degrees from Thomas A. Edison College. We told him we might be interested in doing business together, and we flew to Little Rock for a meeting.

As I came down the escalator at the airport, there at the bottom was this tiny little man, in his late seventies, no more than five-foot-two. He was wearing cowboy boots, black pants, a black shirt with a purple clerical collar, and a big silver cross on a silver chain under his white beard. He was wearing a huge amethyst ring that would have choked a horse. Looking past him, we saw a large dark green Rolls-Royce parked just outside the glass doors. We soon learned he also had a bright red Mercedes parked in his driveway in Benton, Arkansas.

It was my first and only ride in a Rolls-Royce, and on the way back to the airport after lunch, he hit us up for gas money, so we gave him a couple of bucks. It was a fun day. While visiting Lyon, I told him the MD degree that he had previously sold me, signed by Lawrence Weinberg, had been damaged in the mail. And so, in our presence, Lyon took out a blank United American Medical College diploma, forged Weinberg's name on it, and handed it to me. It was a great piece of evidence for court later.

After our undercover visit to Lyon's operation in Arkansas, we had probable cause for a search warrant. When we returned to execute the federal search warrant in the old church he'd bought in Benton, we found and took documents of Edison, the medical school, and thirty-eight other entities, sixteen of them his and the rest from other mills that he was representing.

Lyon was indicted on thirteen counts of mail and wire fraud. He was seventy-eight years old at the time. He entered a Rule 20 guilty plea, which meant he wouldn't have to go back to North Carolina, where the indictment was issued, but would appear before a federal judge in Little Rock. He did so, showing up in cowboy boots, red-and-white checkerboard pants, a red sports coat, and that big silver cross around his neck.

He told reporters, "I have not done anything illegal or improper at all. I never offered a diploma of Thomas A. Edison College. I call it entrapment. It is my word against the person who set me up."

The evidence suggested he had sold between three thousand and four thousand degrees at an average of $500 each, meaning total sales between $1.5 million and $2 million. He also sold State of Maryland medical licenses, which gave the holder permission to practice medicine and perform surgery.

At age seventy-nine, he was fined $2,000 and sentenced to a year in prison, which he served at Fort Worth, Texas. He was a feisty old guy, very sharp. At the end, he declared, "I am being persecuted. My background is without blemish. This is a dirty rotten deal, and I hope God takes care of me."

Alumni Arts, One of the Early Counterfeiters

The FBI received a letter from a concerned citizen about an advertisement in *Soldier of Fortune* magazine, offering a so-called lost diploma replacement service in Grants Pass, Oregon. The ad, which also had run in many other newspapers and magazines, read:

COLLEGE DIPLOMA—1 DAY

Has your diploma been lost or damaged?

Most schools available. Beautiful exacting reproductions including seals & colors. All inquiries confidential. Color catalogue $3.

Alumni Arts
Box 562, Grants Pass, OR 97526

I ordered degrees in two names other than my own—one of the first times I had permission to do that—and as things turned out, I'm glad I did, since the perpetrator had a DipScam newspaper clipping, mentioning my name, tacked to his bulletin board. One diploma was from the University of North Carolina, which I felt would be of special interest to the North Carolina grand jury, where we would seek an indictment.

Based on information I had collected, I prepared an affidavit for a search warrant, flew to Oregon, at which time it was reviewed by the assistant US attorney. Then I appeared before the US Magistrate in Eugene, Oregon, who issued two search warrants, one for a private home and one for a commercial printer, both in Grants Pass, Oregon. The warrants specified exactly which documents could be taken.

It is important that multiple search warrants be executed simultaneously, and it is desirable to cooperate with local law enforcement. As I knocked on the door of an old Victorian house in a residential neighborhood—so residential there were actually goats grazing in the front yard—an FBI agent from Oregon was walking into the print shop. We were each accompanied by local deputy sheriffs.

The first thing you do on any search warrant is secure the premises. First, are there any firearms? Second, is anyone else present? Clearly this was a family home. There was a computer on the kitchen table, and hundreds of shrink-wrapped bundles from the printer lining the long hallway of the house: schools A through M down one side, N through

Until they were closed down by DipScam, the Alumni Arts business in Oregon offered a cafeteria of accurate copies of hundreds of university diplomas for $40 to $65.

Z up the other side. There was a light table, photonegatives, and various seals, ribbons, and lettering devices: all the paraphernalia needed by a counterfeiting service.

We ended up taking more than thirty-two thousand blank diplomas representing more than three hundred legitimate colleges and universities, including all of the "big names"—Harvard, Yale, Princeton, Stanford, and so on—as well as military credentials (Bronze Star, Air Medal, etc.), and certificates for the American Society of Clinical Pathologists. Some, but not all, of the diplomas had a line of tiny print at the very bottom edge, reading, "No degree status is granted or implied."

From the man's computer records, we found evidence of 2,311 clients, so he had major growth plans based on those thirty-two thousand blanks.

The perpetrator, in his late thirties, had no prior record. He was indicted by a grand jury in August 1984, pleaded guilty in December, and was sentenced in February 1985 to five years of probation and 120 hours of community service. Local publicity for the case had caused considerable humiliation to the man's wife and children. To the best of our knowledge, he never engaged in crime again. He later declined an offer to testify before Congressman Pepper's subcommittee.

What kind of a man was he? We had occasion to talk over coffee when I returned to Oregon to oversee destruction of all the confiscated goods. He seemed a very likeable sort of guy. Printing diplomas was simply his job; it was what he did. He'd found a niche, and felt, as illogical as it sounds, that he was filling a need and doing no harm.

His wife, who surely knew what was going on, was never charged, nor was the printer who clearly should have paid closer attention to the things he was being paid to print.

The one interesting "loose end" here is where this man got the originals of the diplomas he copied. We simply didn't know. The perpetrator talked about picking things up at yard and estate sales and getting them from "some guy in California," whom we could not identify at the time. As it happened, new evidence came to light in 2004, and now the source is known.

American National University

A California chiropractor named Clarence Franklin, also using the name John Caraway, operated the fake school of this name, advertising regularly in *Psychology Today, Popular Science,* and other publications. Accreditation was claimed from the National Accreditation Association, incorporated in Maryland by Franklin. Degrees were sold for $2,000 and up, including $2,495 for a combined master's and doctorate.

I answered one of the ads and applied for an MBA. I was asked to write a twenty-page paper, but when I said I didn't have time, I was told that a job description would do. I sort of left out the fact that I was with the FBI. I also ordered a class ring from the university's "jewelry department," which turned out to be the office of a fake degree broker in Miami, Stan Simmons, who represented American National and three other phonies, including American International University, run by Edward Reddeck, where Franklin had once worked.

Within two weeks, I received my MBA diploma and my class ring. I paid a friendly visit to the office in Phoenix, saying I was on a business trip and wanted to have a look at "my" alma mater. I was given a tour of the offices and invited to attend the graduation ceremony later that month.

Back in North Carolina, I prepared three search warrant affidavits, for American National, North American University, and their broker Stanley Simmons's "Off-Campus University Programs" business in Miami.

When I showed up in Phoenix on May 14, 1983, now as an FBI special agent, with a search warrant and a truck, the office manager wistfully said, "I guess you're not coming back for the graduation ceremony next week."

Following their indictment, Franklin and Simmons each pleaded guilty to one count of mail fraud. Simmons went to prison, in part because of his involvements with other schools; Franklin received a suspended sentence and did not go to prison.

Anthony Geruntino, American Western University, Southwestern University, and Others

I responded to an advertisement run by Vocational Guidance Services of Columbus, Ohio, which offered to find the perfect school for me, based on a questionnaire I filled out. When I sent in the questionnaire, they replied that because of my "unique situation and credentials, I have taken the opportunity of contacting American Western University, in Tulsa, Oklahoma, and have been advised that you already have the qualification for the MBA degree."

I purchased the MBA for $485, $25 for a transcript (I earned straight

As), and $97.50 for a class ring. Almost immediately after this, I received an unsolicited offer from Southwestern University in Tucson, Arizona, and purchased a master's in business management and two transcripts.

I then contacted proprietor Anthony Geruntino in Columbus, telling him I was an accountant with interest in this business, and could I stop by when I was next in the area. He took me on a tour of the operation, and then he offered me a job helping him find clients. "Don't look at this as a job," he said, "but as a way to get rich." He told me I would make $100,000 in my first year. So that is what I put in my affidavits for search warrants for the premises in Ohio and Arizona. When I walked into the "university" in Tucson on the morning of October 13, 1982, with several other FBI agents and a search warrant in hand, Tony was there. "I thought you were too good to be true," he sighed.

We had an immense amount of data to review—a fourteen-foot truck full. Two staff members took months to put all the "student" records into a database so that we could ask FBI agents all over the country to interview Geruntino's clients, focusing on federal employees and others in the public sector, such as school principals. There were people with the Federal Bureau of Prisons, the Department of Justice, the Joint Chiefs of Staff, an Undersecretary of State, and so on. We were building what is called a prosecutive case to take to a federal grand jury. We found clear evidence of twenty-two hundred people who bought degrees, with revenues of $1.8 million.

While study of his materials was going on, Geruntino had not yet been charged with anything. However, because of Arizona's new laws governing private postsecondary institutions, he moved his operation to St. George, Utah. He advertised that he would be transforming Utah in general and St. George in particular into a major worldwide educational center.

Many people in St. George seemed enthusiastic about Tony's plans. But some people had concerns about this man, and so a well-attended public hearing was held on the evening of February 7, 1985, to discuss issuing the business license for which he had applied. People spoke for and against him. When the hearing was over, he stepped outside and was arrested based on a thirty-one-count indictment handed down earlier that day by a federal grand jury. He was taken to the local jail and the next day was taken before the US Magistrate at Salt Lake City. He made bond and was released from jail.

After he entered a guilty plea in US District Court, Western District of North Carolina, in Charlotte, but *before* he was interviewed and sentenced, he moved Southwestern University from St. George to the address of an answering service in Salt Lake City. He actually put on a graduation ceremony in Salt Lake City.

Geruntino was fined $5,000 and sentenced to five years in prison. We were on pretty good terms with him. He respected what we did and saw why we did it. While in prison, he testified in a forthright and repentant manner before Congressman Pepper's hearings on degree fraud. A couple of years after his release, he declined a newspaper request for an interview and has been out of the public eye ever since.

Edward Reddeck, American International University, North American University, Dallas State University, and Others

American International was one of the fraudulent activities of a man who appears over and over in the world of fake schools and degrees, Edward Reddeck, also known as John Palmer, John Polmar, and many other names. Reddeck has been imprisoned at least three times for his various fakes. His affiliations include North American University (Utah), the University of North America (Missouri) and Coast University and Gold Coast University (Hawaii), Dallas State University, the Global Church of God, the International Accreditation Association, Success International, and the American Freedom Foundation.

He also worked with degree-mill agent Stanley Simmons in Florida.

I interviewed Reddeck in 1983 when he was in Terminal Island Federal Correctional Institution following his conviction for selling the fake degrees of Dallas State University. He called himself the "grandfather of nontraditional education in America" and said that he could be a huge asset to the FBI in identifying fake schools, but his "fee" would be having all the perceived "wrongs" done to him by the United States government taken care of.

Later, he was indicted by a federal grand jury in Utah for North American University: mail fraud, fictitious name abuse, money laundering, forfeiture, and aiding and abetting. He claimed, among other things, that it was all a government frame-up.

After his conviction and imprisonment, he filed a lengthy rambling suit against John Bear, me, and state officials in Washington and Utah, asking for $1.5 billion (with a *b*). Another suit was filed against the Attorney General of Missouri, citing a "rain [*sic*] of terror" against him.

Reddeck is out of prison again, following his Gold Coast and Coast University convictions, still writing long angry letters, filing *pro se* law suits, and I wouldn't be surprised to learn that he is running yet another so-called school.

Some degree sellers, like Geruntino, Jarrette, and Bishop Lyon, were likable enough, with just a touch of class, but there is nothing charming about Reddeck. He is an angry, hostile man, a con man with no class, all rough edges.

Doc Caffey, National College of Arts and Sciences, Northwestern College of Allied Science, American Western University, South Union Graduate School, Northwestern College of Allied Science, and Others

In 1980, a social studies teacher from New York knocked on the door of the National College of Arts and Sciences in Springfield, Missouri. He was there because of a concern he had about the National College degree being used by his school superintendent. The door was opened by a man in a bathrobe: the Right Reverend Dr. James Robert Caffey, the founder and president of all the above-named institutions.

Caffey first learned about the world of fake schools and degrees while in prison. As one newspaper article at the time put it, "His fondness for cocaine and other people's property earned him several years in the Missouri State Penitentiary at Jefferson City."

In prison, he served as editor of the prison paper, the *Jefftown Journal*. When he got out, he headed for Tulsa, where he opened three diploma mills, and he opened five more in Missouri.

Before Caffey was indicted, convicted (along with Geruntino and others), and sent back to prison for five years, he sold a National College degree to a man named Wiley Gordon Bennett, who was soon to go into the degree-mill business himself.

Wiley Gordon Bennett, Sands University, Great Lakes University

Bennett used a mailing service in Yuma, Arizona, for his fake schools, but everything was run from his Consulting Specialists Inc. business in Memphis. His literature all had the slogan, "Knowledge Today is Success Tomorrow." Degrees, including the PhD, were offered in eighty-one listed subjects, and if you didn't like those, the literature said that he would "be happy to grant the PhD in any subject you want," and with any date.

I bought a Master of Education degree from his Great Lakes University, and two months later, an MBA from Sands University which cost $580. When we got a warrant and searched his premises, we found evidence of 527 customers. He kept meticulous records. The federal grand jury returned an indictment on eleven counts of mail fraud and wire fraud, and an arrest warrant was issued.

When Bennett learned of the warrant, he checked himself into the psychiatric ward of the Veterans' Administration hospital in Long Beach, California, but since he had done this voluntarily, we were able to arrest him there. Like so many of the others, he never resurfaced after this episode was over. He was a pleasant enough fellow.

Roosevelt, DePaul, Northwest London, and Metropolitan Collegiate: The Crook Who Stole from Other Crooks

In 1983, a man in South Carolina, who happened to be the brother-in-law of the local police chief, copied some pages from the literature of other degree mills and started selling them as his own, operating under the name "External Study Program."

He must have had problems keeping things straight, because when I ordered my degree from Roosevelt University, the diploma I actually received was from Northwest London University.

His lawyer claimed that these $940 diplomas were just an expensive novelty and that his buyers knew just what they were doing, which somehow made it all right. He was indicted on six counts of mail fraud; pleaded guilty to one count of title 18, section 1341; and was sentenced to three years' probation and restitution of $1,700 to the US government.

The Fowler Family, Roosevelt, Cromwell, Lafayette, DePaul, John Quincy Adams, Dallas State, Loyola, Southern California University, and Others

The Fowler family, operating from Chicago and Los Angeles, ran one of the more complex and far-flung degree-mill empires and ended up in the only full-fledged courtroom battle of the DipScam era. Brothers Norman, Arnold, and Randall Fowler; their mother; their sister; and her husband operated all of the above-named degree mills, along with three

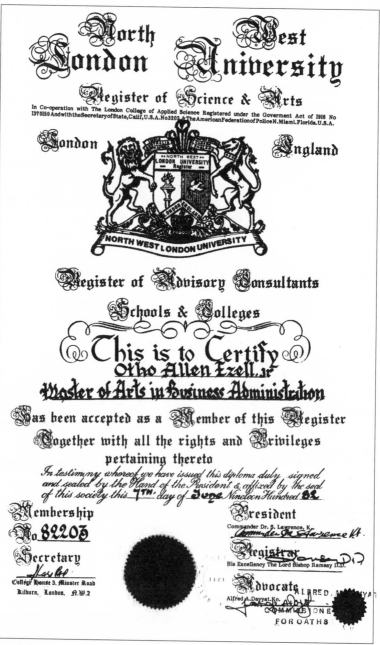

Some of the European fakes have far more elaborate diplomas than their American counterparts.

fake accrediting agencies, using a wide range of addresses in England, France, the Netherlands, Belgium, Germany, and the United States.

Both the FBI and postal inspectors responded to several advertisements placed by "External Degree Program" and purchased degrees from this operation. Later, members of the Chicago police department, in an unrelated criminal investigation, searched the apartment of Arnold Fowler, and in his safe they found evidence of the sale of degrees, which they turned over to us.

The Fowlers had been operating for up to twenty years, taking in millions of dollars. Selling degrees was the family business. They had annual family gatherings, where they would each brag about how well their various "branches" were doing.

The FBI worked with the postal inspectors on this case, each agency buying a variety of degrees in business, law, music, and pulmonary physiology. This was one of the few cases where the phonies had no office, no telephone, and not even a claimed faculty.

We didn't ask for a federal search warrant because we had no place to search in the United States for which we had sufficient possible cause, so we took possession of no records. Even if records had existed, they might have been at any number of locations, in and outside the United States. So we did everything through the "backdoor" approach, rebuilding business records through study of bank evidence.

We presented our findings to a federal grand jury, which returned a twenty-nine-count indictment against the seven family members on mail fraud, conspiracy, and aiding and abetting.

Following quite a complex ten-day trial, with 110 witnesses from the banks, mailing services, and others, the judge dismissed all charges against two lesser defendants, and the remaining five were found guilty by the jury on all counts and sentenced to prison terms ranging from two to seven years.[16]

Rabbinical Academy of America

We generally stayed away from religious schools, sticking with "middle-of-the-road" phonies, but this one really wasn't a school at all. Several people from a congregation in North Carolina came to us with the message "Our cantor is a ringer; please help us." His credential was from the Rabbinical Academy of America (RAA), ostensibly in Brooklyn, New York.

We asked an FBI agent who was fluent in Hebrew to give them a call, and he negotiated for the purchase of a credential. After submitting a one-page paper and a copy of his junior-high report cards from Israel, he received his ordination as a rabbi by return mail. FBI agents visited the RAA in New York. It was not a school at all, just a credential-selling service, that advertised regularly in the Jerusalem *Post* and in a New York Hebrew paper.

We retrieved a list of all their graduates and sent them a form letter asking what work they did for their degree or ordination, how long it took, how much it cost, and how it had been used. We were flooded with letters and phone calls from all over the world, the great majority of them from these graduates' lawyers. When the academy closed down, the decision was made not to pursue matters any further.

Of course, when people used a religious shell to hide a diploma mill, as in the case of LaSalle, that was a different matter.

John Jacob Gordon, the Presidential Candidate

This was a meat-and-potatoes case. The man, who claimed to be a candidate for president of the United States, was wanted for wire fraud for unrelated issues and had tried to run over an IRS agent, and now his picture was hanging in the post office. When we learned that he was helping support his life as a federal fugitive by selling degrees, we reached out to him. He'd always call collect. When he phoned me to sell me a degree, it was from a pay phone in New England. We sent an FBI agent to drive 20 miles in each direction from that phone booth, hitting every motel. At the last motel in the twentieth mile, the desk clerk looked at the picture and said, "Room Fifteen." Gordon pleaded guilty, but then he claimed that he had been kidnapped by Russians and was a political prisoner. He had bumper stickers made that said "Free Jake Gordon."

Because of jail overcrowding, Gordon was held in jail in Rutherfordton, North Carolina, a town of fewer than five thousand people. The matter was heard by Judge Woodrow Wilson Jones in Rutherfordton. Gordon had an observer monitoring his court proceedings and announced he had found judicial misconduct and prosecutorial fraud. Gordon held a press conference on the courthouse steps, where he announced that he liked this area so much that he was going to return and live in Rutherfordton when released from federal prison. Judge Jones was not amused.

Lynetta Gail Williams, Elysion College

Ms. Williams was one of the few women to run a fake school. She apparently inherited her degree mill from her father, Lane Williams, who had operated Elysion and Williams College from Arizona, Idaho, and other locations. Elysion degrees were being sold through a mail drop a few blocks from her apartment in San Francisco.

We didn't make a buy, but Williams was served with a federal grand jury subpoena to produce all the Elysion records. In the apartment house, tenants put their trash into a large cabinet that the manager emptied. The manager called the FBI and said, "You fellows might want to come back." He noted that Williams had deposited twenty large bags of trash in this cabinet right after the subpoena was served.

He surrendered the trash, the courts having ruled that garbage no longer belongs to a person once she has put it in the trash. Pursuant to a federal grand jury subpoena, Williams called the FBI and surrendered all the Elysion records—about twelve pages. But we already had twenty bags of college records. Following our analysis of the Elysion material, Williams was indicted on the charge of obstruction of justice. She pleaded guilty to this charge and got a suspended sentence, since there was no evidence she was selling degrees but only tidying up after her late father. Yet twenty bags of trash suggest that a fairly sizeable business had been in operation.

James Kirk/Thomas McPherson/Thomas Kirk/James McPherson, LaSalle University, Southland University, International University

We first encountered James Kirk as a graduate of Southeastern University, since he had traded a degree from the University of San Gabriel Valley with Jarrette for a Southeastern degree.

By the time we turned our attention to Kirk, he had incorporated Southland University in Louisiana in 1979 under the auspices of the Trinitarian Church. He had been working at the University of San Gabriel Valley in California, which he left, along with its president's wife, and opened Southland University of California in Pasadena in 1980, as a state-authorized school. We were unable to purchase a degree from Southland. We executed a search warrant in 1983, but while we found some irregularities, including claimed faculty members who said they had never worked there, we didn't have enough for the grand jury at that time. At the time, Southland qualified to have its students take the bar exam in California, the last remaining state that permits students from unaccredited law schools to take the bar exam.

After our visit, Kirk moved Southland University to Arizona, along with a fake accrediting agency, the Arizona Commission of Non-Traditional Private Postsecondary Accreditation. The *Arizona Republic* newspaper exposed that activity promptly. Then we received information that Kirk was setting up shop in Florida. We immediately notified Florida authorities, and they didn't even last a week there. Around the same time, Kirk's wife and mother were incorporating International University in Louisiana.

When Arizona invited him to move on, Kirk opened up in a St. Louis suburb shortly after. By then, both he and his school had a new name. He was Thomas McPherson, and the school was LaSalle University. Following certain activity in the Missouri state capital, LaSalle closed in Missouri suddenly one Friday and opened in Louisiana the following week.

Kirk's schools generally had an affiliation with a church of his devising: first the Trinitarian Church, and then the World Christian Church. When the state of Louisiana questioned the legitimacy of the World Christian Church, Kirk/McPherson built a chapel on his land in Louisiana and scheduled some services.

Later, I was happy to be able to cooperate with FBI agents in New Orleans in supplying information that they could use in requesting a search warrant for LaSalle. In addition to the "usual" charges of mail fraud, wire fraud, aiding and abetting, and conspiracy, the New Orleans agents added two new statutes: money laundering and forfeiture, which meant the government could keep the $10 million plus discovered in executing the search warrants, until the case was resolved.

Kirk professed his innocence, claiming the ruthless government was attacking his little church school. He made this claim in a full-page $70,000 advertisement in *USA Today*. But following an eighteen-count indictment by a federal grand jury, Kirk pleaded guilty to one count. Part of the agreement was that Kirk's partner, Stanley Foster, plead guilty to obstruction of justice and tax evasion.

The judge seemed irritated by the agreement and gave Kirk the maximum sentence possible for the one count, five years. Kirk went to the federal prison camp in Beaumont, Texas, and within weeks, literature of the brand-new Edison University, with Kirk's wife as registrar, was being

While Acton University's "campus" was a mailbox service in Hawaii, it didn't require major detective work to learn that it was being run by James Kirk from his prison cell in Beaumont, Texas.

mailed from Beaumont, Texas. (Following complaints from the real Edison in New Jersey, the name was changed to Addison and then Acton.)

Kirk served four years. Since his release, he has had involvements with several unaccredited universities in Louisiana and Mississippi.

LaSalle was allowed to continue in business as long as there were new directors unaffiliated with the World Christian Church. It operated legally for a short while, changed its name to Orion College, then closed for good in 2002.

Because of the many millions of dollars recovered, the US Attorney's office wrote to all LaSalle students and alumni, offering them the opportunity for a refund of their payments. They had to surrender their LaSalle diploma to get the refund. A large number of people chose to keep the diploma and, presumably, continue using the degree.

Bruce Copen, Sussex College of Technology, Brantridge University, University of the Science of Man

Sussex was one of the longest-surviving British degree mills. We thought we should give it a try, since people in the United States were using these degrees on their resumes, and Sussex/Brantridge had used mail drops in both Louisiana and Hawaii.

We had no jurisdiction in England, of course, so the odds of getting prosecution were very low, especially since British authorities were well aware of what was going on there and had done nothing. Still, we felt it would at least be good to have a file on them, to make things easier when their degrees came up in other cases. This is just what happened in the case of the fake medical doctor, Gregory Caplinger, who claimed several of his seven doctorates from Sussex.

I sent Bruce Copen my enrollment form, a cashier's check for $372, a five-page paper I'd written for another purpose on the psychology of the embezzler, and a resume of sorts. I must have fallen short of his high expectations because when I got my degree and my transcript nineteen days later, it showed that I'd gotten four Bs along with my fourteen As.

University Novelty and Engraving Company

One of the last DipScam cases was one of the few disappointing ones. Knowing I was being transferred from Charlotte to Tampa, I entered into communication with this Tampa-based company, which sold counterfeit diplomas. I bought a University of South Florida degree, a B.S. in elementary education, and another agent bought a University of Florida degree in electrical engineering. I thought that subjects relating to teaching children and possibly working at a nuclear power plant would get the attention of a grand jury and judge.

I obtained a federal search warrant and executed it with the assistance of a postal inspector. We took everything, including the proprietor's outgoing mail, which the FBI can't touch, but a postal inspector can. She had been selling degrees for at least eight years and had many, many customers. Hers was the first operation where we found a lot of metal seals with the names of major universities for making imprinted gold seals.

But when we looked at her customer lists and conducted some interviews, we didn't find the clear cases of harm to society that we had elsewhere: the teachers and the government employees. Bottom line: even though we'd made our buys and had plenty of evidence, the US Attorney's office declined to prosecute the case. Still, she was, in effect, put out of business, and as far as I know, she's never done this sort of thing again.

There were other DipScam cases, but that covers many of the highlights. By 1988, most of the big degree-mill cases had been resolved, and with the growing savings-and-loan scandals unfolding, I was spending less time on degrees and more on these other crimes. I retired from the FBI after thirty-one years in December 1991, and, following a thirty-six-hour "retirement," I began my next career as a vice president for fraud at what is now Wachovia Bank.

During the eleven years of DipScam, we purchased forty degrees, executed sixteen federal search warrants, obtained nineteen federal grand jury indictments, and twenty-one convictions, and dismantled forty "schools" with total sales into the many tens of millions of dollars.

At the time, we felt the word was out. The schools were put on notice. We'd closed dozens of them, never lost a case, and put a bunch of bad guys in prison. It seemed as if the problem was largely abated.

And along came the Internet, and it was a whole new ballgame.

THE THIRD ERA: 1991 TO THE PRESENT

Gazing into what proved to be an extremely clouded crystal ball in 1991, Allen Ezell believed the degree-mill problem was in major decline, and John Bear wrote, in the 1991 edition of his book, that the era of the degree mill seemed to be nearly over.

And then an unanticipated series of events transpired.

- The FBI's interest in degree mills, while not ending with Ezell's retirement, took a distant backseat to the savings-and-loan scandal and then to matters of drugs and of security.
- Despite the Pepper subcommittee's pleas, other federal agencies as well as state agencies seemed unwilling or less willing to proceed on their own.
- Far more ambitious criminals were just beginning to discover the potential in selling degrees.

When degree-mill operators of that era went to bed at night, in addition to praying that the FBI would knock degree mills down a few notches on their list of priorities—if they prayed at all—they would have prayed for

- a way to make their catalog available worldwide at no cost whatsoever;

- a way to remain completely anonymous and utterly untraceable, either by their customers or by law enforcement;
- an easily usable electronic banking system that lets them deposit funds in secret accounts in small island nations;
- and for good measure, how about a means of sending their messages to millions of people a day without spending a penny on what used to be their three biggest expenses: advertising, printing, and postage.

Welcome to the era of the Internet.

As we move into the twenty-first century, we are seeing these developments:

- Much bigger operations than those that existed in the eighties and nineties. Mills that took in a million dollars a year were once considered huge; now they are at the low end of the scale.
- There are more international or multinational operations. As one example, the huge phony degree business we call the University Degree Program has offices in Romania and Israel; gets its mail in England, Ireland, and the Netherlands; does its printing in Jerusalem; maintains its Web sites in half a dozen countries; and does its banking in Cyprus.
- Higher technology, including sophisticated computers, enables the very professional manufacturing of diplomas, transcripts, seals, and so on. Skilled telemarketing, state-of-the-art security, privacy and "anonymizer" services, as well as "virtual" Internet campus and Web sites make it difficult, sometimes impossible, to learn where a given mill is really located.
- There is a wider array of ways to reassure customers. Fake accrediting agencies, fake impartial-sounding degree consulting and referral services, fake credential evaluation services, even entire countries make their "accreditation" available for a fee.

These are all the kinds of things that are discussed in the remainder of this book.

NOTES

1. J. M. Wallace-Hadrill, *The Barbarian West: The Early Middle Ages A.D. 400–1000* (New York: Hutchinson's University Library, 1952), p. 93.

2. Barbara Tuchman, *Distant Mirror: The Calamitous 14th Century* (New York: Knopf, 1978).

3. Oren H. Baker, *Theological Education: Protestant* (n.p.: Education for Professions, 1955).

4. Edwin Wooton, *A Guide to Degrees in Arts, Science, Literature, Law, Music, and Divinity* (London: L. U. Gill, 1883), pp. viii–x.

5. Robert H. Reid, "Degree Mills in the United States," (PhD diss., Columbia University, 1963), pp. 82–83.

6. US Senate, *Hearings*, 68th Congress, 1st Session, pursuant to Senate Resolution 61, March 1924.

7. Walter Wienert, *Doktorfabriken*, unpublished MS, 1958, cited by Reid.

8. Benjamin Fine, *New York Times*, February 7, 1950.

9. Reid, "Degree Mills in the United States," p. 29.

10. Reid, undated personal communication, late 1970s.

11. Nothing was done to attempt to close this institution or to prosecute its people.

12. US Congress, House, "A Joint Report by the Chairmen of the Subcommittee on Health and Long-Term Care and the Subcommittee on Housing and Consumer Interests of the Select Committee on Aging: Fraudulent Credentials," 99th Congress, December 11, 1985, Comm. pub. no. 99 (Washington, DC: US Government Printing Office, 1986).

13. Ibid.

14. Fraud by wire (telephone, etc.) must be interstate. Mail fraud does not need interstate action, since the US mail is involved.

15. It came with a cover letter stating, "You have been a credit to our institution and to our country." He was very perceptive indeed.

16. This was John Bear's first appearance as an expert witness in federal court.

2

The Sellers

In addition to the counterfeiting services (described in appendix G), there are four distinct categories of schools, businesses, or individuals who offer degrees that do not meet generally accepted accreditation principles.

Category 1: Too new or too unusual. Schools that are either too new or too unusual or innovative to qualify for recognized accreditation. Recognized accrediting agencies typically want an applicant school to have at least two years of successful operation before applying.

Academic models and fields of specialty are flexible concepts, and so what is potentially accreditable can change from time to time. Less than fifty years ago, there were official government warnings that *any* school offering degrees 100 percent by distance learning had to be a fake. Now, of course, there are many hundreds of properly accredited universities that do this.

In the same vein, there have been times when there was no recognized accreditation for schools specializing in acupuncture, naturopathic medicine, cosmetology, funeral service education, midwifery, or leisure studies. Now each of these fields has its own recognized accrediting agency.

Category 2: Geographical Issues. This relates to schools that operate from, or have a token presence in, states or countries that have less stringent school legislation. These range from places with moderately rigorous systems of oversight (such as California state approval) to places that let just about anyone do just about anything in the way of offering degrees (such as the state of Alabama and the island nation of Dominica).

Category 3: Religious Issues. This category includes schools that have, or claim, some sort of religious exemption. There are hundreds of such institutions, ranging from one-man Bible schools to large campus-based universities that do not believe in the concept of accreditation and/or licensing.[1]

Category 4: Degree Mills. There are degree mills that pretend to be legitimate schools but simply sell their degrees to anyone, man or beast, based on little or, in most cases, no work.

A small number of people find something that meets their needs in schools in categories one, two, or three, but many people have difficulty in knowing exactly where to draw the line between legitimate (or acceptable) and degree mills.

There are unaccredited schools whose degrees qualify people to take the bar or various licensing exams in some states, which some employers accept and pay for. And yet those very same degrees are illegal for use in some other states and have little acceptance in the academic world.

Over the years, we have identified roughly two thousand degree-granting schools that fall in one or more of these four categories. But readers will need to decide for themselves what to call a "degree mill," what to call "acceptable" or "adequate" or "meets our standards," and what to put in between. We offer detailed guidelines for the ways and means of making that decision and, a bit later in this chapter, a detailed list of ninety-two things that some dubious or less-than-wonderful schools do to mislead people.

But we are well aware that if we asked one hundred readers (registrars, HR people, school seekers, alumni, law enforcement officers, news media, et al.) to sort one hundred schools into those four categories, we'd have responses all over the map.

FIVE REASONS THAT PEOPLE HAVE PROBLEMS WHEN DECIDING WHAT TO CALL A DEGREE MILL

The term *degree mill* (or *diploma mill*) is a real pejorative. It is not a term to be used lightly. One can call a school "dreadful" and "dubious" and "non-wonderful" and "suspicious" and "unsavory" (and so on), and that is just a matter of opinion. But if one calls a school a degree mill, phony, or fake, especially if one bases a decision, policy, news story on those words, one must be very confident of the ground on which one is standing.

Here are five factors with which we have seen people struggle when they are attempting to identify and describe degree mills or unacceptable schools in the course of developing personal, business, media, government agency, or legislative guidelines on the problem—in other words, where to draw the line on their own particular continuum.

It is appropriate to explain and discuss these reasons in some detail, since they provide insight into the degree-awarding and -selling situation as it is today.

1. That pesky church-state situation.

Most states are terrified about doing anything that might be construed as restricting the right of a church to do just about anything it darn well pleases, including starting and running a university and handing out degrees of all kinds.

The Universal Life University in California has "awarded" hundreds of thousands of degrees, including the PhD, for "donations" of $10 and up (for many years, their PhD cost $100), and the state Supreme Court has decreed that this is all quite legal *as long as they award only religious degrees* (Doctor of Divinity, Doctor of Theology, etc.).

There are two problems with this reasonable-sounding rule.

One problem is that people don't wear badges saying what their degree is *in*. When a high-school dropout calling himself "Doctor" was busted in upstate New York for running an illegal sex therapy clinic, his *only* degree was a perfectly legal PhD in religious science from the Universal Life people.

A second and equally serious problem is that not every state says that religious schools can grant only religious degrees, as we believe they should. In other words, even though a school may operate entirely through a religious exemption, in some states it can award degrees in physics, psychology, political science, or anything it wishes. Not surprisingly, the church-operated schools that do this sort of thing are not exactly associated with mainstream religions—Catholics, Lutherans, Jews, and so forth—but are typically a one-man (or one-woman) church founded by the school owner and existing primarily as another button on his or her telephone.

One such institution, Hamilton University, operated legally (under Wyoming's minimalist regulations) from a small building in Evanston, Wyoming. It is run by the not-exactly-mainstream Faith in the Order of Nature Fellowship Church. Hamilton made big news in the summer of 2003 when a reporter for *Government Computer News* discovered that a high-ranking executive in the Department of Homeland Security in Washington had "earned" her bachelor's, her master's, *and* her PhD in computer-related fields from Hamilton University.

The Hamilton doctorate, which can take as long as ten days to earn, requires nothing more than producing a four-page paper (on ethics, believe it or not), and, of course, the ability to sign a check or credit card voucher.

Laura Callahan's account of her involvement with Hamilton University appears as an essay in appendix I, the first time she has commented publicly on these matters.

It is clear from the findings of the Government Accountability Office degree audit, discussed on page 159, that a great many other federal employees have degrees from Hamilton and from dozens, perhaps hundreds, of unrecognized and often fake schools. Hamilton is just one drop in a very large bucket.

All degrees are religious degrees because God created everything: How LaSalle University of Louisiana parlayed that argument into selling more than $35 million worth of degrees

For many years, Louisiana was one of the states that did not regulate religious schools as long as they granted *only* religious degrees. The state's assumption was that this would allow church-run schools to train their own clergy in a setting where academic quality was less important than doctrinal soundness.

Along came LaSalle University, prepared to drive its eighteen-wheeler through the loophole in that law. (We refer, of course, *not* to the legitimate LaSalle in Philadelphia but to the operation that had been "invited" to leave California, then Arizona, Florida, and Missouri and finally headed south to the then-friendly bayous of Louisiana.)

As the official university of the Trinitarian Church, later the World Christian Church, a religious entity existing only in the mind of owner James Kirk (also known as Thomas Kirk and Thomas McPherson), LaSalle was exempt from state licensing, as long as it gave only religious degrees.

So it did.

With a straight face, presumably, it declared that because God created everything, *all* degrees had to be religious degrees. God created the
elements, so chemistry degrees were religious. God created the mind, so
psychology degrees were religious. God created numbers, so math
degrees were religious. And so on.

Could anyone in his or her right (God-created) mind take this seriously? For starters, the Supreme Court of the State of Louisiana did. It
twice sustained this argument, deciding against state challenges to the
LaSalle approach.

Fortunately, the feds didn't agree. Following a surprise visit to the
campus with search warrants in hand, agents of the FBI and the IRS and
the postal inspectors found evidence of fifteen thousand students, a grand
total of one faculty member (who had only LaSalle degrees), and more
than $35 million in bank deposits made over the previous four years.

Following an eighteen-count grand jury indictment for mail fraud,
wire (telephone) fraud, tax evasion, and money laundering, LaSalle
owner Kirk/McPherson pleaded guilty and was sentenced to the maximum possible term in federal prison camp—five years—by an angry
judge who said he wished it could have been longer.

As mentioned earlier, within days of Kirk/McPherson's arrival at the
federal prison camp in Beaumont, Texas, advertisements began appearing in *USA Today* and other national publications for Edison University.
Edison's literature was almost identical to that of LaSalle. Indeed, in the
promotional video telling us what a fine place Edison is, one can see,
on a shelf in the background, a framed photo of Kirk's children.

While the "campus" of Edison University was in fact a mail-
forwarding service in Honolulu, Hawaii, the catalogues bore the postmark
"Beaumont, Texas." And the director of admissions and registrar of Edison
University, Natalie Handy, had become Kirk/McPherson's wife while he
was in prison. We've heard of many instances of "university without
walls." This would clearly seem to be a case of "university *behind* walls."

Edison University was promptly accredited by an unrecognized, but
still thriving, agency called the World Association of Universities and
Colleges. Then, when the real Edison in New Jersey got an injunction,
the name was changed to Addison and finally to Acton University.

Kirk/McPherson served his time and became a free man a few years
ago. Can you guess what he's doing now? If you answered, "Affiliated
with a new university in Louisiana," you win an honorary doctorate in
the field of your choice.

2. The Four-Inch-Square Campus

In the course of our three decades of checking out new and suspicious schools, there have been numerous occasions in which one of us arrives at the campus address to discover a mailbox rental store, a secretarial service, or one of those office-services companies that rents cubicles and conference rooms by the hour.

More often than not, this official address of the university is in a state that either has weak licensing laws or doesn't seem to care what people do as long as they aren't defrauding the citizens of *that* state. So the crack they have fallen through is this: state A, where such schools would be illegal, says, "We don't care because they're really run from state B—just look at their mailing address." And state B says, "We don't care because all they have here is a rented mailbox; they are really run from state A; it's *their* problem."

Once in a while, a state will impose some minimal requirements on a school it knows is really operated from its own state, even though the "campus" (i.e., the mailing address) is in another state or even another country. Often, the only requirement is that the school cannot accept students who live in the state from which it is *really* run.

Thus, the attorney general of California is currently saying to a sizeable institution run from California but whose campus (according to a reporter for the *Chronicle of Higher Education*, who made a surprise visit in 2001) comprised, at that time, two clerks working in a basement office in another state, "I don't care what you do with people in the other forty-nine states or in other nations, but you can't do it with people who live in California."

Authorities in Idaho and Alabama have, at times, also ordered several dreadful universities not to enroll people who live in the same state as the school.

It goes without saying (but some people need it said anyway) that when a school tells a potential student, "Sorry, we cannot accept applicants living in your state," there is quite a large red flag waving, even for students who live in another state or country.

Of course, most schools in this situation don't advertise the fact of their geographical problem. They wait until a potential student supplies an address, and *then* the telemarketer (that is to say, the admissions counselor) makes the explanation. And even then, of course, the "counselor" doesn't say, "Sorry, even though we say our campus is in South

Dakota, our location there is actually a four-inch-square box, and we are run from Florida, but the attorney general in Florida has told us that if we accept one Florida student, we're off to prison." No, the telemarketer will, if pressed, provide an elaborate explanation of how the state laws are unfair or restrictive or don't allow innovative schools like theirs to operate or, in the case of an Idaho wonder, that it would "cost millions of dollars" to go through the state licensing process (not true), and so, reluctantly, the school has this policy.

A few states have attempted to be compassionate in writing laws that allow legitimate but low-budget start-up schools to operate from within their borders. They want to see something more than the four-inch-square mailbox "campus"—but not a whole lot more.

Hawaii, for instance, says that an unaccredited school can operate legally if it has at least one full-time employee in the state. But when a tabloid television program, *American Journal*, visited the official Hawaii address of a heavily advertised university that claims to have more than twenty-five thousand graduates, the program found a nearly empty room and a secretary at the law offices next door who apparently was the entire Hawaii employment force of this really-run-from-Los-Angeles university.

California used to have an innovative law that encouraged unaccredited schools to operate while ostensibly maintaining some level of consumer protection: a new university needed to own at least $50,000 worth of property in order to get a state license. While this may possibly have prevented some fly-by-night schools from opening in California, it also served to encourage the better-funded fakes whose operators would simply put their homes in the university name.

In the case of the notorious California Pacifica University—the school whose owner was caught by *60 Minutes*'s camera selling Mike Wallace a PhD for $3,000, no questions asked—owner Ernest Sinclair bought one hundred used high school textbooks and found a corrupt accountant who appraised them at $500 each, thus meeting the state's $50,000 law. When Sinclair went to prison, and for at least a year thereafter, this phony was listed in the official California directory of state-authorized schools.

California Pacifica at least had a two-room office with its name on the door. But some of the people with those four-inch-square mailbox campuses make it as hard as possible for a reporter, a law enforcement official, or a potential student to check them out.

First, they make it sound as if their tiny campus is a real one by using an address designed to deceive. If they rent mailbox forty-seven at their local UPS Store, they might refer to "suite 47" or "building 47" or even "47th floor" in their address.

They can also say anything they darn well please *before* the box number. When John Bear visited a "University Center" on "University Drive" in a rural Louisiana town, he found the institution in question in a double-wide mobile home at the end of a one-lane road, across from a fence with a hand-painted sign reading "Bad Dog."

One of our favorite examples of chutzpah is a degree mill run from a mailbox address whose impressively designed literature and Web site invite potential students to visit the registrar's office, "located on campus in the Office of Institutional Advancement, at the top of the stairs to the right of the Chapel." Presumably one of those extra-large two-story mailboxes.

Another thing some institutions do to obfuscate the lack-of-real-campus situation is to rent their mailbox in a place so remote that they hope that no student, reporter, or sheriff will ever make the effort to visit. A major Canadian start-up, for instance, although apparently run from Toronto, established its mailbox campus in Whitehorse, in the Yukon Territory, which is a mere four-day drive from Yellowknife.

Those accommodating Canadians offer another interesting option for using smoke and mirrors in the matter of a school's actual location. When the owner of the fake Kansas-based Monticello University attempted to escape the authorities who were after him in Kansas and South Dakota, he moved his university to Canada, where he provided what looked like a real street address. But it turns out that in Canada, if you have a post office box, you can use the street address of the *post office* as part of the address, so that "123 Maple Street, Suite 63" is actually box sixty-three in the post office located at 123 Maple.

3. Schools that are undeniably legal—legal, that is, in some place you may never have heard of

The Islands That Aren't Quite Countries

There are a number of islands on our planet—most of them in the South Pacific or the Caribbean—that aren't exactly countries, but they behave like one in some ways, and they seem quite happy to have universities set up on their land or their Internet domain. Consider, for instance, Niue, a tiny dot in the South Pacific we'll bet you've never heard of. This "self-governing parliamentary democracy" of fewer than two thousand people has its own Internet abbreviation—.ni—and is the legal home to at least five less-than-wonderful universities: a ratio of one university for every three hundred inhabitants![2]

Norfolk Island, Puerto Rico, the British and the US Virgin Islands, Turks and Caicos, Barbuda, Sark, and the Isle of Jersey are also not-quite-countries that are or have been home to unaccredited universities.

The champion is Ascension Island in the South Atlantic, whose .ac Internet abbreviation is much in demand, since it is easily confused with the British .ac designation used by academic schools. Several dozen "universities" call this rock outcropping with no indigenous population their home.

Indian Reservations

The argument goes like this: If an Indian nation can run gambling casinos without any interference from the state in which it is located, then why can't they accredit and run their own university without fretting about annoying little things like state approval, much less accreditation?

A California unaccredited university in trouble with the state gave it the old college try by claiming full accreditation from a small Nevada-based Indian tribe. The university did not operate from Nevada, but the tribal council produced an official "letter of accreditation." By the time the laughter in the academic world had died down, that institution had moved: first to Montana, and then to oblivion.

The Special Cases of Liberia, Malawi, and St. Kitts

There are currently at least three countries that have been granting their accreditation to various United States–based institutions that, in some cases, have little or no presence in those countries. This practice has proven troublesome to some gatekeepers and decision makers, who are uncertain how to deal with degrees from such schools.

These troubled decision makers include the publishers of the *International Handbook of Universities* (a UNESCO-related publication), college registrars, human resource professionals, and indeed the authors of this book. For years, such people have said that if the highest education authority in a sovereign nation approves a school, there must be *some-*

thing there. But recent developments have caused significant dilemmas in this regard.

Liberia

In 2003, a representative of the government of Liberia, widely regarded at the time as a corrupt, unstable, and nearly bankrupt country, wrote to a number of unaccredited and less-than-wonderful universities offering them the full accreditation of the Liberian Ministry of Education in exchange for a payment of $1,000, later raised to $10,000, and then $50,000 down and $20,000 a year. In short order, more than a dozen institutions, most of them run from the United States but claiming campuses in various other countries, were proudly showing off their certificate of accreditation, apparently signed by the Minister of Educa-

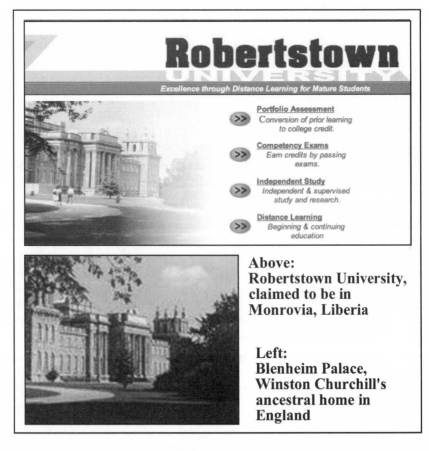

**Above:
Robertstown University,
claimed to be in
Monrovia, Liberia**

**Left:
Blenheim Palace,
Winston Churchill's
ancestral home in
England**

tion of a country that is undeniably a full-fledged member of the United Nations.

This situation caused much consternation at the United Nations office in Geneva, which publishes the huge, expensive, and generally reliable reference book called the *International Handbook of Universities.*

UNESCO's mandate is to accept whatever the highest education officer of a member nation says and does. They are not in the business of evaluating the accrediting or licensing procedures of individual countries and saying to some, "You don't meet certain standards, so you can't be in the book." *Everyone* goes in.

Presumably, no one at UNESCO anticipated that there would ever arise a situation in which a UN member would be openly selling its accreditation, willy nilly, to any school willing to write a check. Being responsible professional educators, how can they possibly put schools into the *International Handbook* that offer ten-day PhDs, sell honorary degrees of all kinds, and appoint anyone as a professor on payment of a fee?

They know what that will mean to the reputation of their book and its usefulness as a reference source in the worlds of education, business, and government. On the other hand, how can they be put in the position of having to say that one UN member is not being treated the same as other UN members?

This particular dilemma seems to have turned out well when it became known that the Liberian National Board of Education had been established by the proprietor of one less-than-wonderful university, and, subsequently, signed by the daughter of the proprietor of some other dubious schools, using a mailbox service in Washington. After this information was revealed on education news groups, and in several in-depth stories in major daily newspapers, the National Board of Education began fading away from the Web sites of schools that had previously featured it.

Indeed, the same perpetrators created what looked like the official Liberian embassy Web site, which assured people of the legitimacy of the school. But when the turmoil subsided in that country, the *real* Liberian embassy in Washington put a notice on the *real* Liberian Web site, making clear that the "other" Liberian embassy site was a hoax, and the real Liberians did not recognize the school.

After this, the editor of the *International Handbook of Universities* wrote that neither St. Regis nor any of the other schools who purchased Liberian accreditation would be included in the next edition of that book.

The Liberian situation remained volatile until October 2004, when the new regime officially renounced it as a fake.[3] It was not a good year for many St. Regis University alumni. On July 8, 2004, the *Atlanta Journal-Constitution* reported that

> The state Professional Standards Commission voted Thursday to revoke the licenses of 11 Georgia educators who bought online degrees from [St. Regis University] a diploma mill in Liberia. The commission voted 11 to 1 to exact its most severe punishment for violating the Code of Ethics for Educators, which amounts to banishment from working in Georgia public schools. The licensing board also passed a rule Thursday that will make it more difficult for educators to get pay raises using bogus foreign credentials, by reducing to four the number of foreign credential verification agencies the state uses for advanced degrees.

In June, WTHR-TV in Indianapolis, Indiana, reported that more than ninety workers at Daimler-Chrysler were facing trouble because of their purchase of St. Regis degrees. The June 2 story said that St. Regis

> offers a degree earned and approved within 30 minutes online. Payment and delivery take just a three-day turnaround, with credentials based on classes never taken, complete with letter grades that give honor society status.
>
> St. Regis calls it a degree by prior learning assessment.
>
> Experts from the Indiana Commissioner on Higher Education call it troubling. . . . [A]fter an Eyewitness News investigation into St. Regis last month, Chrysler said, no more, and St. Regis is feeling the heat.

Malawi

Malawi is a mostly agricultural nation of about 10 million people in southern Africa. Because the country has only two universities and one college, all government-run, there has been no need for a system of higher education accreditation. But in 1999, inexplicably, an unaccredited institution then operating from a small office in Missoula, Montana—which also had a Wyoming license to operate, and a California-based chancellor—declared that it was fully accredited by the Republic of Malawi. Why a small, poor African nation accredits only one university in the world, and one that is not in Malawi but in Montana/Wyoming, has never been clearly explained.

Once again, the question arises: how are the decision makers and gatekeepers, from UNESCO to the authors of this book, to know how to deal with this situation?

St. Kitts and Nevis

The nation of St. Kitts and Nevis consists of two small islands in the Caribbean, with a combined area a bit larger than Washington, DC. An American-owned university that at the time was run from a small office in rural New Hampshire, although not licensed by that state, began holding an optional four-week summer session at a beachfront resort on St. Kitts and proclaimed that the university was now fully accredited by the Ministry of Foreign Affairs and Education.[4]

At the time, and for years after, the ministry was either unwilling or unable to reveal what its rules, standards, or procedures for accreditation might be. On one occasion, when a reporter for the Portsmouth, New Hampshire, *Record* inquired, he was told, "We have just as many votes in the United Nations as you do. What's your problem?"

One problem was that soon after this, St. Kitts also granted full accreditation to something called Eastern Caribbean University, an institution that issued doctorates based entirely on study of a few James Bond films and was run from the home of its owner, a teacher in Smithville, Texas.

A few years later, in 1999, St. Kitts passed a law formalizing the accreditation process and describing a reasonable set of criteria for granting accreditation. As a result, Eastern Caribbean University is no longer accredited, but four others, including the university with the small New Hampshire office and at least two medical schools, are.

As a result of these matters, we would not call a school with post-1999 St. Kittsian accreditation a degree mill, although other writers on popular education Web sites continue to do so.

4. The Matter of Having Hundreds of Sets of Laws

Each state and each country has its own body of laws, and they often conflict with those of other states or countries. A man having four wives? OK in Saudi Arabia but illegal in Connecticut. Driving eighty miles an hour on the interstate? OK in Nevada but illegal in Minnesota. Owning an assault rifle? OK in the United States but illegal in Canada.

It is when people from one place end up in another place that problems may occur and lawyers start earning their fees. This is as true in the area of degrees as it is in bigamy, speeding, or gun ownership, a fact that clouds the issue of which schools can properly be called degree mills.

Consider a person who earns a degree from an unaccredited but entirely legitimate distance-learning school that is officially approved by the state of California. Many people in California and worldwide have and use that degree. The law degrees of this university enable graduates to sit for the state bar exams, and the psychology degrees may qualify students to take state licensing exams. So of course we would never consider calling such a degree mill.

And yet if an alumnus of this university takes up residence in Oregon, New Jersey, North Dakota, Nevada, or Illinois and uses that degree, then he or she technically becomes a criminal. Use of a California-approved but unaccredited degree (as well as most other unaccredited degrees) in those states is a criminal offense, punishable by a stiff fine and up to six months in prison. So while Oregon puts hundreds of such schools on its official state site at http://www.osac .state.or.us/ oda/diploma_mill.html, some of those illegal-in-Oregon schools would be legal elsewhere. We find it inappropriate to call such schools "degree mills"—but others do so.

There is, in effect, a continuum of strictness of school laws, from places like Liberia, Wyoming, and Alabama, where just about anything goes, to places like Oregon, New York, and Canada, where things are very strict indeed.

5. Who makes the decision as to whether a school is good or bad, legal or illegal, degree mill or not?

The question of whether any given school is a "good" school is one that has been debated for many years. We are *not* referring to the classic debates that rage in clubs, locker rooms, and the pages of *U.S. News* as to whether Harvard is better than Yale, Cal is better than Stanford, or Michigan is better than Michigan State. Those debates are mostly over reputation. No one challenges the legality, legitimacy, and value of such schools and their degrees.

When the issue at hand is whether to call a school a degree mill, things get more complicated. We provide our definition of "degree mill" in the introduction, but it has a lot of flexibility, a lot of "wiggle

room" in it. And we discuss the methods that bad or fake schools use
to fool or mislead the public later in this chapter.

Whenever anyone publishes a list *called* "Degree Mills," as the US
government did in 1959 and many others have since, there are always
people who disagree with those lists in *both* directions: believing that it
includes schools that it shouldn't have or that it *doesn't* include schools
that it should have. It is up to each reader to decide whether any given
school meets his or her definition of *degree mill* or *innovative educational
provider* or anything in between.

THE KINDS OF SCHOOLS THAT
SOME PEOPLE CALL DEGREE MILLS

They run the gamut from modest "mom and pop" (or just "mom" or just
"pop") operations run from the family home to huge international cartels.

The DipScam case histories presented in chapter 1 gave a taste of
the kinds of people and schools that were in operation at that time. The
main changes since are that many of the entities have grown bigger
(dozens of, even a hundred or more, employees) and are using advanced technology, aggressive marketing (on the Internet as well as the
"old-fashioned" ways), and their sales are in the many millions of dollars each year.

The People Who Run the Schools

We're talking about a very small number of people here, in the general
scheme of things. All the people who have run unrecognized schools of
any kind in the past half century wouldn't even fill a single lecture hall
on a university campus, so it is hard, perhaps impossible, to generalize.

Many people who run schools that we believe are bad or fake are
"loners," working by themselves, or with some hired hands to stuff
envelopes, enter data, or take messages.

Some are friendly, likeable, affable, even charming. Others are hostile, angry, and abrasive. Some are so secretive that literally nothing is
known about them. Others are genial, even jolly. Ernest Sinclair lit up
like a Christmas tree when *60 Minutes*'s Mike Wallace walked through
his door at California Pacifica with the cameras rolling. Ronald Pellar
(Columbia State University), while officially a federal fugitive, wel-

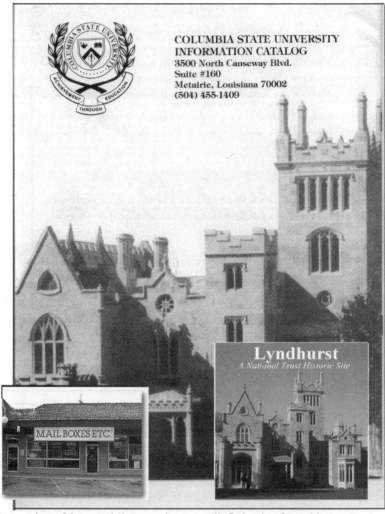

COLUMBIA STATE UNIVERSITY
INFORMATION CATALOG
3500 North Causeway Blvd.
Suite #160
Metairie, Louisiana 70002
(504) 455-1409

Lyndhurst
A National Trust Historic Site

MAIL BOXES ETC.

The catalog of America's biggest degree mill, Columbia State University.
Right inset: the mansion in Tarrytown, NY, that bears a striking resemblance
to the university. Left inset: the actual "campus" of the university.

comed ABC's *20/20*, after the show found him living on his yacht in
Mexico and gave quite a charming interview.

Some are career criminals who add selling fake degrees to a resume
already filled with other scams and even violent crimes.

There is an interesting subset of academics gone bad: people with
earned doctorates from properly accredited schools who end up running

their own dubious or fake institutions. There are even a few cases where they played both sides of the street simultaneously. When authorities finally discovered who was running the fake Pacific Northwestern University, it turned out to be an officer of a traditional university in Seattle. And it was the Rector of a traditional Peruvian university who set up a fake school with the same name to offer PhDs to Americans.

And some are simply opportunists who seem to see selling degrees, or counterfeit diplomas, as just another way to earn a living by supplying something that people want and are willing to pay for.

Most mill operators practice what might be called a "hands-on" management style. They simply don't trust other people to run their business. There have been, however, more than a few family-run operations, involving either a husband and wife or extended family members.

There are many more men than women who start and run degree mills, but there have been a handful of women-run ones. Many of the operators are middle-aged, but there have been some quite young ones (the founder of the dreadful Ratchford University was in his twenties) and some well into their dotage. Ronald Pellar of Columbia State University was in his seventies when he was indicted for that fraud, and "Bishop" Lyon of Thomas Edison University (and others) was past eighty at the time of his last arrest.

In North America and Europe, most of the people who start degree mills are Caucasians, but at least three have been run by African-Americans and a few by Chinese-Americans. Most of the many degree mills in Africa, India, and Asia are run by people from the region in which they operate.

From Where the Mills Are Run

There is a very wide range of kinds of "campuses." Some ambitious fakes have actually purchased buildings, sometimes former school buildings. Southwestern University had a very large building in Tucson, even if only two or three people worked there. At the time that LaSalle's founder was indicted, the "university" had four large and attractive buildings in a New Orleans suburb.

At the other end of the location scale, the Internet has made it possible for a degree mill literally not to exist in any physical space other than the mind of its owner. With a Web site and an electronic banking arrangement using credit cards, online payment services such as PayPal, or Western Union, there does not need to be an office or even a tele-phone. Many are somewhere in between: typically a few rented rooms or even a small house. When John Bear visited a multischool operation in New Orleans, he found a tiny house, with one university in one bed-room, a second university in the other bedroom, and four or five others on the dining table in between.

It is also common for mills (as well as some legitimate schools) to operate from so-called executive suite facilities, which can function just as mail, phone, and Internet handlers or can rent little cubicles by the month or conference rooms by the hour.

How They Get Their Customers

Selling degrees is a business with many things in common with tradi-tional, legitimate businesses. You have a product to sell. You have to figure out who your potential customers are. You need to make them aware of your product. You need an infrastructure in place, so they can reach you and place an order. You may need salespeople to encourage them to buy. You need a fulfillment function, to get them what they ordered, and possibly a follow-up "customer service" function to assure that they are happy with what they bought.

While the Internet is clearly the tool of choice, the tens of millions of people who are *not* online, or have limited use, are not being neg-lected by the degree sellers. We'll look first at the "old-fashioned" methods, then the electronic ones. Any given degree mill may use a combination of approaches.

The "Old-Fashioned" Methods

Print Advertising

The "old-fashioned" methods are still selling degrees. The surest sign that advertising works is if it is regularly repeated. Although fewer than in pre-Internet days, the number of ads for unaccredited schools appearing in major consumer, military, and business publications is holding strong. A little classified ad in *USA Today* costs about $200 a day. A one-third-page color ad in a major airline magazine (which some of these guys have used) costs about $10,000. You can work out how much business they need to do to keep those ads running.

Of course, not every advertisement comes from the "bad guys." On many occasions, we've seen a Harvard ad and a degree mill ad side by side in *The Economist* and other well-regarded publications.

Direct mail

Before spam, there was "junk mail": unsolicited letters and brochures, sometimes sent to "Occupant" and sometimes meticulously personalized, as "Dear Mr. Ezell." Names can be acquired from list rental companies for about ten cents each, and they can be carefully selected by age, sex, income, religion, occupation, education, and so on. If you want names of men in their thirties with no bachelor's degree and living in middle-class neighborhoods, there are hundreds of thousands available. Even if most letters are thrown away unopened, the institution only need to make one sale per thousand letters to show a profit.

One degree salesman told us his most productive mailing lists are people called "self-improvers"—people who have already bought weight-loss gimmicks, get-rich schemes, and find-inner-peace programs, and now they might like to have a degree or two. Mailing packets of advertising postcards, with one advertiser on each card, is another form of direct mail used by these people.

Telemarketing

"Inbound" telemarketing (they call you) is little used in the era of the national "don't call" list, but it has been effective in the past. One operator of unaccredited schools reported that a skilled salesperson working on commission and making "cold" (unsolicited) calls to people in carefully chosen neighborhoods can make two or three sales a day, more than enough to make the practice pay. "Outbound" telemarketing, where skilled telephone salespeople call those who have returned coupons or left messages on machines, is very popular and very successful. An "insider" at one large degree mill told us that one-third of people who are called back after leaving a message end up buying a degree.

Bogus referral services and misleading reference books

Elsewhere we have described the seemingly impartial degree referral services that only refer clients to one fake school (their own) and the mostly reliable school guides that nonetheless include some less-than-wonderful schools.

Resales to old customers and alumni referrals

There's an advertising adage that "your best new customer is an old customer." Some mills routinely mine the names of their alumni, offering special deals on higher or different degrees. In the same vein, alumni are invited to tell their friends and associates about the degree opportunities available and are sometimes offered a referral fee or commission or even another degree for themselves for so doing.

Miscellaneous methods

Signs on buses, trains, and train stations; radio spots; flyers put under windshields at malls; billboards—they've all been tried, although not often. The one thing we haven't seen is a television "infomercial" for a degree mill, but somehow it seems inevitable.

The Internet and Electronic Methods

Unsolicited e-mail

Some of the biggest schools, real and fake, send "spam" in huge quantities, even millions a day. Anyone can hire a spam-sending service, typically in central Europe, Asia, or other less-regulated places. The cost can be as low as $100 per million messages sent. At that rate, even if there is only one customer for each five million spams, the business is profitable. The actual rate of success is probably a good deal higher: perhaps one customer for every ten thousand spams. The spams are not designed to sell but only to encourage the recipient either to go to a Web site or to make a telephone call to ask for more information, and then the skillful telemarketing comes into play.

Banners and pop-ups

Anyone who uses the Internet is well aware of the "banners" that regularly appear at the margins of the page you really wanted to look at, and pop-ups, the entire screens full of something other than what you wanted, which you have to close manually or choose to ignore. (Ignoring is difficult when they are flashing or otherwise annoyingly competing for your attention.) Real and fake schools are major users of these banners and pop-ups, paying to have them appear either randomly or on pages related to education and degrees. The companies that sell and place banners pay little or no attention to the content. One of the most inappropriate events imaginable happened in 2003, when *USA Today* ran quite a good article on the menace of degree mills. And when one read that article online, there were two large degree-mill advertisements flashing away on the same page.

Search engine advertising

Much the same thing as banners and pop-ups, the major Internet search engines routinely sell advertising that will appear on the same page as your search results. The more ethical ones, like Google, at least clearly identify the paid advertising as such. But even if you search for Harvard, Yale, or Oxford, you may well see bad or fake schools advertising on the same search screen.

Search engine placement

While advertising at least usually *looks* like advertising, many people seem not to realize that advertisers can pay the search engine companies to appear near the top of the list, just as publishers pay bookstores to put their books in more prominent locations. When we searched in Google for "MBA by distance learning," we found 646,000 sites. Obviously, no one is going to look at even a small fraction of those, so there is a great advantage to being in the top ten. As it happened, in our Google search, the top ten included six properly accredited schools and four others: two gray-area ones and two degree mills, all of them probably paying for that preferred location.

What Is Required to Get a Degree-Mill Degree?

The majority of degree mills require no work whatsoever, although they often *talk* about certain requirements, which can then be waived for a given student because of his or her excellent life experiences. Each of these customers may well believe that nearly everyone else is required to do work, but they are not.

A few mills have very minimal requirements, perhaps so the customers will feel they have done *something* to earn the degree. A common method is to require a book report. Some mills send customers a book in (or related to) their field, telling them to read it and write a ten-page book review, which no one ever reads.

Since many mills use the artifice of basing the degree on career experience, they will ask for a resume or for customers to fill out a form telling about their life. No matter what they say, whether fifty words or five thousand, they will be complimented on their excellent achievements and told they have qualified for the degree they wish. Some mills add a bit of apparent authenticity to this process by asking a question about the resume: "How many years did you work at [such-and-such a place]?" or "What were your duties?"

Testing

There are legitimate accredited universities where a bachelor's degree can be earned entirely by taking examinations. The University of London, for instance, requires thirty to forty, or more, hours of exams. Some mills say they have adopted this well-accepted procedure and give exams of their own. A University of Illinois professor, intrigued with this process, reported on the news forum at www.degreeinfo.com (August 19, 2003) that he had taken the online multiple-choice degree exams of several schools claiming Liberian accreditation. It turned out that a score of twenty-six out of one hundred on the absurdly easy test, which required about ten minutes, was enough to be offered the degree. He cheerfully pointed out that a pigeon, pecking randomly at such a test, would have achieved a similar score and "earned" the degree.

Pay

The only certain requirement to get a degree-mill diploma is that payment must be made, although there have been some schools, such as the Clayton Institute in California and another in the state of Washington, that would award the degree for free, but then you would have to pay to get the diploma and transcript.

From the sophisticated telemarketing script used by the University Degree Program in Romania (see appendix B), it is clear that prices are highly negotiable. If the salesperson senses hesitation, the price is likely to come down. The Romanian degrees have had a $3,000 price, which is reduced in various ways, including, ultimately, the offer to allow four payments of $600 each, with the diploma and transcript sent after the first payment, knowing full well that no one will make the later payments.

NINETY-TWO DECEPTIVE TACTICS

Degree mills have come up with an extraordinary number of ways in which they attempt to fool the public, ranging from the absurdly simple (choosing a name that can be confused with that of a legitimate university) to the fiendishly complex (claiming accreditation from another country and then setting up a large and elaborate counterfeit Web site pretending to come from that country).

In attempting to decide if a given school is a degree mill, some of these tactics are of the "all or nothing" sort. When a school offers to backdate the diploma to the year of your choice, there is no gray area, no "in between" possibilities: that school is unequivocally a fake. But many of the tactics are on a continuum from "definitely fake" to "probably OK" and even includes things used by legitimate and well-known schools, some of which are extremely aggressive in their advertising and marketing.

For instance, when a school claims its accreditation from an agency that is not recognized by the authorities in Washington, it could be a sincere and reasonable accreditor that has not yet been recognized, a nonexistent accreditor that is just another button on their telephone, or something in between.

No one entity will use all of these tactics, of course, but it is not uncommon for dozens, even scores, of red flags to be waving from the same flagpole.

The annotated list that follows is as complete as we could make it. Yet hardly a week passes in which some new tactic or a variation on an old one appears—a reminder to be thorough, to be careful, and if there is some possible evidence of chicanery, to delve deeper until the truth is known. At the end of this section, we offer a checklist of the ninety-two items in condensed form, which can be copied and used to help evaluate schools.

Accreditation Claims

1. *Accreditation is claimed from a fake or unrecognized agency.* In the United States, accreditation is useful only if the accrediting agency is recognized by the US Department of Education (www.ed.gov) and/or the Council on Higher Education Accreditation (www.chea.org). Unfortunately, many popular press articles on choosing schools mention the importance of accreditation but fail to point out that there is such a thing as fake or worthless accreditation. That we have identified more than two hundred unrecognized accreditors suggests that this may be the most popular way in which degree mills pretend to be legitimate.

2. *The fake or unrecognized accreditor also accredits legitimate schools.* A common tactic is for such accreditors to claim to accredit traditional universities such as Harvard and Stanford, so that their list of members might include many well-known schools, thus camouflaging the appearance of one or more degree mills on the list.

3. *The accreditor offers a confirming telephone service or "hot line" to assure people that a given school is accredited.* Some people presumably are reassured if they can reach the accrediting agency by telephone and are told that yes, such-and-such a school is indeed accredited. Some fake accreditors take messages and return calls; others have an outgoing message that says, for instance, in the case of one large mill, "We are proud to accredit such fine schools as Notre Dame, Yale, and Columbia State University."

4. *The school claims that, as a global or international university, it doesn't require accreditation and/or government approval from any single government agency.* Every legitimate school has some form of recognized accreditation and/or government approval from the country, state, or region in which it operates.

5. *The school explains at length why accreditation is not important or is relevant only for student loans.* Some mills correctly state that they are not accredited, and then go on to explain, sometimes for two or three pages, why accreditation isn't all that important anyway, unless a student wishes to apply for a federal student loan.

6. *The school claims that Harvard and Oxford aren't accredited either.* Harvard is indeed properly accredited. Oxford was founded in the eleventh century under a Papal Bull, predating introduction of the royal charter. Nonetheless, each constituent college of Oxford has its own royal charter, the British equivalent of accreditation.

7. *Accreditation is correctly claimed but from a place where the word is used in quite different ways.* One example is Australia, where the word "accreditation" refers to a self-study process schools may go through, which has nothing to do with approval from an outside agency. When a school based in Australia, or one of its territories or protectorates, says, "We are accredited," it means only that they regard *themselves* as worthy. Outside recognition there comes from the Australian Qualifications Framework.

Another example comes from Great Britain, where one university, or department within a university, can accredit another university, even in another country. All this means that the university will accept the credits or degrees of the second school. But because the word *accredited* is used, there have been situations in which, for instance, a US institution claimed British accreditation after one department in one British university agreed to accept the American institution's credits.

8. *The school claims that accreditation is impossible because of the separation of church and state.* Some religious or church-owned "schools," especially those that also award nonreligious degrees, maintain that accreditation is impossible for them because religious schools can't qualify for accreditation. This is nonsense. Not only are there four properly recognized religious school accreditors, but also the regional accrediting agencies routinely deal with church-owned or operated institutions, ranging from Notre Dame to Southern Methodist to Yeshiva University.

9. *The school lists approval or accreditation from a fake or unrecognized country.* From time to time, people or groups establish what they claim is a new sovereign nation, whether for political, social, or nefarious purposes. When they do, one of the first things that often happens is the establishment of a university, either run by or recognized by said "country." Recent examples include:

- The Dominion of Melchizidek, located either in central Europe or an out-island of Fiji or both, established, according to an article in *The Economist*, primarily to sell bank charters that the magazine called "worthless" but also to operate its own "university," Dominion University, and to give its blessing to others, such as a "Russian" university run from California.
- International University of Advanced Studies, established by the privately run nation of New Utopia, ostensibly located on a

seamount beneath the waters off Honduras but actually run from a dryer location in Texas.

- Sealand, a World War Two installation in the North Sea off Britain, occupied and claimed by "squatters" decades ago, whence come postage stamps, passports, and the degrees of the University of Sealand.

Other not-exactly-real countries with universities include the Republic of Anodyne (Anodyne International University) and the Washitaw Nation (City University Los Angeles).

10. *Dubious accreditation is claimed from a real country or national agency.* In 2003, impressive-looking Web sites appeared, claiming that they were official sites put up by Liberian and Russian authorities. These sites confirmed and described the accreditation of various universities. It subsequently turned out that the sites of the Liberian National Board of Education, the Liberian Embassy, and the Russian Academy of Sciences were not the real sites but had been established by people associated with the various unrecognized schools.

11. *The school claims accreditation and the right to confer degrees due to wording in the school's articles of incorporation.* A common tactic is for a school to incorporate as a business in a place where one can say anything one wants in a corporate charter, which turns out to be almost anywhere. Thus the school bestows upon itself both accreditation and the "right" to award degrees. And then it advertises that it is "chartered" to grant degrees. Sometimes it adds the name of the country of incorporation for added credibility: "We are chartered by the Republic of Ireland as an accredited university with the power to grant degrees."

Other False or Misleading Claims

12. *The institution is certified by disreputable or incompetent credential checking services.* There are several dozen legitimate and reputable credential evaluation services where people can learn about the validity and equivalency of credits and degrees from both non-US and US schools. These services, described on page 179, are nongovernmental and unregulated, and there are some bad apples in the basket. Whether run by the fake schools, or just cooperating with them, they will confirm the legitimacy of the dreadful schools.

13. *The school misuses the concept of state licensing.* There are a few US

states that will license just about any school that applies, with no evaluation involved. In one of these, Alabama, this "rubber stamp" licensing process even permits schools to use the term *state approved*. The bad guys milk this for all it's worth. At the very least, they make statements of the form, "We have met all legal requirements set for private universities by the state." And in Alabama, even if they operate from a mailbox service and are really located in another state, they can trumpet their "state approval."

14. *The institution points to inclusion on an impressive-looking compiled list of universities.* There is a gag item one finds in gift catalogs: a poster titled "The World's Ten Best Golfers." The well-printed list includes the names of nine famous golfers and, usually at number six, the name of the person buying this item or his designee. The bad or fake schools will create such a list of the "best universities," either in print or on what looks like an impartial Internet site, always with an impressive title at the top (example: "The International Association for Quality Education," for instance), with their own name appearing, probably at number six, between Princeton and Stanford.

15. *The "school" lies or misstates its age.* Since longevity is felt to be reassuring to customers, some phonies just out-and-out lie. Created in 2004, they will fabricate a story of offering quality education since 1927. Others, more creatively, build on a shred of truth. One, in a southern California building that was on a Spanish land grant, said "Since 1843." Another that rented an old church for its graduation invited people to "come join us, where people have gathered since 1829."

16. *An institution writes about an earlier use of its building as if it were its own.* An Australian-owned university rented a building that had once been used by Oxford University. In what may well be the most creatively misleading such statement ever made, the university wrote: "It is here on [our] terraced lawns that some of this century's great innovators have conceived great thoughts. Mahatma Gandhi, Bertrand Russell, Albert Einstein, Madame Curie, Bernard Shaw, H. G. Wells, Gilbert Murray, and many others, have all walked the halls, and found a place of inspiration amongst [our] 13-acre woodland campus."

17. *The school confuses the city with the university.* Some well-known universities take the name of their city: Cambridge, Princeton, Chicago, and so forth. And so a school that rents a room or a building in that city may say, for instance, "Come to Oxford. Come to [our] college." When a US state attorney successfully sued this place, he had found students who genuinely believed they were enrolling in Oxford University.

18. *The school provides information about the legitimacy of awarding life/work experience credit then abuses that process.* Many unrecognized schools correctly explain that schools like Thomas Edison State College award credit and even degrees based entirely on experiential learning, and "just like Edison, we follow that process." But while Edison might give three semester units for a given experience, the bad guys will offer an MBA or even a PhD.

19. *The institution claims that its critics (individuals, Web sites, and authors of books) are out to get it because they are run by fired employees or by people who secretly own fake schools and are afraid of the competition.* John Bear is regularly accused, in print and on Internet news groups, of being a disgruntled former employee of criticized schools or the secret owner of "dozens" of degree mills. The man who founded a Web site that exposes degree mills (www.degreeinfo.com) has been accused of being a wanted criminal. In an extreme manifestation of this phenomenon, the owner of a fake California school sent hundreds of telegrams to the media claiming that his fine university was called a degree mill in *Bears' Guide* because he had rejected the author's homosexual advances.[5]

20. *The school pretends to be bigger than it is.* The catalog or Web site has long lists of staff. The only real person involved calls himself "vice chancellor" or "vice president," as if there were a chancellor or president. Dozens of e-mail addresses or phone extensions are given using different names but all going to the same place. Some low-budget or noncreative mills have the same distinctive voice at each of many extensions: "The dean is busy with students"; "The registrar is on another line."

False or Misleading Memberships and Affiliations

21. *Membership in real organizations—but ones that don't screen members.* It is common for mills to list memberships in a long list of legitimate and relevant-sounding organizations, suggesting there is some approval process here, when in fact the organizations have open membership. Even some recognized accrediting agencies have a membership option open to all.

22. *The school implies legitimacy through United Nations–related organizations.* There are many nongovernmental organizations (NGOs) that have a tenuous affiliation with the United Nations for educational, scientific, or humanitarian purposes. Some of these have open membership or do not screen members carefully, leading the mills to claim that they are "affiliated with" or even "approved by" the United Nations.

23. *The institution claims affiliations with real schools.* Degree mills love to be able to associate their names with that of legitimate schools. Sometimes they simply lie about being, for instance, a member of the (fictitious) Northeast University Alliance, along with Harvard, MIT, and Dartmouth. Sometimes they make a small donation to a legitimate school's scholarship or building fund, and, when they appear on a list of donors, they state that their institution "is featured prominently in the literature of Stanford University."

24. *The institution cites membership in nonexistent or bogus organizations.* Some degree mills put out long lists of organizations to which they claim to belong. While they always have impressive-sounding titles ("The International Alliance of Universities," "The World Society of Scholars"), in reality they rarely can be located.

25. *The school rents space from an organization, then implies an affiliation.* Many legitimate colleges rent out their buildings for special events. So a bad or fake school that rents space for a day may claim that its graduation ceremony has been held "in association with the University of London." One unrecognized accrediting agency once advertised an event "at the United Nations in New York," but it turned out they had simply rented a room at the unaffiliated United Nations Plaza Hotel.

26. *The school puts out a list of businesses and agencies that have accepted and paid for its degrees.* Some schools simply lie; it is not easy to confirm this information, even if a prospective student tried to. But others report the truth. When the fake LaSalle University in Louisiana published such a list, it turned out that many of the companies had confused it with the real LaSalle in Pennsylvania, while others were misled by the fake accreditation claim and did pay for employees' degrees. Some mills have offered their graduates a small cash bonus if they can get their degree or transcript accepted by a traditional school.

Fake or Meaningless Documents

27. *Use of Apostilles and notarized statements of all kinds.* As discussed on page 163, Apostilles are simply a form of federal notarization, and notaries validate only signatures, not the content of the document. Many mills claim that their Apostille shows that their school is approved by the government of the United States, which is simply untrue. Some go even further and charge their students as much as $700 for the Apostille statement, which costs less than 10 percent of that.

28. *Claims to have International Standards Organization 9002 certification.* A small number of schools, accredited and otherwise, promote their certification under the rules of the International Standards Organization (ISO). Even if the original ISO distance education standard hadn't been written by an unaccredited California school, it holds no weight in the world of higher education.

29. *Misstatement of nonprofit status.* Because of the belief that the public has more trust in a nonprofit organization, and because the Internal Revenue Service has not always been as careful in policing matters as one might wish, some degree mills and at least one major unrecognized accrediting agency have falsely claimed to be nonprofit section 501(c)3 entities.

30. *Misusing the certificate of incorporation.* Some mills show a small picture of their certificate of incorporation, complete with gold seal and ribbons, as they state that they are "Officially chartered by the State of California, as shown by this document signed by the governor."

31. *Misusing other kinds of certificates.* Almost every city council, board of supervisors, chamber of commerce, and even congressional office will issue a handsome certificate of honor or thanks, when asked, especially by a member, donor, or politically connected person. An entire wall of the little office of a dubious university in Los Angeles was covered with such documents. They were also shown in the literature as evidence of quality and acceptance.

32. *Misusing a "certificate of good standing" (CGS).* A part of many "graduation packages" from bad schools is an actual "CGS," which affirms only that a corporation or business may be in "good standing" in terms of a corporate charter or business license—but has nothing to do with the quality or legality or usefulness of the degrees awarded.

Misleading Recommendations and Links

33. *Better Business Bureau membership.* As discussed on page 181, some completely phony schools have joined the Better Business Bureau and benefited from promoting that affiliation. Many other unaccredited and less-than-wonderful schools have also been accepted as members.

34. *BBB imitations.* Schools that either cannot or choose not to join the BBB have created their own sound-alike entities, such as the American Business Bureau, which, in turn, gives them a glowing testimonial.

35. *Business organizations.* It is not uncommon for degree mills to

join otherwise respectable business organizations that often have few membership requirements other than holding a business license or a corporate charter. Thus, some mills trade on the good reputations of chambers of commerce, Rotary, Kiwanis, Civitan, and other such groups by mentioning their membership in their literature.

36. *Inclusion in "official" directories that list everyone.* Being included in the directory of the government's National Center for Educational Statistics sounds impressive, until one realizes that at one time this directory listed everything that called itself a college or university, regardless of legality. It was as much of an achievement as being listed in the telephone directory.

37. *Inclusion in the official Norwegian Higher Institution Registry.* In a classic example of how a well-intentioned plan can go wrong, the Norwegian Ministry of Education, in turn affiliated with the United Nations, posted an online directory of distance-learning schools worldwide. Those trusting Norwegians permitted any school not included to add itself to this Higher Education Institution Registry. Predictably, more than a few degree mills did this and promptly advertised their inclusion and, by association, their UN affiliation. We tested this in 2003 by adding to the list our own creation called Truly Awful University, located atop Devil's Tower, Wyoming—and promptly notified the Norwegian authorities of the problem. But at press time, Truly Awful University and the other truly awful universities were still on the list.

38. *Fake referral services.* Over the years, some degree-mill operators have discovered the scam of setting up an allegedly independent school referral service. But when well-meaning clients fill out the necessary forms, they are told that the only school on earth that precisely meets their needs is the degree mill run by the same people. First to use this method was Tony Geruntino, whose Vocational Guidance company in Columbus, Ohio, referred all clients to his fake Southwestern University in Arizona and several other schools where he had an interest. Others have included an allegedly impartial referral service in Kentucky linked only to a dubious school in Hawaii, and another such service in Chicago linked only to a dubious school in Wyoming.

An added problem is that some publications that have set up good defenses against accepting advertisements for bad *schools* have accepted ads for these spurious *services*, not realizing their true purpose.

39. *Bogus or self-interest reference books.* It seems most ambitious to publish an entire comprehensive-appearing school guide solely to pro-

mote one school, but this has happened at least four times. The owners of the degree mills called American International University, Columbia State University, and the University de la Romande each produced and sold or gave away their own guides to distance learning, 99 percent copied from John Bear's books, with 1 percent devoted to what they called "the best school in the United States," which was, of course, their own. A currently sold book comes from a man associated with two now-operating dreadful schools.

A variation on this theme is to produce a single page featuring one's own "school" and make it look as if it had been copied from a book. A variation on the variation is to take an unfavorable listing from a legitimate book and rewrite it to make it positive. This was done, for instance, by a widely promoted unaccredited university in southern California, which rewrote its listing in *Bears' Guide*, printed it to look like the real pages in that book, and distributed it to prospective students, stating that it had been copied from *Bears' Guide*.

40. *Offering legitimate certifications along with fake degrees.* There are companies such as Microsoft that license other schools or companies to offer training courses, available from third-party vendors leading to certification, for instance, as a Microsoft system engineer. Some bad schools have gained permission to run these certification courses and feature those in their advertising, to give legitimacy, by association, with their useless degrees.

41. *Testimonials.* Testimonials from happy customers are a tried-and-true marketing tool. Degree mills make frequent use of testimonials in four ways:

- from co-conspirators—comments from colleagues, partners, or people who knew they were buying a fake degree.
- from fooled people—customers who may not yet have realized that their degree is fake and may possibly even have benefited (albeit temporarily) from it. One mill offered huge cash prizes for the "best" testimonials submitted, undoubtedly inspiring buyers of the fake degrees to write fake stories. Fittingly, the offer of prizes *also* turned out to be fake.
- from nonexistent people—glowing endorsements from names plucked from thin air, accompanied by smiling faces cut from clip art collections.
- from real people, but they didn't really say that—statements

from well-known people who might never know what they were supposed to have said (one phony concentrated on Nobel laureates) or even from recently deceased celebrities.

42. *Posting positive comments on Internet newsgroups.* The operator of a mill, a colleague, or a graduate joins an Internet newsgroup or forum, sometimes lying low or making innocuous comments, but as soon as someone says he or she is looking for a certain kind of school, the so-called "shill" or "troll" awakens with a glowing recommendation of his degree mill.

Degree-mill operator Les Snell was a master of the "multiple personality" approach. Under one name, he would ask, "Hey, has anyone ever heard of Monticello University?" (One of his mills.) Under a second name, he would reply, "Yes, they're terrific," and in a third voice he would add, "I got my degree there, and my employer paid for it all," and so on.

Some forums are carefully moderated, so this kind of behavior is difficult or impossible. Some, such as www.degreeinfo.com, are moderated *after* items are posted, so objectionable messages can be removed. A few have no moderation at all, and needless to say, the degree-mill operators thrive there, badly confusing and misleading the well-meaning people who stumble onto such sites. The huge educational publisher Peterson's once operated such an unmoderated site, and when the degree-mill people began to dominate it, the publisher took it down rather than try to sort the bad from the good.

The People Involved in These Schools

43. *The faculty.* All legitimate schools and many fake ones provide a list of their faculty members, often with credentials—their degrees and the sources of them—and some biographical information. If no faculty information is provided, or if most or all of the faculty members have their degrees from the school in question, that is probably all one needs to know.

Five kinds of faculty can be found in degree-mill literature.

1. Co-conspirators: people who are either owners or otherwise share in the revenues. Some may well have legitimate credentials of their own. An ivy league degree is no more a guarantee of honesty in education than in business or politics.

2. Real but naive: A common degree-mill tactic is to run help wanted ads, offering lower-level faculty at legitimate schools the opportunity to earn a good side income as adjunct faculty. In reality, they rarely, if ever, are given students, but they have given permission for their names to appear on the faculty list.

3. Ones who don't know they are on the faculty: Another degree-mill tactic is to run enticing help wanted ads, receive many applications, never respond, but add those people to their faculty list, hoping they won't find out or won't pursue legal action if they do. Since the ads are often "blind" (no school is mentioned), these people may only learn they are listed as faculty months or years later, if at all.[6]

4. Hijacked faculty list: simply copied from the catalog of a legitimate school.

5. Made-up names: Since most of their other "facts" are fiction, why not the faculty list. Some mills choose common names ("Douglas Ford," "Robert Wilson") to frustrate Internet searches for such people.

44. *Administrators.* The chancellors, deans, provosts, vice presidents, trustees, and such, are typically found in the same five categories as just listed for faculty. A few quirky mill owners seem to enjoy throwing down the gauntlet by selecting obscure but once-prominent names. For instance, the fake Calgary Institute of Technology was ostensibly run by a man identified as a Canadian hero of World War One, while another mill identified its president as Austen Henry Layard, who was in fact a prominent nineteenth-century anthropologist.[7]

Advertising and Marketing

45. *Paid search engine placements, often appearing along with legitimate schools.* When one does an Internet search for a degree program ("MBA" or "PhD in psychology," for instance), the result will be hundreds or thousands of "hits." No major search engine makes any effort to weed out the bad and fake schools, so you will get them all, mixed together. Adding "accredited" to the search is useless, since most of the fakes claim to be accredited.

Compounding the problem is that the search engines (Google, Lycos, Yahoo, etc.) sell top-of-the-page advertising to anyone willing to pay. While such ads are often, if subtly, identified as such, it is also the case that the search engines sell placement, so that any school, real or fake, willing to pay will show up in the top ten or twenty-five listings. Even if you search for a very specific program, such as "M.S. in engineering, CalTech," the search engine, seeing what you *think* you want, may entice you with ads or banners for bad or fake schools that offer the same degree, but cheaper, faster, and easier.

46. *Banners, pop-up ads, and spam.* Once a person has been electronically identified as a possible degree seeker, whenever she is "surfing," she will see banners and pop-up ads from good schools and bad, and of course her e-mail box will be getting offers to "become the envy of your friends" by acquiring a degree.

47. *Advertisements in prestigious magazines (and use of "as advertised" labels elsewhere).* As we lament in chapter 6, more than a few prestigious magazines gladly accept advertising dollars from fake schools as well as real. While some bad guys advertise in almost every issue of *The Economist*, for instance, others may just run a small ad once and then be able to say and show, in all future promotional materials, "As advertised in *The Economist*."

48. *Stating that the university is not a diploma mill because "diploma mills are illegal."* It is the mark of many scam artists to warn their intended victims, while setting themselves apart. "Some used-car dealers turn back the odometer and put axle grease in the transmission, but here at Honest Eddie's. . . ." Some degree mills go out of their way to warn people not to deal with degree mills but only with fine schools like theirs. One currently advertising referral service, which refers clients only to a degree mill, says "Watch out for diploma mills. . . . We help you obtain a degree from an accredited school with a full campus. No classes required."

49. *Persuasive and aggressive telemarketing skills.* Read the actual degree-mill telemarketing script in appendix B, and marvel, with us, at the skill these people have in using the telephone as a sales tool.

50. *Offering a long menu of opportunities—the package deal.* Some mills offer not only a choice of two or more schools and up to five accrediting agencies but also a credential-evaluating service, transcript service, verifying services in case an employer tries to check, guaranteed letters of recommendation, and, if you want some evidence of your achievement, a term paper or thesis writing service. The fake Sussex College of Technology even used to offer its diplomas in three designs, two sizes, and a choice of English or Latin wording.

51. *The "loophole."* Many scams suggest that the purveyor has found some long-lost or secret or clever way to cure the disease, remove stains, buy gold at bargain prices, and make the engine last a million miles. Similarly, some mills hint or simply say that they have found a legal loophole that can be exploited to earn a medical, law, or other degree.

52. *Photographs with prominent people.* Many politicians and celebrities are willing to have their photographs taken with people they don't know or don't know enough about. One large unaccredited California school invited a well-known congressman to speak to a luncheon meeting of European businessmen, each of whom was photographed shaking his hand. The congressman did not know that the Europeans had paid $5,000 for a weekend in California, during which they would visit Disneyland, be "awarded" their degree, and have their picture taken with a congressman.

A man associated with Southwestern University in Arizona was photographed presenting a certificate to the mayor of Tucson, and that picture was subsequently used to promote the fake university. And in 2003, the proprietor of an online university promoted in Asia used photographs of himself standing next to what was clearly a cardboard cutout of the US president.

Misleading or Fake Internet Presence

53. *Flaunting the ".edu" extension.* The company called Educause has fallen asleep at the wheel (and down on the job). Not only are the scores of bad and fake schools permitted to keep their ".edu" that they managed to get before Educause took over the process in 2002, but also new and dreadful unaccredited schools are still being granted the ".edu" extension. We have thus far identified seventy-one schools using the ".edu" suffix that would not qualify to have it, if the rules were followed. So of course those that have it flaunt it, and unless retroactive standards are initiated, the ".edu" will never be a guarantee of quality or legitimacy.

54. *Fake .edu and fake .ac addresses.* Because the public has some awareness that ".edu" is supposed to be an indicator of legitimacy, some of the newer phonies are coming up with misleading but legal alternatives, such www.SchoolName-edu.com. Another variant is registering in a country that does not regulate the ".edu" and ending up, for instance, with www.SchoolName.edu.li. And a third variant is for a defunct school that already has an ".edu" designation to sell it on the open

market. Even though this is prohibited, it happens, with asking prices as high as $40,000.

The other suffix that is associated with recognized schools is ".ac," which, in Great Britain, means "academic" and is restricted to legitimate schools. However, ".ac" is also the Internet suffix for the Ascension Islands, which aggressively advertises the "highly sought after" (www.nic.ac) domain name. As a result, this tiny outcropping in the South Atlantic ocean has an indigenous population of zero but dozens of universities.

55. *Spoofed Web sites.* "Spoofing" is computerspeak for creating a Web site that looks like something legitimate but is in fact an imitation or counterfeit. Degree mills have created spoofed sites that look like the sites of countries, agencies, or accreditors, which, in turn, say positive things about them. Links to the spoofed sites are provided on the school's site.

56. *Similar or identical names to real schools.* Degree mills routinely select names that are either identical to those of real schools (there have been fakes named LaSalle, Stanford, Harvard, and the University of Wyoming), slight variations (Stamford, Cormell, and Berkley, for instance), and slight variations in wording (e.g., the fake "Texas University" instead of the real "University of Texas").

57. *Setting up fake discussion forums and chat rooms.* They look like legitimate sites, with impartial-seeming names, but they exist to lure well-meaning potential customers who get dangerous advice from school operators and apologists.

58. *Selected legitimate links to convey respectability.* Many links are offered, typically to ".gov" sites, where there are lengthy explanations and articles on experiential learning processes, accreditation, and so forth. The degree-mill site surrounds the real links with misinterpretation and misrepresentation, just in case anyone actually does read them.

The Trappings of Real Schools

59. *School paraphernalia.* Traditional items with the school logo, including T-shirts, coffee and beer mugs, and, typically, school rings "made by Jostens, the same company that makes school rings for many prestigious universities." Some of the schools have their diplomas printed by the same companies that do the work for major universities and make them available with the same leather or leatherette holders (at additional cost, of course).

60. *Scholarships offered.* Even at a legitimate school, awarding a scholarship rarely means that money is given to the student, only that tuition is reduced. The telemarketers for degree mills almost always have the option of offering "scholarships" to hesitant customers, sometimes being authorized to settle for an amount that is 20 percent of the original price. The mill still makes a handsome profit.

61. *Fake course lists.* Degree mills typically offer their degrees in dozens, even hundreds, of fields of study. To back this up, they sometimes show long lists of courses, these lists typically copied verbatim from the catalogs of legitimate schools.

62. *Map to a nonexistent campus.* Legitimate schools often provide a map showing how to find their campus. Carrying deception in a new direction, some mills, such as Concordia College and University, actually provide a fictitious map to their nonexistent campus.

63. *Claim to offer a student loan program.* Many mills feature what they call a student loan program. In reality, this simply means that they offer the opportunity to pay on the installment plan. Some, such as LaSalle, have required students using their loan program to send in a bundle of twenty-four to sixty checks made out to the school and dated at one-month intervals. The checks are cashed one per month. Because the checks in schemes like this are typically written on federally chartered banks, the schools may call this process a "federal loan program."

64. *Detailed accounts of campus life.* To support the fiction that there really is a campus, some degree mills provide glowing descriptions of campus activities, fraternities and sororities, community involvement programs, the chapel services, the university theater, and the sports programs.

65. *A nonexistent "on-campus" option.* Again, to support the fiction that there is really a campus, some mills offer the option of earning the degree through residential on-campus study, knowing full well that no one will (or could) take them up on this opportunity.

66. *Nonexistent alumni association and alumni gatherings.* The prospect of joining an alumni organization and participating in its events is held out as a further indicator of the legitimacy of the school.

67. *Picture of the diploma and transcript.* While a few legitimate schools show a picture of the diploma in their literature, this is rare. On the other hand, the majority of bad or fake schools do so, often accompanied by a picture of the transcript, to show the potential customer what a fine product they are acquiring.

68. *Support for charities.* A few of the currently operating bad guys hope to attract students by claiming that a portion of tuition received goes to charitable causes.

69. *Unnecessary follow-up questions.* Some mills ask applicants some gratuitous questions, such as providing the phone number of an employer or the address of a school, simply to show that the application is really being evaluated (which, of course, it isn't).

70. *"Branch campuses" worldwide, which are really alumni homes.* Some schools offer international graduates the opportunity to establish a "branch campus" in their home country, at best by putting a small sign on the door of their home or office.

Links with Well-Known People

71. *Claims of famous alumni.* There are three ways in which degree mills associate themselves with well-known people or ostensibly well-known people:

A. Real people who don't know they've been given a degree. The mills actually send a diploma to prominent people, and unless they get a letter of rejection (which rarely happens), they go ahead and state that that person is a graduate of their "school." In this way, a non-wonderful school in Los Angeles claims Ethel Kennedy, Coretta Scott King, and Muhammad Ali as alumni, while others have listed Jonas Salk and various Nobel laureates.

B. False claims. Knowing that it can be very difficult for a skeptic to get in touch with some famous people, the mills simply list some celebrities as graduates, hoping they won't be caught lying, and knowing that if they are, there will almost certainly be nothing more than a demand to remove Prince Charles, Bill Cosby, or whomever from the list.

C. Fake people with impressive titles. Since it is the titles not the names that are designed to impress, sometimes names are not even used: "A senior vice president of General Motors." "Two Saudi Arabian princes." "An Olympic gold medal winner." And so on. Hard to check and unlikely to be protested.

72. *Inviting (and paying) a prominent person to speak at a gathering or graduation, then misstating the connection.* After paying a speaker, they say

things like, "Yale University sent a delegate to address our convocation." An unaccredited California institution once hired a former British prime minister to speak at its graduation and dined off that for years.

73. *Big names as chancellors.* It is common in British universities to have a well-known person in the largely honorary role of chancellor. Some unrecognized institutions in Britain and in the United States have discovered there is apparently no shortage of naive, impoverished, or senile (or possibly all three) titled people willing to accept this job. That is why various lords, ladies, barons, duchesses, and so forth, have been listed as the chancellor of some less-than-wonderful institutions.

Misleading Acceptance of Degree Claims

74. *Lists of businesses and organizations who have "accepted" the school for tuition reimbursement.* Some did in error; some never did. In some large companies, degree acceptance is a local option, so that a branch manager might accept and pay for a degree that the home office would never recognize.

75. *Misusing the Sosdian and Sharp study.* In 1978, the National Institute of Education published a study that demonstrated the obvious fact that regionally accredited undergraduate degrees had a high level of acceptance in the business world and that graduates were happy with these degrees. Dozens of schools have misinterpreted the findings of Carol P. Sosdian and Laure M. Sharp, claiming that *unaccredited* degrees through the doctoral level have this level of acceptance.

76. *Claims of reciprocal, automatic recognition due to being a dependent territory of the motherland.* Degree mills and other unrecognized schools have claimed that because they are located or have an address in a dependent territory, they are "automatically" recognized by the home country. The claim has been made, for instance, that institutions associated with Turks and Caicos, Barbados, and Barbuda have recognition in the United Kingdom; that Norfolk Island licensing is concomitant with Australian licensing; and similarly that the US Virgin Islands is just the same as the United States. For schools in British dependencies, the claim is sometimes made that their incorporation grants "derivative full European Union acceptance of the degrees."

Misleading or Fake Physical Evidence

77. *Fake pictures of the school's building(s).* In these times of easy-to-copy Internet images, it is commonplace for degree mills to "borrow" photographs of real universities and other impressive buildings and claim them as their own. A university that claimed to be Liberian, whose "campus" was a mailbox service, depicted Winston Churchill's stately home in England as its campus. Columbia State University, run from a California warehouse, depicted Lyndhurst, a historic mansion in Tarrytown, New York, as its main building.

78. *Doctored photos of real buildings.* By making use of computer photo-editing techniques, it is possible to change the look of an impressive building to make it appear as one's own. A California-approved university once showed a photograph of a large office building with the university's sign at the top. When a colleague visited that building and found no such sign, the school, which actually did rent a small office in that building, claimed the sign had not yet been installed, and the doctored photo in their catalog was "anticipating it."

79. *Prestigious-sounding address.* The postal service essentially looks at the last two lines of an address and doesn't worry about what comes before it. A school in rural Louisiana informally named their driveway "University Circle" and made that part of their address. A mill whose mailbox was in the North Point district of San Diego referred to their "North Point campus."

80. *A private mailbox (PMB) presented as "suite" or "floor" or "building number."* At one time, businesses renting private mailboxes were required to use "PMB" as part of their address. This valuable consumer law was revoked by presidential order in 2002, permitting schools to use misleading addresses, as discussed on pages 64 and 75.

81. *Facilities rented once, or rarely, portrayed as the campus.* A currently operating Swiss school rents a city-owned castle for some meetings and shows it in the school's literature as if it were the campus. One dubious school, run from the suburban basement of its owner, rented a cathedral in Washington for a graduation ceremony and showed only that picture in their catalog. In an almost charming case, a degree mill called the College of Applied Science in London was asked to stage a graduation ceremony for a wealthy industrialist who had bought his PhD. The degree mill rented a fancy girls' school for a day, rented costumes portraying dukes and duchesses for their friends, and staged an impressive ceremony.

82. *Depicting a large building in which the school either rents one room or uses a mailbox or an "executive suites" service, as if it all belonged to the school.* Sometimes the school name is pasted onto the photograph to make it seem as if it really is its building.

83. *Illegal activity associated with a legal school.* There have been instances when dishonest employees or executives at a legitimate university had a degree-mill sideline associated with their school. For instance:

- A medical school in the Caribbean was sending four-year-trained MDs out the front door at the same time as it was selling MDs to unqualified people for $28,000 out the back door.
- A traditional South American university signed up more than one thousand Americans for a $10,000 nonresident doctoral program, but it turned out to be run by an executive of the university without the knowledge or permission of the school.
- A fake doctor in California turned out to have bribed a computer room employee at a major university to alter all the records to make it appear as if he had earned the degree. The university believed there were no other such cases but could not be certain.

Misleading Policies

84. *Claiming exclusivity: stating that only 5 percent of applicants are accepted.* With degree mills, the actual number is generally 100 percent.

85. *Not specifying which classes are required or how many units are required to graduate or saying that "rare exceptions can be made."* The mill might list dozens of "required" courses but then tell every applicant that because of his or her extraordinary experience, the course work has been waived.

86. *Backdating diplomas.* No legitimate school backdates diplomas. Degree mills regularly do the date of the client's choice, sometimes using the argument that the diploma can be dated as of the time the knowledge was actually gained.

87. *Selling graduate honors and the GPA of choice.* Some degree mills charge extra if the client wishes to graduate "with honors" or "summa cum laude." The "summa" or "magna" designation is also sold for masters' and doctoral degrees, a practice rarely if ever done in the real world. Amusingly, while mills offer to make the fake transcript up showing any grade point average the customer wants, they often recom-

mend against a perfect 4.0 as being too suspicious, suggesting instead a more modest 3.79.

88. *Assuring the customer that "we'll always be here for you."* Mills typically offer a "degree verification service," suggesting they will always be available to answer employers' inquiries and confirm the "earning" of the degree. In reality, the way many innocent victims learn they've been had is when they attempt to make contact with their alma mater a year or two later and find it is no longer there.

Sometimes the "verification service" takes the form of a secure Web site listing the names of graduates, so that employers can go there directly to confirm the degrees.

89. *Using names of real universities no longer in existence.* An average of a dozen or so properly accredited colleges and universities go out of business each year. Mill operators sometimes "harvest" those names— Eisenhower University, Nasson College, Beacon College—for their own purposes and even claim or imply that they are a legitimate successor to the original school. One Louisiana operator of many schools listed a legitimate defunct school in the telephone book, then fielded calls and fabricated transcripts for alumni, who didn't realize they were dealing with an interloper.

90. *More than one degree at a time.* Some mills offer package deals: a bachelor's, master's, and PhD at the same time for a single payment, backdating them to different years so that it does not appear all three degrees were "earned" on the same day.

91. *Multilevel marketing combined with a degree mill.* The "deal" is that one buys a bachelor's degree. Then, when one signs up another person for a bachelor's, he gets a "free" master's, and so on. Georgia Christian University offered a multilevel faculty scheme: with your degree came appointment as assistant professor. When you signed up three people to buy degrees, you became an associate professor. When your "down line" people signed up others, everyone rose in rank: full professor, dean, and so on up the academic ladder.

92. *"Order by midnight tonight."* Big discount if you sign up quickly. The telemarketer offers a special discount for people who buy their degrees immediately, "before this special offer expires." More than a few legitimate schools also use this kind of marketing. Some fake schools offer to send a courier to the door to pick up the tuition check—quite possibly the same courier who will deliver the diploma a week or so later. To date, no "university" has offered miracle-blade

Ginsu steak knives with every diploma, but we will not be surprised when it happens.

On the following page, we summarize these ninety-two red flags into a single checklist, which can be copied and used as a means to help evaluate any given institution.

NOTES

1.   Bob Jones University, a totally legitimate school that does not believe in secular accreditation, is an often-cited example of this category. But even they are now pursuing accreditation through a recognized religious accreditor.

2.   The island of Niue was nearly destroyed by a cyclone in 2004. It remains to be seen if its "universities" will remain there or head for the canoes.

3.   The official message appears at http://www.embassyofliberia.org/news/item_a.html. And St. Regis is already claiming to be an Indian university. It never ends.

4.   The university in question claims that the thirty-day residency is mandatory, but we have three letters sent to potential students who said that they were unable to come to St. Kitts. The letters assure them that visitation was not necessary.

5.   The question often arises, "Why not sue people like this?" Apart from the time and cost, there is the tiny likelihood of collecting. In this instance, an assets trace revealed that the man had considerable assets—all banked in a tax-haven country.

6.   For instance, "Major university seeks adjunct faculty in business, psychology, and engineering for high-paying part-time assignments."

7.   An extreme example of this was the fake East Missouri Business College (EMBC), set up by the Missouri attorney general in a sting operation to check out a suspicious accrediting agency. Good old EMBC was duly accredited despite the presence on the faculty of Moe Howard, Curley Howard, and Larry Fine, better known as the Three Stooges.

CHECKLIST: 92 THINGS BAD AND FAKE SCHOOLS DO TO MISLEAD PEOPLE

Accreditation Claims

☐ 1. Accreditation is claimed from a fake or unrecognized agency.

☐ 2. The fake or unrecognized accreditor also accredits legitimate schools.

☐ 3. The accreditor offers a confirming telephone service or "hot line" to assure people that a given school is accredited.

☐ 4. The school claims that, as a global or international university, it doesn't require accreditation and/or government approval from any single government agency.

☐ 5. The school explains at length why accreditation is not important or is relevant only for student loans.

☐ 6. The school claims that Harvard and Oxford aren't accredited either.

☐ 7. Accreditation is correctly claimed but from a place where the word is used in quite different ways.

☐ 8. The school claims that accreditation is impossible because of the separation of church and state.

☐ 9. The school lists approval or accreditation from a fake or unrecognized country.

☐ 10. Dubious accreditation is claimed from a real country or national agency.

☐ 11. The school claims accreditation and the right to confer degrees due to wording in the school's articles of incorporation.

Other False or Misleading Claims

☐ 12. The institution is certified by disreputable or incompetent credential checking services.

☐ 13. The school misuses the concept of state licensing.

☐ 14. The institution points to inclusion on an impressive-looking compiled list of universities.

☐ 15. The "school" lies or misstates its age.

☐ 16. An institution writes about an earlier use of its building as if it were its own.

☐ 17. The school confuses the city with the university.

☐ 18. The school provides information about the legitimacy of awarding life/work experience credit then abuses that process.

☐ 19. The institution claims that its critics (individuals, Web sites, and authors of books) are out to get it because they are run by fired employees or by people who secretly own fake schools and are afraid of the competition.

☐ 20. The school pretends to be bigger than it is.

False or Misleading Memberships and Affiliations

☐ 21. Membership in real organizations—but ones that don't screen members.
☐ 22. The school implies legitimacy through United Nations–related organizations.
☐ 23. The institution claims affiliations with real schools.
☐ 24. The institution cites membership in nonexistent or bogus organizations.
☐ 25. The school rents space from an organization, then implies an affiliation.
☐ 26. The school puts out a list of businesses and agencies that have accepted and paid for its degrees.

Fake or Meaningless Documents

☐ 27. Use of Apostilles and notarized statements of all kinds.
☐ 28. Claims to have International Standards Organization 9002 certification.
☐ 29. Misstatement of nonprofit status.
☐ 30. Misusing the certificate of incorporation.
☐ 31. Misusing other kinds of certificates.
☐ 32. Misusing a "certificate of good standing" (CGS).

Misleading Recommendations and Links

☐ 33. Better Business Bureau membership.
☐ 34. BBB imitations.
☐ 35. Business organizations.
☐ 36. Inclusion in "official" directories that list everyone.
☐ 37. Inclusion in the official Norwegian Higher Institution Registry.
☐ 38. Fake referral services.
☐ 39. Bogus or self-interest reference books.
☐ 40. Offering legitimate certifications along with fake degrees.
☐ 41. Testimonials.
☐ 42. Posting positive comments on Internet newsgroups.

The People Involved in These Schools

☐ 43. The faculty.
☐ 44. Administrators.

Advertising and Marketing

☐ 45. Paid search engine placements, often appearing along with legitimate schools.
☐ 46. Banners, pop-up ads, and spam.
☐ 47. Advertisements in prestigious magazines (and use of "as advertised" labels elsewhere).
☐ 48. Stating that the university is not a diploma mill because "diploma mills are illegal."
☐ 49. Persuasive and aggressive telemarketing skills.
☐ 50. Offering a long menu of opportunities—the package deal.
☐ 51. The "loophole."
☐ 52. Photographs with prominent people.

Misleading or Fake Internet Presence

☐ 53. Flaunting the ".edu" extension.
☐ 54. Fake .edu and fake .ac addresses.
☐ 55. Spoofed Web sites.
☐ 56. Similar or identical names to real schools.
☐ 57. Setting up fake discussion forums and chat rooms.
☐ 58. Selected legitimate links to convey respectability.

The Trappings of Real Schools

☐ 59. School paraphernalia.
☐ 60. Scholarships offered.
☐ 61. Fake course lists.
☐ 62. Map to a nonexistent campus.
☐ 63. Claim to offer a student loan program.
☐ 64. Detailed accounts of campus life.
☐ 65. A nonexistent "on-campus" option.
☐ 66. Nonexistent alumni association and alumni gatherings.
☐ 67. Picture of the diploma and transcript.
☐ 68. Support for charities.
☐ 69. Unnecessary follow-up questions.
☐ 70. "Branch campuses" worldwide, which are really alumni homes.

Links with Well-Known People

☐ 71. Claims of famous alumni.
☐ 72. Inviting (and paying) a prominent person to speak at a gathering or graduation, then misstating the connection.
☐ 73. Big names as chancellors.

Misleading Acceptance of Degree Claims

☐ 74. Lists of businesses and organizations who have "accepted" the school for tuition reimbursement.
☐ 75. Misusing the Sosdian and Sharp study.
☐ 76. Claims of reciprocal, automatic recognition due to being a dependent territory of the motherland.

Misleading or Fake Physical Evidence

☐ 77. Fake pictures of the school's building(s).
☐ 78. Doctored photos of real buildings.
☐ 79. Prestigious-sounding address.
☐ 80. A private mailbox (PMB) presented as "suite" or "floor" or "building number."
☐ 81. Facilities rented once, or rarely, portrayed as the campus.
☐ 82. Depicting a large building in which the school either rents one room or uses a mailbox or an "executive suites" service, as if it all belonged to the school.
☐ 83. Illegal activity associated with a legal school.

Misleading Policies

☐ 84. Claiming exclusivity: stating that only 5 percent of applicants are accepted.
☐ 85. Not specifying which classes are required or how many units are required to graduate or saying that "rare exceptions can be made."
☐ 86. Backdating diplomas.
☐ 87. Selling graduate honors and the GPA of choice.
☐ 88. Assuring the customer that "we'll always be here for you."
☐ 89. Using names of real universities no longer in existence.
☐ 90. More than one degree at a time.
☐ 91. Multilevel marketing combined with a degree mill.
☐ 92. "Order by midnight tonight."

3

The Buyers

WHY ACQUIRE *ANY* DEGREE?

Let's start with the broader question of why people would spend the time and the money to acquire *any* degree, real or fake, and then look at the reasons someone might choose "fake" instead of "real."

Legitimate degrees typically represent one of the three or four most expensive and most time-consuming things a person will do in a lifetime. There must be persuasive reasons to consider doing such a thing, and indeed there are.

Years ago, John Bear ran a consulting service, offering advice to people who wished to earn one or more degrees. That process began with a questionnaire asking, among many other things, the reason that the client wished to have a degree. The multiple-choice question had these six options:

1. My employer/potential employer says I must have a degree.
2. I plan to look for a new job, and the degree will help.
3. I would like to advance/get higher pay in my current job.
4. I wish to learn more about my field of interest.
5. I plan to start or expand a business, and I want my customers or clients to have more confidence in me.
6. For personal satisfaction, and/or to earn the respect of others.

The responses, based on several thousand clients, were pretty evenly distributed among the six choices, with a fair number of people checking two or more boxes.

The first three are all pretty much different ways of saying the same thing: many jobs either require degrees or reward degree-holders with higher pay and the possibility of promotion. That, of course, is a persuasive reason to want a degree. And for some people, it is a persuasive reason to short-circuit the process by purchasing a degree in the hope of getting away with it. (The matter of people who are, themselves, genuinely fooled by a degree mill will be discussed later in this section.)

The fourth choice is usually combined with one of the other choices, since a person who *only* wants to learn more about a subject, whether business or astronomy or Greek history or whatever, could simply take one of the thousands of online or home study courses available from hundreds of legitimate colleges and universities, without the need to commit to a full degree program.

Choices five and six are both concerned with image: being seen as a person with a certain credentials and the level of knowledge that it suggests to friends, family, business associates, or potential clients. While a marriage counselor doesn't *need* to have a doctorate in most states, or a financial planner an MBA, or a contractor a degree in engineering, the fact of those degrees may attract more customers and inspire confidence in them.

One of the especially scary subsets of the matter of image, or being seen as an expert, is the matter of expert witnesses. Some courts have been quite remiss in verifying the claimed credentials of a proposed expert witness. To the best of John Bear's knowledge, almost no one has ever checked to see if he has the credentials and publications he has claimed.[1] But sometimes attorneys for the "other" party *do* check, and so John Bear has done expert witness work in cases where he was not relevant to the main topic but was only there to help discredit an expert witness for the other party. One case, for instance, involved a tree expert, calling himself a forensic arborologist, whose only degree was a doctorate from an unrecognized British school.

Other so-called experts who were found to have bogus degrees include

- a self-styled automotive engineer who testified on behalf of an auto manufacturer that the brakes "could not have failed" in a fatal accident. This man was exposed on the witness stand as having bought his engineering degree from a notorious degree mill.

- an asbestos removal "expert" whose degrees in environmental sciences came from a worthless source.
- a burn expert, who always seemed to conclude that horribly disfigured burn victims had somehow brought it on themselves through carelessness and that his corporate clients were in no way responsible. When his fake PhD in safety was exposed, it triggered a review of decisions in which his testimony had been a factor.

There are these two general categories of people who buy degrees from degree mills: Category one are those who hope and plan to use them with employers and potential employers, and category two are those who simply want to impress people.

An essential difference between these two categories is that in the first, the person *knows* that a third party is going to have to approve the degree, while in the second, the person concerned is not only the one who *wants* the degree but also the one who finds a supplier and decides whether to go ahead—deciding whether any given school and degree is likely to meet her needs.

This suggests that people who know that the degree will have to get past a gatekeeper—another person or a committee—may be less likely to deal with a degree mill.

But people in both categories *do* sometimes deal with degree mills. In asking why they do so, it is appropriate to ask the crucial question that every human resources person, law enforcement agency, potential customer or client, and even the media, should ask when people with degree-mill credentials are discovered: Did they know it was fake, or were they genuinely fooled?

DID THEY KNOW IT WAS FAKE, OR WERE THEY FOOLED?

Give us an infallible mind-reading machine for just a few minutes and we would use it to get to the heart of one of the most perplexing and, sadly, unanswerable questions of all: What is *really* going on in the mind of the person who purchases a degree from a degree mill? There really are only these two possibilities:

1. They knew exactly what they were doing, and they bought the fake degree for the sole purpose of using it to fool others.
2. They genuinely believed they were earning a legitimate degree from a legitimate institution that recognized their excellent career achievements and said those achievements were equivalent to a degree. (After the fact—after a degree mill is exposed or the person gets in trouble—there are some who will say that they really did have some concerns or doubts but decided to go ahead anyway. There may well be a small subset of such people.)

To be sure, there are people in each category. But is it 90-10 percent, 10-90 percent, or somewhere in between? Our hunch is that it is nearer to the former than to the latter. Common sense tells us that most people with an IQ higher than room temperature must at least *suspect* that a doctorate that can be earned in two weeks, no questions asked, or a bachelor's degree that can be backdated to the date of one's choice, cannot be legitimate.

And yet, when a place like Columbia State University with its twenty-seven-day degrees or Concordia College and University with its twelve-hour degrees, is exposed, inevitably we will hear from some people who sound absolutely truthful and genuinely astonished. One victim wrote, "I can't believe I did this. I earned a master's degree from the University of Wisconsin. I know what graduate school is like. But these sellers were so persuasive, so soothing on the phone, and of course I really *did* believe that I had the knowledge and skill of person with a doctorate in my field."[2]

If we were sitting on a jury, we'd probably give some of these people the benefit of the doubt, but not a whole lot of them. And, in our experience, the more people talk about what they did and why they did it, the deeper the hole they dig. Consider the following case history for a textbook example.

Case History

John Bear was an expert witness for one state's department of professional regulation in a case involving a psychologist who worked for the state prison system in a job that did not require a PhD but had a significantly higher salary for people who did have doctorates. The employee in question had a legitimate bachelor's and master's degree, and then

The Fowler Brothers made millions with one crudely simple school catalog after another: a new name every few years.

he purchased his PhD for $600 from the University of England at Oxford, one of the many fakes started and run by the notorious Fowler brothers (see page 47) of Chicago and Los Angeles. Allen Ezell had earlier helped bring them to justice in a trial where John Bear testified as an expert witness.

This psychologist, predictably, had insisted that his colleagues and underlings call him "doctor." He started out on the witness stand by expressing astonishment that this school could be anything other than the excellent long-established institution they claimed. Why, he even wrote and submitted a doctoral dissertation, he said.

The prosecutor introduced the school's badly designed and poorly printed little six-page catalog. Was the defendant familiar with graduate school catalogs? Yes. Have you seen one for the state university where you earned your master's? Yes. Did it look anything like this? No.

The prosecutor pointed out that the university had no telephone and operated from a post office box. Does that sound like a real university? The defendant mumbled that he had never had any need to telephone the school. Do you mean you earned a Doctor of Philosophy degree without ever speaking to anyone from the university, even once? Yes.

Next, the prosecutor noted that the "university" offered to backdate the diploma to any date of the graduate's choice. Have you ever heard of any school that will state that you earned their degree years before you even heard of them? Does that seem right to you? Well, when you put it like that. . . .

Then the prosecutor asked what sort of due diligence the defendant had done before choosing his school. Had he looked it up in any directory? No. Had he asked any friends or colleagues about it? No. Had he checked with the registrar of any of the state universities to see if the degree would be acceptable? No.

Finally, the prosecutor explained that he had had the defendant's doctoral dissertation read by several experts in the field. They all agreed that it was at best at the level of a high-school term paper. There was a strong suspicion that he had cobbled it together *after* he had been subpoenaed to appear.

The outcome was that the defendant lost his license to practice as a psychologist, despite his tearful appeal that this was literally his meal ticket, his only way to earn a living.

And the office of the attorney general was seriously considering a criminal suit, based on the fact that this man had "stolen" tens of thousands of dollars from the state, by collecting, for years, the much higher salary paid to psychologists with a doctorate, as compared to those with a master's degree.

While there may not always be a clear answer to the "Did he or she know?" question, in many situations *either* a yes or a no answer can be useful and provides a course of action for the person asking the question.

If he *did* know that he was buying a fake degree, then what else does one need to know?

And if he genuinely *didn't* know, what does this say about the intelligence, judgment skills, and decision-making ability of the employee, job applicant, public figure, and so forth?

HOW PEOPLE RATIONALIZE BUYING DEGREES: THE ISSUE OF SUMPTUARY LAW

No one would challenge the notion that robbing banks or shooting people is a criminal act, deserving of punishment of some kind. But we still hear a lot of people saying, with regard to their fake degrees, "Well, what harm is really being done here. I already knew how to do the work; I just needed that piece of paper to get the job." Alternatively, the argument goes, "This job did not require that particular degree. I just wanted the self-satisfaction and the respect that went with being identified as a master or doctor in my field."

When we try to understand their motivation and explain their behavior, we move into the realm of sumptuary law.

Sumptuary law relates to matters of law that attempt to regulate human behavior, typically on social, religious, or moral grounds. The concept arose in ancient Greece and Rome, dealing with everything from dress codes (slaves must not wear clothes similar to that of their masters) to behavior in public places.

In the twentieth and twenty-first centuries, we have seen numerous attempts to regulate human behavior in areas such as gambling, drugs, prostitution and sexual behaviors, clothing (as with high school and college dress codes), and of course the "great experiment" of Prohibition, making alcohol illegal in the United States during the 1920s.

The simple fact is that all of these activities survive and often thrive, despite attempts to regulate them, because of the law of supply and demand. If enough people want those products or services and are willing to take the risks involved, then they will somehow become available. As a sarcastic advertisement of the 1970s said, "Drive over fifty-five. Fiddle your income taxes. Smoke marijuana. If you don't like a law, ignore it. It's the American way."

All of this is relevant to degree mills because the simple if distressing fact is that they survive and prosper *solely* because there are enough people who want and are willing to pay for their product and are either unaware of the risks or willing to accept them.

"I will drive ninety miles an hour on the freeway because I am a good driver, and I am late for an important appointment."

"I will use cocaine because I know I can handle it, and anyway I'm so discreet that I'll never get caught."

"I will buy a PhD and call myself 'doctor' because it will help my career, and I already know a great deal in my field, and I don't have time to go back to school."

That is why we acknowledge, with sorrow, that the scourge of fake schools and fake degrees and diplomas, a problem, as discussed in the introduction, since at least the eighth century, will probably always be with us.

Like drugs, prostitution, gambling, and other so-called victimless behaviors, the selling, buying, and using of fake degrees and credentials has been with us for long enough to suggest it will be around forever, no matter how stringent the laws, no matter how widespread the publicizing of dangers and prosecutions, and no matter how effective the "gatekeepers" or decision makers on degree acceptance may be.

There is no better evidence of the willingness of people to buy degrees—even people who know the dangers—than what happened on CBS television in 1978. That year, *60 Minutes* did its one and only segment on degree mills, focusing on a major phony then operating in Los Angeles. Mike Wallace visited California Pacifica University and was shown on camera buying a PhD for $3,000. While the cameras were rolling, the sheriff arrived with an arrest warrant for school owner Ernest Sinclair and took him away.[3] After the program aired on Sunday evening, according to segment producer Marian Goldin, more than eight hundred people telephoned CBS to learn the address and phone number of that school so they could buy a degree "just like Mike Wallace did."

Oh, dear.

WHY PEOPLE DEAL WITH MILLS: SOME ACADEMIC RESEARCH

The academic world has been surprisingly apathetic in looking at degree-mill matters. Searching academic records for the last half century, we found only three doctoral research projects and one master's thesis specifically addressing the issues: a historical look at the problem (done in 1963 and discussed in chapter 1), a 2003 survey of what human resource managers know about degree mills and how they deal with them (discussed in chapter 6), an in-depth look at whether three "virtual universities" operating in Australia are "a guise for degree/diploma mills to thrive," and the only experimental study—some charming if modest introductory research by Robin Calote for her doctorate in education in 2002, under the title "Diploma Mills: What's the Attraction?"

Dr. Calote's purpose was to look at the effect of four factors on the decision to choose a degree mill: time (degree mills are fast), credit for life experience (degree mills are exceedingly generous), tuition on a per-degree basis (degree mills are cheap), and institutional licensure (degree mills rarely have a license to operate as a degree-granting school).

Her experimental subjects were students enrolled in an accredited community college. Each was asked to view Web pages created by Calote for sixteen fictitious colleges. They varied only in the presence or absence of the four variables: time, credit for experience, cost, and licensure.

After viewing each Web page, the subjects were asked to rate their likelihood of enrolling in the college on a five-point scale. Then they were asked to reflect on their choices and to rate the effect each of the four variables had on their decisions.

There was no relationship between the variables of time, credit for life experience, or tuition and the decision to choose that institution. But there was a statistically significant relationship between the assertion that an institution was licensed and the decision to choose it.

Intriguingly, the subjects *believed* that they had been influenced by all four variables, but in fact only licensure really influenced them.

The results offer a persuasive argument why so many bad and fake schools choose locations, from Wyoming to Alabama to Liberia, where they can claim to be licensed and even approved. It also points out why such places are doing a real disservice to the public through their weak licensing laws and regulations.

In her dissertation, Calote concludes that "accredited colleges should partner with the media to build public awareness of diploma mills as a form of consumer fraud. In addition, academic counseling should include instruction regarding the meaning of accreditation, the difference between accreditation and licensure, the definition and legal status of diploma mills, and the professional risks taken by those who acquire diploma mill degrees." We could not agree more.

THE RISKS

Human beings take risks all the time. Nearly every aspect of human behavior involves some risk, whether or not we think about it at the time.

There are high-risk behaviors, such as smoking, climbing Mount Everest, or unsafe sex, and there are low-risk behaviors, including driving, flying, and walking down the sidewalk (even though people have been killed by falling debris).

Then there is the matter of results or consequences.

A high-risk activity can have very small consequences. Most tax cheats, if caught, get relatively minor penalties. Playing the lottery is extremely high risk, but for most people the downside means only losing a few dollars.

A low-risk activity can have very big consequences. Not many people are hit by lightning on the golf course, and most people who drive fifty miles an hour through a school zone don't have incidents. But for the golfer who is hit, or the driver who kills a child, the consequences are extreme.

The two important questions, then, are these: Is buying a diploma from a degree mill a low- or a high-risk activity? And are the consequences small or large?

Is Buying a Degree High Risk or Low Risk?

It comes down to a matter of odds. If one knew that 98 percent of people who fiddle their taxes get caught, they'd be crazy to try. But if it were 3 percent? Or 17 percent? Might be worth the risk.

Our best answer is that buying and using a fake degree *used* to be very low risk. Twenty years ago, the Pepper Subcommittee estimated there were half a million people with fake degrees. How many of those have suffered? Very few, indeed. But we believe the winds are shifting. Fake degrees are getting more and more attention. Human resource people, law enforcement people, and the media are paying closer attention than ever before.

People who buy a degree are truly putting a time bomb in their resume. More time bombs have exploded in the last few years than ever before. Every one that *hasn't* exploded is ticking away. There are no exceptions, no other categories.

Bottom line: we believe this formerly low-risk activity is well on the way to becoming high risk.

What Are the Consequences?

As with the risk level, we think things are changing. Thirty, twenty, even ten years ago, people found to be using fake degrees were often seen as amusing scoundrels at worst. Some degree abusers achieved the status of folk heroes. There have been popular books and movies about Ferdinand Waldo DeMara (*The Great Imposter*) and Frank W. Abagnale (*Catch Me If You Can*).

Things seem to be changing. When a popular television advice guru who called herself "The Love Doctor" was found (by the media) to have a degree-mill PhD, she was promptly fired. When a college professor in Michigan had his fake degree exposed on *Good Morning America*, he was promptly fired. When a fairly high state official in Colorado was found to have a fake degree, not only was he fired, but also his "green card" was revoked and he was deported to his native country.

In addition to the obvious matter of general embarrassment and humiliation, the risks of fake degree use would seem to be:

1. loss of job (or reduced chance for advancement)
2. loss of professional license or security clearance
3. deportation
4. criminal prosecution

The first three are clear and are persuasive reasons not to take a chance. The fourth seems to be an area of growing risk. While any state can theoretically prosecute a fake degree user under general fraud statutes, it is only recently that some states have begun to address the precise problem by passing laws specifically punishing the use of unrecognized or fake degrees.

Will what began in Oregon and has now spread to half a dozen other states become a national trend? Even if no one is actually imprisoned on the offense of fake degree use in North Dakota, for instance, the very fact that people *could* be is a major deterrent to using such a degree or indeed to hiring an employee with one.

How Do People Feel, and Behave, after They Are Caught?

Social scientists are fascinated by what people do when something they really thought was true turns out not to be (for instance, that smoking is relatively harmless or that Richard Nixon was a totally honest politician), or when an event they truly believed was going to happen didn't happen (such as the religious leaders who name an exact date for the end of the world and go onto a mountain top with their followers to see it happen).

Since the category of "I really believed it was a legitimate university" fits here as well, the findings on how these people react has relevance here.

Essentially, in most cases, the "aftermath" can be fitted into one of these four categories:

Acceptance: I see now that I was fooled. I shall renounce and stop using my degree(s); apologize to all concerned, make amends to colleagues, coworkers, and clients; and seriously consider pursuing a legitimate degree program.

Denial: There simply is no way Lexington University can be a fake. I have seen photographs of the campus. I have talked to the dean. I have confirmed its accreditation. This is an attempt by [villain of choice: "my political enemies," "the left- (or right-) wing press," etc.] to discredit me. When the facts are known, I will be vindicated.

Rationalization: Well, the accrediting agency may not be recognized, but accreditation is voluntary anyway, and they are state licensed, and those two famous authors have degrees from there, and my employer paid for it, so what's the problem?

Dysfunction: No comment. This topic is off limits. The facts speak for themselves. There is nothing more to say.

Needless to say, we believe the first category of response is the only healthy and realistic one. But people who have fake or dubious degrees, and others who must deal with such people, should recognize that responses might fall into any of these categories.

NOTES

1.   He does.

2.   The actual telemarketing "script" of a very successful degree mill is given in appendix B. It is enlightening to read the text as if you were an honest person in search of a degree to see if you might be persuaded. One out of three people who received this call ended up buying a degree.

3.   Sinclair was convicted of mail fraud and sentenced to Terminal Island Federal Correctional Institution. While there, he started and ran his next phony school, Hollywood Southern University, selling degrees to inmates, guards, and the general public. Then he signed up for a "work furlough" program to attend a cake-decorating class. He walked in the front door of the school and out the back door, and he has never been heard from again.

4.   The research was published as a master's thesis by George M. Brown, "Are Virtual Universities in Australia a Guise for Degree/Diploma Mills to Thrive?" Flinders University of South Australia, 2001.

4 Legal and Ethical Issues

What's wrong with buying a degree from a degree mill?

How should employers and others think about and deal with this issue, both legally and ethically?

From the employer's point of view, these two questions are not quite as simple as they might seem at first glance. There are, for instance, many cases in which the buyer of the degree is performing well, sometimes in a job that does not require that particular degree. But at the same time, there may well be legal, ethical, and public relations issues to consider.

A well-publicized case is that of Laura Callahan, a senior employee of the Department of Homeland Security, discovered in 2003 to have fake degrees. Her response to her employer was fivefold:

- She did not seek out this fake but responded to an advertisement for a school referral service, not knowing it was secretly linked only to one fake school.
- She believed she was dealing a properly accredited school, apparently not knowing there were such things as fake accrediting agencies. She even used a "degree-mill checklist" to avoid being a victim.
- The job she held did not require any college degree.
- No one denied that she was doing a good job.
- She had listed the three degree-mill degrees on her official resume for several years.

An essay by Callahan relating to this situation appears as appendix I.

Is there an issue here? Is there, in fact, a problem if the person with the fake degree is doing a good job?

Many people would suggest there are two factors to consider in formulating an answer:

- What the degree purchase says about that person, and his or her judgment, as well as the possibility of causing problems for the employer.
- The potential liability for the employer.

Some feel that it is situational: dependent on the person, the field of endeavor, and the circumstances. A psychotherapist, however competent, with a fake doctorate in psychology, is inappropriate, while a successful real estate broker with a fake MBA may not be as much of a problem.[1]

These issues are regular fodder for coffee shop discussions and for ethics classes. Would you rather have your jet piloted by a man who flew jumbo jets for the Air Force but then bought a fake bachelor's degree in order to get his airline job or man who barely scraped through at an accredited aeronautics school? Would you rather have a compassionate marriage counselor with a fake degree or a less-caring person with an Ivy League degree?

These issues arise commonly in the workplace, often causing anguish among the decision makers, who are uncertain how to find the best answer: whether to take drastic action, punitive action, or no action at all.

These three different options—major penalty, some penalty, or no penalty—were each exercised in recent cases involving the top officers of three large corporations. Each was found to have a fake MBA degree. None was accused of doing a bad or unsatisfactory job.

At Veritas Software, the chief financial officer was summarily fired.

At Bausch and Lomb, the chief financial officer was penalized more than a million dollars by having his promised bonus withdrawn, but he was allowed to keep his job.

And at the third company, whose situation never reached the public eye, the chief financial officer was neither fired nor penalized, and no public announcement was ever made.[2]

With increased public and media awareness of degree mills, and with new public disclosure rules and practices in the post-Enron era, it is probably wise for any organization to have in place a policy to deal with newly discovered fake degrees and to try to keep the problem from arising in the first place.

WHO IS HARMED BY USE OF FAKE DEGREES?

It saddens us that the question even needs to be asked. But when we wrote to a reporter for a big-city daily to alert him to a school psychologist with a fake PhD in his area, and he replied, "And I should care because?" we were reminded there is a problem here.

In fact, that "So what?" response comes all too often, as in the case of the publisher of *The Economist* magazine who, when alerted to the fact that the magazine has run hundreds of advertisements for degree mills, replied, "Our readers are smart enough to make their own decisions."

Who, then, is harmed by degree mills?

- The truly innocent victims who unknowingly acquire a degree from an illegal university, perhaps one they saw advertised in *The Economist* or *USA Today*, and then get in trouble with their employer or with the law.
- The employers who have potential liability for bad publicity and for damages attributed to employees with fake degrees
- The customers or clients of bogus doctors, lawyers, therapists, architects, accountants, and so on. When someone defiantly declares that no one is being harmed, as longtime degree-mill operator Ronald Pellar said to ABC's *20/20* a few years ago, we point, among many others, to patients at Lincoln Hospital in New York who were treated by an accountant who bought a medical degree and was employed as an emergency room physician, or the couples who divorced following their "treatment" at a New York "sex therapy" clinic run by a high school dropout whose only degree was a PhD purchased from a California degree mill.
- The taxpayers who are paying the salaries of federal, state, and local government employees with unrecognized degrees, from teachers and principals to elected officials to military officers to a senior undersecretary of defense.

WHAT TO CONSIDER IN DEALING WITH FAKE DEGREES

I. Legal Issues

Can hiring or harboring an employee with a fake degree cause legal problems for the employer, quite apart from any problems the employee may face? There are at least two areas where this is a possibility.

One relates to an organization's potential liability for things done by employees with fake degrees or even things that have not yet caused evident problems. Consider bridges built under the supervision of people with fake engineering degrees, therapy from people with fake psychology degrees, medical treatment from a fake MD, and so on.

Inspection of resumes posted on Monster.com found thousands of people with fake degrees who should give corporate officers and their insurance companies cause for alarm: a quality control officer at a controversial tire plant, a safety official at a nuclear power facility, the head of a clinic for a national health-care organization, a missile control officer for the army, and so on. Every person listed in the extensive "Time Bombs" section (appendix F) is a potential insurance disaster.

One relevant area of the law in this matter is the rule of *respondeat superior*, or "let the master answer." It says that an employer is liable for harms done by employees while acting within the scope of their employment.[3]

The second legal issue deals with the way various federal regulations may be interpreted, especially in the "full disclosure" post-Enron era. Such matters have not been clearly resolved in the courts, but one attorney for a Fortune 500 firm, wrestling with the problem of a senior officer discovered to have a fake degree, expressed concern that the company's filings with the Securities and Exchange Commission, including the credentials of this officer, could be construed as a violation of Sarbanes-Oxley Public Accounting Reform and Investor Protection Act of 2002.

2. Financial Issues

Discovery of a fake degree problem can have a significant, even a dramatic, impact on the value of a company. The stock of two large American companies where a degree scandal surfaced declined sharply in the aftermath, and in Hong Kong, Richard Li, the tycoon often called "the

Bill Gates of Asia," saw the value of his companies drop by a billion dollars after his fake degree was revealed.

Sales can be affected through loss of confidence in the company, as can possible mergers and acquisitions. In what was known as the Fermenta Affair, a several-hundred-million-dollar sale of an industrial company to Volvo was canceled when the fake degrees of the seller became known to the buyer.

There is also the matter of companies that pay tuition for employees to acquire degrees from fake schools and pay them higher salaries once they have their degrees. Degree mills often publish lists of companies that pay tuition for their employees, and many of these claims turn out to be correct: the companies had simply failed to do the most minimal "due diligence" in checking whether a given school was properly accredited.

3. Publicity Issues

Public disclosure of a fake degree, especially when it is a person in a high profile and responsible position, has the potential to be a public relations nightmare.

Publicity can affect reputation, which can result in losing customers or clients, even if the person or people with fake degrees are dismissed. A big-city daily newspaper suffered a decline in readership and advertising revenue when the fake law degree of its publisher was disclosed by a rival paper. A national organization of health-care professionals lost members after its national director was found to have her highest degree from a California mill.

4. Business Development Issues

There are a great many people with fake MBA degrees. How many of these, as employees or consultants, may have produced flawed business plans, whether for small-business clients or departments within large organizations?

5. Logistical and Personnel Issues

As a practical matter, a person with a degree-mill degree, as well as most other unaccredited degrees, faces the risk of prosecution if he or she uses that degree in Illinois, New Jersey, Oregon, and other states, whether by working there or possibly attending a convention or sales meeting there.

There are the practical matters of whether such degrees should be included on personnel records, either with comment or without, and, if the employee keeps his or her job, whether the degree should be mentioned when a potential employer asks for references.

6. Ethical Issues

What about whistle-blowing? Should other employees be encouraged to report possible bad or fake degrees or even be rewarded for so doing? What about members of the public? When we have reported particularly egregious fake degree use to executives of organizations, sometimes we receive grateful thanks, and sometimes, as with a division of Brunswick that had paid for at least three fake degrees, we are told to mind our own business.

The role of an ethicist in these matters. Sometimes people who are faced with the decision of whether to fire, punish, or ignore a person with a fake degree turn to professional ethicists for advice and counsel. Marina Bear, coauthor John Bear's wife, earned her doctorate in philosophy from Vanderbilt University and has helped clients work through these issues. Here, for instance, is one of those cases.[4]

Case History

In a medium-sized American city, a job of school principal unexpectedly became available after the death of the incumbent. The school board decided to appoint a woman who was several years from retirement to reward her for many years of outstanding service. The problem was that the job required a master's degree, and this woman did not have one.

The school board apparently "looked the other way," while the woman purchased a master's degree from a degree mill operating from a mailbox rental address in another state. The degree, ostensibly based on her life experience, cost her about $1,000 and was delivered ten days after she applied.

After the new principal had served successfully for a year, the local newspaper discovered her fake degree and ran a story on it. At that point, a teacher in the district who had a legitimate master's degree, and had been in line for the job of principal, brought a suit against the school board, claiming it did not act appropriately.

The attorney for the woman who brought the suit was troubled. He was required to oppose a woman who was well liked, who by all accounts was doing a good job as principal, and who seemed to believe she was fulfilling the school board's wishes in acquiring this degree.

The attorney engaged Marina Bear's services to help him work through the complex ethical situation surrounding these matters. An abridged version of the report is provided in appendix A. It offers a detailed and useful way to look at and deal with the issues involved.

SHOULD JOB DESCRIPTIONS EVEN INCLUDE DEGREE REQUIREMENTS?

Many employees or job seekers feel they are compelled to deal with a bad or fake school in their desperation to secure a job where the degree is a requirement. Whether many job descriptions *should* have a degree requirement is a big and complex matter, beyond the scope of this book.

Certainly there are some situations where a degree is *essential*: a psychology degree for a therapist, a business or finance degree for a financial planner. But there are also many situations in which people have the necessary knowledge and skills without benefit of a degree. It is these latter situations that often motivate people, such as that school principal, to deal with degree mills.

A landmark Supreme Court decision, *Griggs v. Duke Power Company*, established that it is illegal to set an unnecessary job requirement, including a degree, solely to exclude certain people, typically minority groups, from applying.

The big question, then, is, just what is an "unnecessary" degree requirement? An important study by Ivar Berg, charmingly titled *The Great Training Robbery*, suggests that the degree requirement may be regularly abused.[5] Berg looked at jobs where some employers require degrees and others do not, ranging from air traffic controllers to operators of a fabric-cutting machine at a clothing factory. People without a degree were found to perform as well as, or better than, those with the degree. Berg suggests many employers have inappropriately been persuaded that degrees should be rewarded with higher salaries.

Why do so many jobs either require or reward degrees, forcing employees or job seekers to earn legitimate ones, or buy fake ones?

Reassurance that there is likely to be a certain knowledge or training level.

If a job pool at a brokerage firm included fifty applicants with Ivy League MBAs and fifty with no master's degree, the probability is high that most of the former group, and a much smaller number of the latter group, would be capable of doing the work. So why take chances? It is probably much more efficient to shortlist a subset of the MBAs and reject the others.

For every accomplished non-degree-holder, from Harry Truman and Eleanor Roosevelt to Bill Gates and Steve Jobs, there are many more who simply don't have the skills or training of a person with the appropriate degree or credential.

Simplifying the recruitment process. If one can reasonably expect hundreds of applications for a given job, it is much more efficient for the employer to reject automatically those persons who do not meet a certain criterion. It is illegal in most places to reject people based on their race, religion, or gender. However, one can have a degree requirement, as long as it can be defended as desirable for a given job.

Things have reached the point where many major employers use automatic resume-scanning software, and so the person without a degree may get the rejection letter without a human being even having looked at their otherwise impressive C.V. But the software is not nearly as likely to "know" that Trinity University can mean either the real one in Texas or the bogus one that operated from South Dakota.

Case History

John Bear once surveyed the personnel or HR departments of twenty airlines, all of which, at that time, required that pilot applicants have at least a bachelor's degree, although most did not specify that the degree be in a field related to aviation, science, or engineering. As one non-degreed applicant so charmingly put it, "I've flown four-engine jets for the Air Force for ten years, and I'm passed over for a Cessna-flying kid with a bachelor's degree in English poetry."

It makes the selection process faster and more efficient. If there are a great many applicants for an advertised pilot job, it is much simpler (although, of course, not necessarily fair) to reject automatically all those with no degree, since there will almost certainly be enough qualified people among the degreed subgroup.

Earning *any* sort of degree, even one in poetry, shows a certain level of gumption, of ability to follow instructions, play by the rules, and complete a major endeavor; as one personnel officer put it, "a demonstration of 'stick-to-it-iveness,' which is a quality we like in pilots." Of course, a degree in avionics or mechanical engineering might be a bit of icing on this particular cake.

Note: Not surprisingly, in times of major airline growth, and concomitant pilot shortage, these degree requirements tend to be removed or overlooked.

The bottom line here is for employers to look seriously at any degree requirements that are written into job descriptions and employment and union contracts, and for employees and potential employees to resist going out and buying a "time bomb" solely to meet some employer requirement, no matter how inappropriate or unfair it seems to be.

NOTES

1.   There are more than a few people who believe that credentials are irrelevant, that skill or knowledge is the only relevant consideration. Louisiana state senator Woody Jenkins opposed *any* school licensing in his state for this reason. He put his career where his mouth was. Even though he graduated from law school with highest honors, he refused to take the bar exam, claiming that the state had no right to decide who could give legal advice and who couldn't.

2.   John Bear consulted with the attorneys for the company, who were trying to decide if they should take any action in the matter.

3.   For instance, Supreme Court of the Unied States, *Faragher v. City of Boca Raton*, 524 US 775 (1998).

4.   A few nonessential facts have been changed to hide identities.

5.   Originally published in 1974, it was revised and updated in 2003; things hadn't changed all that much.

5

The Enforcers

HOW CAN DEGREE MILLS CONTINUE TO EVADE THE LAW?

This is a question we hear all the time. As John Bear once said in a speech at an accrediting agency convention, "If you hold up a convenience store for $50, you'll probably be in prison before your Slurpee melts. But if you steal millions of dollars from thousands of people by selling fake degrees, no one seems to be able to do anything."

That's a bit exaggerated, but there is almost always a triage situation going on in law enforcement. With a limited budget and limited personnel, which crimes or potential crimes are going to be dealt with? Degree mills often don't make the cut because they are much less visible and rarely involve violence or urgent matters of life and death.

Further, there are at least these four other factors:

- the complex issues of federal *versus* state jurisdictions, as well as the international complications;
- problems of enforcement, especially across state or national borders;
- issues of overlapping agency functions: the notion that degree mills have been dealt with by state attorneys general, other state and even county and local consumer protection agencies, the FBI, the FTC, the postal inspectors, the IRS, and others. Who makes the first move? Do they work together?

The US Department of Justice's *Prosecution Manual* suggests that prosecutions of mail and wire fraud "should not be undertaken if the scheme employed consists of some isolated transactions . . . involving minor loss to the victims. . . . Serious consideration, however, should be given to the prosecution of any scheme in its nature which is directed to defrauding a class or persons, or the general public, with a substantial pattern of conduct."[1] This is presumably why the FBI, the FTC, and the postal inspectors only choose to get involved if there is a likelihood of a large number of victims.

- The potential time and effort required to convince a judge to issue a search warrant, a grand jury to issue an indictment, or a jury to convict.

Here's an extreme but relevant example. The degree mill called Dallas State University began operating in the early 1970s. State officials in Texas took years to shut it down. But the mill reopened almost immediately as Jackson State University in California. The postal service eventually shut off its mail, whereupon the school resurfaced as John Quincy Adams University, with an Oregon address. And on and on and on. It was nearly two decades, and millions of dollars in revenues, before the FBI finally brought the perpetrators to justice. Nowadays, neither the FBI nor any other agency seems to have the time, the budget, or even the interest to pursue situations like this.

This became sadly clear recently when Allen Ezell discovered a flagrantly illegal degree mill operating in his home state of Florida. He collected a good deal of information and shared it with the appropriate regulatory authorities in the state capital who said, in effect, "Yes, we agree it is a degree mill, but we simply aren't going to be able to do anything about it at this time." A year later, the phonies were still in business.

WHICH LAWS ARE BEING BROKEN?

This is not a law textbook, and we will not go into great detail here. It is emphatically the case that there are ample laws on the books in every state and federal jurisdiction to deal with the selling, buying, and using of fake degrees. While not every jurisdiction has laws that specifically mention either degree mills or degrees, they all have laws dealing with fraud and other deceptive practices.

- Laws relating specifically to the *selling* of fake degrees: All fifty states have some laws governing school licensing and degree-granting behaviors, although a few are notoriously weak or vague.
- A handful of states have laws relating specifically to the *buying* and using of degrees, and we suspect an ever-growing number of states will move in this direction.
- All states and the federal government have laws dealing with fraud in general, which can include fraudulent behavior with regard to selling, buying, or using fake or misleading degrees.

As one example of this, there is a section of the United States Code that deals with fraud by wire (which includes telephone and Internet).

> Whoever, having devised or intending to devise any scheme or artifice to defraud, or for obtaining money or property by means of false or fraudulent pretenses, representations, or promises, transmits or causes to be transmitted by means of wire, radio, or television communication in interstate or foreign commerce, any writings, signs, signals, pictures, or sounds for the purpose of executing such scheme or artifice, shall be fined under this title or imprisoned not more than five years, or both. If the violation affects a financial institution, such person shall be fined not more than $1,000,000 or imprisoned not more than 30 years, or both.[2]

Other general fraud provisions are found in sections dealing with unfair or deceptive acts and practices by individuals or businesses that affect commerce in any way.

The Federal Trade Commission has made good use of this concept in its May 2003 action against a seller of fake degrees, part of which said:

> Defendants provide to others phony academic degrees, including but not limited to, doctoral degrees in medical related fields, and associated verification and backup materials, including, but not limited to, university transcripts, letters of recommendation, and other verification materials.
>
> These materials are used to facilitate deceptive activity, including, but not limited to, falsely representing that the recipient has completed and shown proficiency in a curriculum recognized as necessary to earn the academic degree, and that the diplomas are issued by established colleges or universities. By providing the academic degrees and associated verification and backup materials, Defendants have

provided the means and instrumentalities for the commission of deceptive acts and practices.

Therefore, Defendant's acts and practices, as outlined above, constitute deceptive acts and practices in violation of Section 5(a) of the FTC Act, 15 USC § 45(a).

Since there are no federal laws regulating degree mills per se, following is the "shopping list" from which an investigator, regulator, or prosecutor can choose where fake-degree selling or usage fits into the body of the frauds described. All but the last listing are sections of the United States Code, title 18:

section 2, Aid and Abet
section 371, Conspiracy
section 1028, False Identification
section 1030, Computer Fraud
section 1341, Mail Fraud
section 1344, Fraud by Wire
section 982, Forfeiture
section 1956, Money Laundering
section 1961 and 1963 (forfeiture 3554), RICO (Racketeer Influenced and Corrupt Organizations)
section 2320, Trademark Violation
United States Code, title 26, section 7201, Tax Evasion

SHOULD ALL DEGREE BUYERS BE PROSECUTED?

If there were a simple answer that all could agree on, of course we would not need lawyers or juries. But many write about the "art and science" of law. Some of each. We like the answer that a scholar of these matters posted on an education forum when the question arose.

If I buy a jar of pickles, then I own a jar of pickles. If I wanted to, I could *call* it a jar of diamonds, but that wouldn't make it anything other than pickles. It would be a stupid, but harmless thing to do. However, if I try to sell my pickles as diamonds, I'll be doing something dishonest. Buying a $500 jar of pickles that sits on a shelf in the garage is stupid. Buying a $500 doctoral diploma that sits on a shelf in the garage is stupid but not a fraud. But if I hang it on my office wall, and it plays any kind of a role in solicitation of business, then I would argue that both I, and the seller of my diploma, are in violation of the fraud provisions of the US Code.

HOW TO CHECK OUT A SCHOOL

The good news is that in a great many cases, the work has already been done, and one can rely on other people's research and opinions. The extent of checking depends largely on the purpose at hand: Is it simply a matter of whether to accept a given degree by an employer or other decision maker? A decision whether to consider a business venture with a school? Whether to recommend it to others or to enroll oneself? Whether to consider writing about it or prosecuting it?

Relying on others may be sufficient for most purposes, but doing one's own due diligence can be satisfying and, at times, especially informative.

Information Already Available

1. *Other people's lists.* As we have made clear throughout this book, there are institutions we choose not to call degree mills, but others do. In appendix H, we give the coordinates for the lists of schools without generally recognized accreditation, available from several states, one other country, and other useful sources. The most complete and most used list is the one maintained by the state of Oregon (see page 225).

2. *Ask a professional.* We often point out that many people who claim to have been fooled by a degree mill could have done the necessary "due diligence" for free in about one minute by telephoning the registrar or admissions office of any nearby college and asking if they accept the credits or degrees of such-and-such a school.

One can also hire, at modest cost, an expert: one of the reliable degree evaluation services that are members of the National Association of Credential Evaluation Services (NACES, www.naces.org) or use the services of the American Association of Collegiate Registrars and Admissions Officers (AACRAO, www.aacrao.org), or one of the private commercial services that do this kind of evaluation.[3]

3. *DegreeInfo.com.* This free Internet forum has more than one hundred thousand postings relating to schools good and bad. It has a good

search function, and it is also a place to ask questions. While the information is usually reliable, there are, of course, no guarantees.

4. *Agencies, directories, and reference books.* The legitimate agencies and reference books provide information on legitimate schools but rarely offer information or opinions on the others.

Agencies

Each state has its higher education agency or equivalent. Agencies rarely comment on the *quality* of schools, only on whether they are properly licensed, but there are exceptions. A complete list, with all contact information, can be found on the US Department of Education site at http://bcol02.ed.gov/Programs/EROD/org_list.cfm?category_ID=SHE or by typing "State Higher Education Agencies" into a Google search box.

We call various state agencies fairly often. We have found that once we get through the voice mail, the basic answers are generally correct but often incomplete. A lot depends on who happens to answer the phone.

For instance, one time when we called Alabama to check on a dubious school operating there, we were told, "Oh, we've been trying to close them down for years. At least we got them to agree not to accept students from the state of Alabama." But on another call to the same office, we were told (by a different person), "The state of Alabama has no official position with regard to this school."

In another example, we called the proper California agency to ask about a school that we had heard had just lost its state approval. The helpful person on the phone confirmed this and gave us the exact date it had happened. But then we found out, a few days later, that the school had gone to court and secured a writ that prohibited the state from enforcing its decision until further hearings were held, and thus the school continued legitimately in business.

The inconsistency from state to state, the level of knowledge of state personnel, and the volatile situation with regard to many schools and many laws makes our job a harder one—and yours as well.

Reference Books

The reference book we use the most is the *Higher Education Directory*, which lists every school with recognized accreditation, as well as all the recognized (by the Council on Higher Education Accreditation [CHEA] and the Department of Education) accreditors, the state agencies, and hundreds of higher education associations. A new edition comes out every November.

A list of all recognized accrediting agencies can be found on the Web site of the Council on Higher Education Accreditation, www.chea .org. A list of a great many unrecognized accrediting agencies can be found in appendix E.

Developing Your Own Information

1. *Hunches, intuition, and experience.* It may not easily be teachable, but we know with certainty that people who regularly check on educational claims develop a very strong sense of whether a school is likely to be good or bad, based on some combination of its name, location, the way it presents itself, the kind of address it has, and so on. It is not to be relied on as a sole reason for a decision, but it is an interesting and useful skill. Reviewing and becoming familiar with our list of ninety-two things degree mills often do and say (page 81) is one good way to start.

2. *Telephone the school.* If there is nothing but an answering machine during business hours, that is a clue. If a sleepy person answers when you phone at three in the morning their time, that is a clue.

3. *Determine who owns or manages the Web site.* This can be a very rich source of information, especially when the information conflicts with information the school publishes about itself. For all but ".edu" sites, two reliable sources of ownership of URLs are www.betterwhois .com and www.whois.net. For ".edu" sites (remembering that this suffix is no guarantee of legitimacy), the information is available at http:// whois.educause.net/edudomain/whois.asp.

4. *Determine what is at the "campus" address.* While a visual inspection is nice, it is often not essential. Typing the complete street address into the Google search box very often provides information on whatever is at that address. If it is a mailbox service or "executive suite" service—or, in the case of one especially dreadful school, a Holiday Inn hotel—you know what you need. If the listing is for a university, it still can be anything from one shared room to a major campus. Degree mill expert Steve Levicoff writes that local fire departments can be very helpful in telling what is to be found at a given address.

5. *Use reverse telephone information.* Typing a telephone number, with area code, into a search engine will often produce the name or names of

A University Without Wall, Off Campus........

American M&N University
(𝔏𝔬𝔲𝔦𝔰𝔦𝔞𝔫𝔞)

Current Catalog

𝔉𝔬𝔯 𝔐𝔦𝔡 ℭ𝔞𝔯𝔢𝔢𝔯 𝔄𝔡𝔲𝔩𝔱𝔰 : 𝔞𝔫 𝔞𝔩𝔱𝔢𝔯𝔫𝔞𝔱𝔦𝔳𝔢 𝔱𝔬 𝔢𝔡𝔲𝔠𝔞𝔱𝔦𝔬𝔫

"An alternative to education." Our favorite university slogan from this school whose Louisiana campus is a mail-forwarding service.

the school (or person or business) with that number. This is how we learned, for instance, that the Calgary Institute of Technology was actually a pizza parlor. The search engine at Google.com works well for this, and sometimes the free site at www.reversetelephonedirectory.com works even better.

6. *Business information.* Most schools, good and bad, are incorporated, and incorporation is a public action, with information available, usually online, from each state's secretary of state or comparable office. Some states' corporate records can be searched by name of people as well as organizations, which is how we learned, for instance, that one of our favorite scoundrels was involved, either as an officer or a director, with a couple of "schools" we'd not heard of before.

What If There Is No Information Whatsoever Available?

In the very unlikely but not impossible event that none of the eleven steps just described result in learning *anything whatsoever* about a given school, you may well be the first person ever who wishes to check it out. This sometimes happens. If it does, here are two suggestions.

Learn more (or try to) about the school.

If you have already learned that the school is not known to the relevant accrediting agencies or state or national departments of education, that very likely is all that you need to know. However, if it is important to know more about who the school is and how it operates, here are some

CURRICULA OF THESES AND AWARDS

CALGARY COLLEGE OF TECHNOLOGY
Caisse Postale 5481
Chinook Ridge
Calgary, Alberta, Canada
T2H 0L0
Tel: (403) 242-0444

At the Calgary College of Technology, the telephone is answered, "Hello, Spiro's Pizza."

questions you may wish to ask. It is safe to suggest that no legitimate school would decline to respond to such questions.

How many students are currently enrolled? Curiously, quite a few schools seem reluctant to reveal these numbers. Sometimes it is because they are embarrassed about how large they are, as, for instance, in the case of one alternative school that at one time had more than three thousand students and a faculty of five! Sometimes it is because the school is embarrassed about how small it is, as is the case with one heavily advertised school that has impressive literature, extremely high tuition, and fewer than fifty students.

How many degrees have been awarded in the last year? Some bad schools are embarrassed, either because there are so many (typically with few or no faculty), or so few.

What is the size of the faculty? How many of these faculty members are full-time and how many are part-time or adjunct? From which schools did the faculty members earn their degrees? From which school(s) did the president, the dean, and other administrators earn their own degrees? There is nothing inherently wrong with faculty staff members earning degrees from their own school, but when the number doing so is 25 percent or more, as is the case at some institutions, it starts sounding a little suspicious.

May I have the names and addresses of some recent graduates in my field of study and/or in my geographical area? Most, but not all, legitimate schools will supply this information.

May I look at the work done by students? Inspection of masters' theses and doctoral dissertations can often give a good idea of the quality of work expected and the caliber of the students. But you may either have to visit the school (not a bad idea) or offer to pay for making and sending copies.

Will your degree be acceptable for my intended needs (state licensing, certification, graduate school admission, salary advance, new job, whatever)? This sort of information is often specific to the state or country where the student lives and/or the field of study.

What exactly is your legal status, with regard to state agencies and to accrediting associations? If accreditation (or candidacy for accreditation) is claimed, is it with an agency that is approved either by the US Department of Education or the Council on Higher Education Accreditation? If not accredited, are there any plans to seek accreditation? Is the school listed in any major reference sources used by registrars and admissions?

No legitimate school should refuse to answer questions like these. Bear in mind, however, that alternative education does not require all the trappings of a traditional school. Legitimate schools may not have a big campus with spacious lawns, an extensive library, or a football team.

You definitely cannot go by the Web site, the catalog, or other school literature alone. Some really bad schools and some outrageous degree mills have hired good writers and designers and produced very attractive catalogs that are full of lies and misleading statements.

2. Ask us.

One of the ways we learn about new degree mills and other dubious schools is when people ask us.

If you have failed to learn about a new school after doing appropriate due diligence, as just discussed, *including pursuing the matter on* www.degreeinfo.com, then please let us know, and we'll do what we can. If you write or e-mail us, tell us what steps you have already taken to try to learn more. Please communicate in writing, either to info@degreemills.com or to P.O. Box 1575, El Cerrito, CA 94530.

HOW TO CHECK OUT A PERSON
WITH A SUSPECTED DEGREE

There are many variables to consider in this situation. The flow chart on page 140 makes the various paths clear.

The first variable is whether you want people to know that you are checking up on them.

If it is all right that they know, then of course, you can simply ask them. If they don't answer or are evasive or reluctant, this is useful information.

We are aware of more than a few situations in which a person simply declines to state. When John Bear asked the president of the unaccredited Somerset University (and several other schools) the source of his PhD, he replied, "That's for me to know and you to find out."[4] So not all "refuse to say" situations refer to fake degrees; some might just be embarrassing.

There is an interesting subset of prominent politicians who have properly accredited doctorates yet seem reluctant to reveal this in public. Most of the public seemed unaware, for instance, that Newt Gingrich, Phil Gramm, George McGovern, Woodrow Wilson, and others had legitimately earned doctorates.[5]

There is no simple way to find out where someone other than a well-known person earned her degree. A search of the Internet, or of the LexisNexis database of newspaper articles, may discover a news story or press release or governmental document that lists the school.

While the LexisNexis database is huge, it is also rather pricey. An excellent free alternative is the news search feature at http://news.google.com. The good news is that it searches millions of articles in nearly five thousand newspapers and magazines. The bad news is that at this time, it can only search for articles appearing in the past sixty days.

Another option is to use one of the relatively inexpensive document search services. For instance, www.knowx.com can search records of professional licensing, DEA registrations, Dun and Bradstreet reports, Experian business reports, and a large database of executive affiliations. There is no guarantee that degree sources will be given, but they could be. KnowX will tell you if the name you're checking on is in any of their sources, but then the actual information will cost between $5 and $10 in most cases.

In asking a person where he got his degree, it is prudent to do so in

FLOWCHART FOR CHECKING A DEGREE

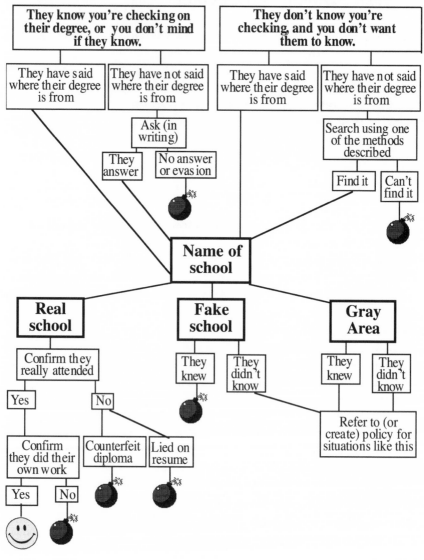

writing. There are more opportunities for miscommunication, intentional or otherwise, in speech. For instance, a person might be heard to
say the legitimate "Western Reserve," when in fact there is a fake school
also claiming to be in Cleveland called "Weston Reserve." Similarly,
there are fakes called "Concoria" (not Concordia) and "Stamford" (not

Stanford). And we read one report of someone replying "Southern Cal," which means "University of Southern California" to nearly everyone in that state, but which referred to the unaccredited but state-approved "Southern California University for Advanced Studies" in this instance.

Further in this vein, some people use initials intending to deceive. If a person in Arizona says a degree is from "ASU," it is assumed to be from Arizona State but may in fact be from the unrecognized American State University. An extreme case of deception by initials was the man in a medical profession whose business card said "John Smith, BA, MD." When authorities came for him, he explained that the listing really meant that he had earned his BA degree from the University of Maryland, the state whose official abbreviation is "MD."

Once the name of the school is known, from whatever method, the next step is to decide whether the school is real, fake, or in a gray area.

If it is either a degree-mill or a gray-area school, then the next question is whether the person knew or suspected it was fake.

If the school is legitimate, then the next step is to determine whether the person really attended and earned the degree(s) claimed.

Next, one may wish to get a copy of the transcript. Most registrars and many HR people will no longer accept a transcript that comes from the graduate. With technology ranging from white-out fluid and color copiers to complex computer programs, it is all too easy to modify or create a transcript. Most decision makers ask that the transcript be mailed directly from the registrar's office of the school.

Some fake transcript "services" (and there are many of them) are so sophisticated that they can reproduce most or all the forgery-preventing devices that are often used. Common ones are special-quality paper with a distinctive watermark, use of ostensibly noncopiable colors, a metallic strip embedded in the paper, use of microprinting (as on US currency), "secretly" embedded individual serial numbers, embedded holograms, and whatever new technology the transcript printers have come up with to try to defeat the forgers and have revealed only to their clients or, in some cases, to no one outside the company.

It is common practice to save and file the envelope in which a transcript arrived, first to make sure it was postmarked in the city where the school is located and sometimes even to go as far as analyzing the postal meter indicia to learn if the serial number matches that of the meter actually used by the school.

Inspecting the diploma itself. This does not necessarily provide useful

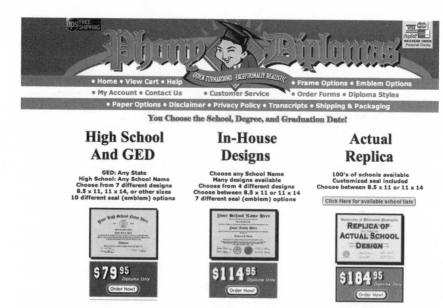

"Phony Diplomas" offers a cafeteria of choices: high school diplomas, degrees of their own design for $115, and authentic replicas for $185.

evidence, since there are so many "services" that sell counterfeit diplomas, and it is so easy for people to make changes in their own legal diplomas and then have them rephotographed or copied on a digital copier. In one case, for instance, a man who had been practicing law in California for quite a few years turned out never to have gone to law school, but he did take the nice certificate he was given after doing a weekend workshop on the law for businesspeople, pasted on new wording giving himself a law degree, and had a good color copy made of the finished product.

Asking the school. Nearly all legitimate schools will give out what is called directory information, which can include name and degree awarded and year. But some don't even do that without permission of the student or the student's Social Security number or a letter explaining the reason for the request. Some need to know the year the degree was awarded in order to confirm whether a given person received one.

If there is no apparent record of the degree, there could be an issue of a name change, whether through marriage or another reason, or a computer or clerical error. Some schools have lost records through fires or war-related events. Hundreds of legitimate, properly accredited schools have gone out of business. In most cases, they will have deposited their alumni records with the state education agency or, in the case of religious schools, with another school run by the same church or religious order, but there are exceptions.

Finally, a reminder that no detection method is perfect, and there are scoundrels with great skill or great luck who break through the defenses. One such example is the staff physician at a prestigious university's campus hospital who had never been to medical school but had the same name as a distant relative who had a legitimate medical degree. He was able to secure an authentic diploma and have authentic transcripts sent to his employer. He got away with it for years, until an uncomfortable family member reported him.

WHAT (IF ANYTHING) TO DO WHEN YOU FIND A PERSON WITH A FAKE DEGREE

This is a very complex issue, with legal, interpersonal, psychological, and other ramifications. And it is generally beyond the scope of this book. People who work for, or have involvement with, an organization and discover a "time bomb" in that organization are often in a different situation from members of the general public, because they need to think about the welfare of the organization as well as the common good. At least two questions merit consideration:

- Is the person with the bogus degree a danger to others or society, such as a medical practitioner or therapist or a mechanical engineer?
- If so, is the danger immediate, because he or she is seeing clients or flying the plane or building the bridge right now?

Even when the common good does not appear to be a major factor, as with discovery of an accountant or a warehouse manager with a fake degree, there is still the factor that ensuing publicity could affect the employer's reputation and possibly, if a publicly traded company, its share value.

It is essential to be on very firm ground when making an accusation, to avoid recriminations or legal repercussions. Conduct a *thorough* investigation before making any public accusations. Some whistle-blowers have themselves been criticized or even attacked for meddling in something that was not their business.

Finally, many whistle-blowers are disappointed by the nature or lack of response from the employer of a person with a questionable degree or the news media. We have that feeling all too often. How can anyone fail to be concerned about a NASA scientist, an engineer at Three Mile Island, or a senior army officer with a fake degree? But in these and many other cases, it happens regularly to us.

NOTES

1. *Federal Criminal Code and Rules* (Eagan, MN: West Group, 2000), pp. 423, 489, 663, 730.

2. Title 18, part 1, chap. 63, sect. 1343.

3. The largest of these is a company called United States Investigations Services (USIS), which was formed through the privatization of the investigative services branch of the Office of Personnel Management. USIS performs millions of checks every year for both government and private industry human resources departments. The authors of this book consult with USIS from time to time.

4. Eventually we did. It had come from an unaccredited school at one time approved by the state of California, which later lost that approval.

5. Columnist Herb Caen suggested this reluctance exists because many people don't want to vote for someone they think is smarter than they are.

6

What Can Be Done about Degree Mills?

What can be done? What can *we* do?

Those are the questions that we hear most often from law enforcement professionals, from government regulators, from educators, from journalists, from human resources professionals, from degree-mill victims, and from the general public.

There is no one single answer, but there are many possibilities that we discuss in this chapter.

Despite the gloomy state of affairs with regard to the proliferation of fake-degree sellers and users, we really feel there is hope of making a major dent in their activities. As discussed in chapter 1, we came so very close to eliminating degree mills in the 1980s, and maybe, just maybe, the time is right once again in this decade to try again to make a significant dent in the problem. It is possible that a combination of effective laws, effective enforcement, and effective publicity could increase the size of the dent.

The problem is vastly bigger than it was in 1991 when Allen Ezell retired from the FBI and DipScam ended. But there are many things that can and, we feel, *should* be done to address the problem today. Every phony that is closed, every scam artist who decides *not* to open a school, every company and government agency that improves its credential-checking activities, and every citizen who decides *not* to buy a degree is a step in the right direction.

This is the longest chapter in the book because there are so many things to suggest in the hope that even one might attract the attention and interest of each reader. We have identified more than one hundred things that could be done to address the problem.

And before we get to them, we need to acknowledge a few things that *are* being done as we go to press, which represents a situation very much in process.

In 2004, a diploma-mill summit was convened in Washington, with representatives from the Department of Education, the FBI, the FTC, the Office of Personnel Management, the Government Accountability Office, and some investigators representing the House of Representatives. Their announced goal was to protect the federal workforce from the scourge of degree mills. To this end, the Government Accountability Office has conducted a "degree audit" at the Pentagon along with a similar audit of six government agencies that was previously requested. The depressing results of this audit are discussed on page 159.

The first summit discussed the notion of putting out an "official" list of properly accredited schools. While it could do no harm to collect this information in one well-publicized and easily accessible official location, there are already such lists readily available in various published directories as well on the Web sites of the various accrediting agencies and others.

At least two significant problems arise about such a list, however.

One problem is the matter of the federal government suggesting that state-licensed schools are not acceptable, since they would apparently *not* be on such a list.

Should the federal government be in a position of saying that, for instance, a California-approved degree—one that qualifies its holder to sit for the bar exam and various state licensing exams—is unacceptable?

Can the federal government say, as *we* are happy to do, that some states' school laws are good ones, and others are terrible?

The even bigger problem is that of schools based in other countries that make their programs available to US students. The public would turn to such a list hoping to learn about the legitimacy of a given school. Presumably neither the venerable Oxford University nor the totally fake Harrington University would be on such a list, nor would any of the degree mills run from the United States but making use of registration or a mailbox in another country.

Far more useful, we suggest, would be an official list of schools that do *not* meet generally accepted accrediting principles.

Here now our thoughts on the many things that could be done to deal with degree mills.

WHAT THE FEDERAL GOVERNMENT COULD BE DOING

Federal Bureau of Investigation

The FBI has two ways of functioning with regard to potential crime: reactive and proactive.

Reactive

For many matters, the FBI waits until a crime has been committed or a complaint has been received. At that time, a regional field office will open a case and assign it to a special agent to investigate. If the investigation is of sufficient magnitude and involves other agencies, then a task force can be formed that includes investigators from the other agencies.

This task force can then deal with the matter locally, regionally, or nationally, with the nature of the crime most likely governing the scope of the investigation.

Proactive

When a problem is felt to be of sufficient importance, the FBI can be aggressive in addressing the matter, not necessarily waiting for a complaint to be filed. An agent writes a report for his or her supervisor, who decides if an investigation will proceed, if a US attorney should be consulted, or if the matter should be filed away for reference.

Thus, the FBI can become involved in the investigation and discovery of *potential* crimes. This is what is done, for instance, with terrorism, child pornography, Internet stalking, and so on. And, for ten years (1980 to 1990), it was done with diploma mills. During this time, Allen Ezell and colleagues, based in North Carolina and, later, Florida developed their own leads, pursued information submitted by the public, and worked closely with other agencies, grand juries, and federal prosecutors.

With Allen Ezell's retirement, DipScam was also retired. Now the FBI treats degree mills on a case-by-case basis, in the reactive model, as earlier described. There is little or no investigative work leading to the discovery of degree mills.

While this approach has resulted in a few significant accomplishments in the post-DipScam era—LaSalle University in Louisiana, Columbia State University in California, and the fake MD, "Doctor" Caplinger in North Carolina—activities in the field have been drastically curtailed in the last decade and a half.

Here are three suggestions for the FBI:

1. Best of all, of course, would be a revival of DipScam or something comparable, as a national priority. FBI people have suggested that in the post-9/11 world, new issues unrelated to terrorism must take a backseat. Well, even the backseat gets to wherever the car is going. And there are these two matters as well:

   • clear evidence that some unaccredited and possibly fake schools have somehow gotten permission to issue I-20 student visas, permitting foreign nationals to enter the country, and
   • clear evidence that one of the largest degree mills ever— hundreds of millions of dollars in revenues—is owned by an American living overseas, whose demographic profile suggests at least the possibility of a concern with terrorist matters.

2. A nationally designated specialist in degree fraud who can work with FBI regional offices, advise other law enforcement people, and be a liaison with the media.
3. A hot line and/or a Web site where people could learn about degree fraud and fake schools and leave information on potential abuse.

Federal Trade Commission (FTC)

The FTC's Bureau of Consumer Protection is mandated, as it says on its Web site (www.ftc.gov), "to protect consumers against unfair, deceptive or fraudulent practices. The Bureau enforces a variety of consumer protection laws enacted by Congress, as well as trade regulation rules issued by the Commission."

There was a time, half a century ago, when the FTC was on the front lines in dealing with fake degrees and the schools that issued them. But in the last few decades, the FTC has done little, even though some senior administrators there have knowledge of, and concern for, degree mills.

As with so many government agencies, the FTC operates in a triage model. With limited budget and investigative staff, the agency has decided to focus on claims for foods, drugs, dietary supplements, and other products promising health benefits; health fraud on the Internet; weight-loss advertising; marketing directed to children; performance claims for computers; tobacco and alcohol advertising; protecting children's privacy online; and claims about product performance. But with a few notable exceptions, there has been nothing related to fake degrees and their sellers.

In the mid-1990s, the FTC did a terrific job in the initial investigation that led to the closing of Columbia State University by the FBI and the postal service. The FTC maintains a "spam database"—spams forwarded by the public at www.ftc.gov, which the FTC monitors for themes of abuse and fraud. In October 2002, that database contained 15 million spams, of which 64,000 (about .05 percent) related to degree and driver's license fraud from the same American-owned, Romanian-based operation. Working with British authorities, the FTC secured temporary, then permanent, restraining orders to close down the Web sites and domestic voice mail and message drops, and, with British authorities, enjoined the entities involved from sending out these spams.

Sadly, this was only a temporary roadblock in the path of the Romanian juggernaut, which, undeterred, promptly moved them to service providers in other countries. (The FTC action is described at http://www.ftc.gov/opa/2003/01/idpfinal.htm.)

The good news is that the FTC has provisions for Priorities, Enforcement, and Rules in place to strike a major blow to the degree mills.

The bad news is that it hasn't exercised those priorities or enforced those rules. Here are the details.

Priorities

The stated priorities of the FTC's Division of Marketing Practices, available on its Web site (www.ftc.gov), include "shutting down high-tech Internet and telephone scams that bilk consumers out of hundreds of millions of dollars annually" and "halting deceptive telemarketing or direct mail marketing schemes that use false and misleading information

FEDERAL TRADE COMMISSION

Guides for Private Vocational and Distance Education Schools

PART 254 (as revised August 1998)

§ 254.0 Scope and application.

(a) These Guides apply to persons, firms, corporations, or organizations engaged in the operation of privately owned schools that offer resident or distance courses, training, or instruction purporting to prepare or qualify individuals for employment in any occupation or trade, or in work requiring mechanical, technical, artistic, business, or clerical skills, or that is for the purpose of enabling a person to improve his appearance, social aptitude, personality, or other attributes. These Guides do not apply to resident primary or secondary schools or institutions of higher education offering at least a 2-year program of accredited college level studies generally acceptable for credit toward a bachelor's degree.

(b) These Guides represent administrative interpretations of laws administered by the Federal Trade Commission for the guidance of the public in conducting its affairs in conformity with legal requirements. These Guides specifically address the application of section 5 of the FTC Act (15 U.S.C. 45) to the advertising, promotion, marketing, and sale of courses or programs of instruction offered by private vocational or distance education schools. The Guides provide the basis for voluntary compliance with the law by members of the industry. Practices inconsistent with these Guides may result in corrective action by the Commission under section 5 if, after investigation, the Commission has reason to believe that the practices fall within the scope of conduct declared unlawful by the statute.

§ 254.1 Definitions.

(a) Accredited. A school or course has been evaluated and found to meet established criteria by an accrediting agency or association recognized for such purposes by the U.S. Department of Education.

(b) Approved. A school or course has been recognized by a State or Federal agency as meeting educational standards or other related qualifications as prescribed by that agency for the school or course to which the term is applied. The term is not and should not be used interchangeably with "accredited." The term "approved" is not justified by the mere grant of a corporate charter to operate or license to do business as a school and should not be used unless the represented "approval" has been affirmatively required or authorized by State or Federal law.

§ 254.2 Deceptive trade or business names.

(a) It is deceptive for an industry member to use any trade or business name, label, insignia, or designation which misleads or deceives prospective students as to the nature of the school, its accreditation, programs of instruction, methods of teaching, or any other material fact.

§ 254.3 Misrepresentation of extent or nature of accreditation or approval.

(a) It is deceptive for an industry member to misrepresent, directly or indirectly, the extent or nature of any approval by a State agency or accreditation by an accrediting agency or association. For example, an industry member should not:

    (1) Represent, without qualification, that its school is accredited unless all programs of instruction have been accredited by an accrediting agency recognized by the U.S. Department of Education. If an accredited school offers courses or programs of instruction that are not accredited, all advertisements or promotional materials pertaining to those courses or programs, and making reference to the accreditation of the school, should clearly and conspicuously disclose that those particular courses or programs are not accredited.

to take consumers' money." Such as, may we suggest, fake-degree schemes bilking Americans out of many tens of millions of dollars a year.

Enforcement

The FTC's enforcement division has the power to enforce "federal consumer protection laws by filing actions in federal district court on behalf of the Commission to stop scams, prevent scam artists from repeating their fraudulent schemes in the future, freeze assets, and obtain compensation for scam victims."

Rules

Most significantly, the FTC already has a rule in place dealing with false claims made by schools about the nature of their degrees and their accreditation.[1] The reason the word *Rule* has a capital R is that Rules are a very specific aspect of what the FTC can do. But the kicker is that the FTC has a bit of Pollyanna philosophy: the FTC hopes and expects that everyone will do the right thing. And so it depends heavily on "voluntary compliance" with its Rules. This is a little bit like leaving your store unlocked at night and hoping that the crooks will practice "voluntary compliance" with burglary laws and leave you alone.

Rule § 254.3 is extremely clear and unequivocal. It says that "an industry member should not . . . represent, without qualification, that its school is accredited unless all programs of instruction have been accredited by an accrediting agency recognized by the US Department of Education."

The Rule appears on page 150.

Our recommendations for the FTC could hardly be clearer or simpler.

1. Enforce your own Rule 254.3! It would have dramatic and instantaneous effect tomorrow morning. Every one of the thirty unaccredited schools that have advertised in the past year in *USA Today, The Economist,* and other major publications is in violation of this Rule. If they couldn't make their useless accreditation claims, these unaccredited schools would get far fewer customers. And if they made the claims on the Internet, or through mail or telemarketing, it's time for your enforcement division to act.
2. Add degree mills to your enforcement priorities.

3. Put up a warning on your otherwise excellent Web site at www.ftc.gov. The site provides useful consumer advice on automobiles, investments, credit privacy, diet, products and services, e-commerce, scholarship services, energy, telemarketing, franchise opportunities, telephone services, tobacco, identity theft, and travel. Information on degree and credential fraud would be a fine addition. Now, a search of the FTC site for "diploma mill" finds one "hit" (and that not too helpful), while "telemarketing" yields 2,493 hits and "identity theft," 1,151.

Internal Revenue Service

The IRS is always interested in criminals and scam artists: people who, in addition to their ill-gotten gains, don't always pay their taxes. But there have been situations in which the IRS inadvertently helped out some fake schools and agencies by being remiss in the matter of monitoring their nonprofit status.

When a school or an accrediting agency identifies itself as nonprofit, there is a certain marketing advantage. The public, rightly or wrongly, sees a nonprofit as more legitimate, less likely to be raking in huge profits for greedy owners. When the IRS allows a for-profit entity to call itself nonprofit, it is contributing to the deceit.

To be tax exempt, an organization, as described in section 501(c)(3) of the Internal Revenue Code, must be set up so that none of the earnings or profits go to any individual, and if the organization goes out of business, all its assets must go to other nonprofit causes or to the government.

Several mills actually reproduced a copy of a 501(c)(3) nonprofit IRS form as part of their literature, but apparently they never had that status or even applied for it.

The IRS participated in the search of LaSalle University in Louisiana, ostensibly run by a non-profit church, because of these concerns. The concerns were valid, and tax fraud was one of the many counts on which LaSalle's owner was later indicted. He had taken a "vow of poverty," and so the tiny "church" he started owned his sports cars, his million-dollar riverfront mansion, and so on.

And the unrecognized accreditor called World Association of Universities and Colleges attracted member schools in part by featuring their nonprofit status. But a successful legal action brought against

WAUC by a disenchanted member school determined that the association was, in fact, a for-profit organization.

We appreciate that the IRS cannot do a detailed investigation of every 501(c)(3) applicant to be certain each is a true nonprofit. But we hope the IRS will pay close attention to some of the multi-million-dollar mills that may be hiding their profit-making status and under-reporting or not reporting their ill-gotten gains, sometimes through banking chicanery involving off-shore or other foreign accounts.

United States Postal Service and the Postal Inspection Service

Both the USPS in general, and the Postal Inspection Service in particular, have had a modest role in dealing with degree-mill issues.

The Postal Inspection Service is the primary law enforcement arm of the United States Postal Service (www.usps.com/postalinspectors). Postal inspectors are federal law enforcement officers who carry out investigations, make arrests, and serve federal search warrants and subpoenas. But there are only about two thousand postal inspectors for the entire United States, and with the huge increase (and high profile) of identity theft crime, and other matters, there has been little focus on degree mills.

Perhaps there is also the factor of overlap with other law enforcement agencies, as well as the fact that many degree mills specifically avoid using the postal system in order to escape the jurisdiction of postal inspectors, resorting instead to the unpoliced Internet and the more anonymous overnight delivery services.[2]

Like the Federal Trade Commission, the Postal Inspection Service generally does not deal with individual cases of mail fraud, but, as its Web site says, "it can act against a company or individual if there is a pattern of activity suggesting a potential scheme to defraud."

The postal service can, however, stop delivery of mail to a given customer when there is ample evidence that the customer is behaving in an illegal manner. The postal inspector prepares an affidavit in which he or she describes probable cause of illegal activity through the US mail. The inspector then appears before a US magistrate in US District Court. If the magistrate feels there is probable cause, a temporary restraining order (TRO) is issued. The TRO enables the inspector to stop mail delivery. Mail is returned to the sender with a notice that mail service has been suspended for illegal activity.

This very relevant tool has been applied to diploma mills only rarely, and even then, not necessarily permanently. While mail to the phony John Quincy Adams University was permanently stopped in the 1970s, mail to the currently active University of Berkeley (run, according to the FBI, from a shed in the owner's backyard in Erie, Pennsylvania, but claiming a "campus" which is really a mail box service in Michigan) was temporarily stopped in the late 1990s, but later resumed.

The USPS Web site suggests that the main current concerns of the Postal Inspection Service are identity theft, senior sweepstakes victims, spam, home improvement schemes, phony inheritances, unsolicited merchandise, prison pen pal money order fraud, and fraudulent health and medical products. There is nothing said about degree-mill fraud. It would be an appropriate addition to this site.

There have been a small handful of occasions in the last decade when the Postal Inspection Service *was* the lead agency in a degree-mill issue, most notably in the cases of Gold Coast University (also known as Coast University) in Hawaii, John Quincy Adams University (address in Oregon, actually run from Illinois), and the fake medical degrees sold by a man in Virginia representing two Caribbean frauds, CETEC and CIFAS. In these cases, the postal inspectors did the investigation and prepared the brief to secure the search warrants that led to the "raid" on the premises. They also worked with the FBI and the IRS in collecting evidence in several other cases, including participating in the execution of search warrants.

While dealing with degree mills themselves is a matter that can be handled by a number of different law enforcement agencies—local, state, or federal—there are two degree-mill matters that are solely related to the United States Postal Service, and both, unfortunately, have had recent law and policy changes that immeasurably benefit the fake schools.

Private Mailboxes

There are more than ten thousand private mailbox services, about a third of them UPS stores (formerly Mail Boxes Etc.) at which individuals and businesses can rent a box to receive their mail. Many degree mills receive their mail in this fashion, in the United States, Great Britain, and elsewhere. They wish to fool their customers and potential customers into believing they have a campus, or at least offices, and so they wish to have an address that cannot be clearly identified as a mailbox service.

For many years, private mailbox services permitted their customers to use the street address plus almost any sort of number, which actually identified their rented box.

> 123 Main Street, Suite 23 (or Apartment 23)
> 123 Main Street, Building 23
> 123 Main Street, 23rd floor

Then, in 2002, the postal service passed a consumerist regulation, which required businesses using a private mail box to use "PMB" and a number for their address:

> 123 Main Street, PMB 23

While not everyone knew what a PMB was, many did, and it certainly waved a major red flag for anyone checking out a school.

As the Federal Trade Commission's Shirley Rooker wrote when this PMB regulation went into effect, "Recent amendments to postal regulations will make it harder for criminals to victimize innocent consumers by using mail drops. . . . The second line of the address block on mail going to mail drops must carry the designation PMB, which stands for private mailbox. It also must be on the return address of outgoing mail. These changes are significant because crooks, hiding behind private mailboxes, have ripped off seniors, traded in child pornography, operated lottery scams, and conducted a host of other frauds" (http://www.ftc.gov/bcp/conline/audio/private_mail_box.htm).

But a year later, the postal service was ordered by the Bush administration to end this requirement, since it was felt by the government to be hostile to small businesses: it prevented them from having a "presence" as an actual business with real offices. The degree-mill operators (and, presumably, the child pornographers) could not have been more pleased with this decision.

The Freedom of Information Act and P.O. Boxholders

A great many degree-mill and unaccredited-school operators have used post office boxes (as contrasted with private mailboxes) as their primary or sole address. It is important for people checking out a school, whether as a potential student or as an investigator, to learn where the school is *really* located. It has been not uncommon for a school to have a box in one state but to be located in another state or even in the home of the owner.

For many years, the Freedom of Information Act was specifically made applicable to the postal service (39 USC 410(b)(1)), requiring any local postmaster to make available to any member of the public the actual physical location of any holder of a commercial post office box as the customer reported it on Form 1583. On many occasions, important information was learned about a degree mill's real location, its real owner, and links with other businesses, through this use of the Freedom of Information Act.

In 2002, this all changed. It is no longer possible for an individual, whether student, potential student, journalist, or other interested party, to learn the real location of the holder of a post office box rented for business purposes. Postal Bulletin 22018 states that "information contained in Form 1583 will be disclosed only to a government agency upon written certification of official need or pursuant to a subpoena or a court order. . . . USPS will ignore civil subpoenas."

Once again, the degree-mill operators could not have been more pleased.

Even when the postal service was required to give the street address of commercial box holders, the system was abused by degree mills, since the postal service either did not confirm that the street address provided on Form 1583 was a real one or that the business in question was actually there. For instance, when a colleague, using the Freedom of Information Act, got the street address provided by a New Orleans "university" that was (and still is) heavily advertised, he found nothing but a totally empty and apparently abandoned room in a small office building. The institution seems to have lied in filling out Form 1583, itself a federal crime.

The use of private mailboxes by degree mills does have its amusing moments. When one currently operating wonder (then run from Connecticut, now claiming to be in Moscow or possibly in Liberia) was using a private mailbox in South Dakota, it insisted that its multi-thousand-volume university reference library was located at their South Dakota "campus."

Summary of Recommendations for the USPS

- Include degree-by-mail fraud information on the USPS Web site.
- Require any entity calling itself "college" or "university" to identify its address as a private mail box (PMB).
- Make the actual addresses of any post office box renters calling themselves "college" or "university" available to the public under the Freedom of Information Act.
- Make more active use of the power to stop mail delivery to degree mills.

Office of Personnel Management (OPM)

OPM calls itself "the Government's personnel agency" (www.opm.gov). As such, it is very much interested in and concerned with the matter of degree mills, fake credentials, and resume fraud. In 1998, we were invited to put on a two-hour workshop on degree mills for an OPM conference in Pittsburgh. And when the senior official in the Department of Homeland Security with three degree-mill degrees was discovered by the media in 2003, OPM, under pressure from Capitol Hill, convened two half-day workshops where we had the pleasure of speaking to nearly five hundred senior federal human resources executives and investigative officers. This event was repeated in 2004.

There were suggestions in the press that OPM may bear some responsibility for problems such as the one at homeland security, primarily by not having clear procedures and guidelines in place for the hundreds of federal agencies and thousands of federal offices to deal with issues of hiring and promotion that might involve fake schools and degrees. In fact, there *are* such guidelines in print, and they were given to participants in the 2003 workshops.

The problem seems to lie in area of encouragement and motivation to *use* these guidelines, since the kinds of comments we heard from well-meaning HR people are ones like:

- I didn't appreciate the scope of the fake degree problem.
- I didn't realize there were fake accrediting agencies.
- I didn't know how easy it is to get counterfeit diplomas and transcripts.

The process of checking people out seems remarkably informal. When a federal agency, whether NASA or a Bureau of Indian Affairs field office in Arizona, has a question about the school claimed by a job applicant, it can ask the OPM Investigative Services Office in Pennsylvania whether such-and-such a school is legitimate. Often, the diligent and hardworking staff members will know. From time to time, they ask us.

But there are problems with this system.

- The various federal HR departments may not see a red flag and may not even ask OPM.
- The system does not directly address employees with counterfeit credentials with the names of legitimate schools.
- The system does not address people who simply falsify their resumes.
- With nearly two million federal employees, there are bound to be some, perhaps many, who have slipped through the net.

Since "the Director of OPM is the President's principal advisor in matters of personnel administration . . . and for the improvement of human resource management and human capital practices," there is ample opportunity to make information on fake degrees and credentials available not only to federal agencies but also to others who may come to the OPM Web site (www.opm.gov) and archives to gain information on how "the government's personnel agency" deals with these issues.

But no information is to be found there. A search of the large and well-designed Web site for the terms *degree, diploma, credential,* or *resume* comes up with nothing. The site index, with more than five hundred listings, from "Access America" to "Zipped File Help," has nothing. Nor does a search of OPM's list of hundreds of publications, periodicals, operations manuals, CDs, and videotapes.

It could be very helpful, both to federal agencies and the human resources world in general, if OPM had its clear guidelines on checking out schools and credentials available.

OPM maintains millions of personnel records at its investigative center, deep in a limestone mine in eastern Pennsylvania. An investigative reporter in Washington has told us that he has fantasies about the number of "time bombs" that may be ticking away there, but he acknowledges they are just about as inaccessible as the gold in Fort Knox.

Government Accountability Office (GAO)

The GAO is the audit, evaluation, and investigative arm of Congress. Its mission, as stated on its Web site (www.gao.gov), is "to help improve the performance and ensure the accountability of the federal government for the American people." The tools of the GAO are financial audits, program reviews and evaluations, analyses, legal opinions, and investigations. The GAO has recently had two significant involvements in the world of fake degrees.

In early 2003, Sen. Susan Collins of Maine was concerned about the proliferation of degree mills on the Internet. Contact was made with GAO's investigators, who then purchased two degrees for $1500 from the fake Lexington University, in the name of Susan M. Collins.

Further testing the system, these investigators then established their own fake school, the Y'Hica Institute for the Visual Arts, ostensibly in London, England. Then they made application to the Department of Education for authority to obtain federal student loans. They were all too successful. As the Associated Press reported, the GAO had little trouble gaining US certification of the school by the Department of Education and obtaining loan approvals for three students (including Susan M. Collins) from two of three major lending institutions contacted (Nellie Mae Student Lending Inc. and the Sallie Mae Servicing Corp.) Only the Bank of America became suspicious and did not offer the more than $50,000 in requested loans.

Under instructions from the Senate Committee on Governmental Affairs, the Government Accountability Office conducted a "degree audit" of eight federal agencies, looking for employees at the GS (General Schedule) 15 level and above who had degrees from unrecognized schools.

GS-15 is quite a high-level position, with salaries typically over $100,000 a year.

The GAO found twenty-eight senior-level employees with highly dubious degrees. Further, in records obtained from three unrecognized California and Wyoming schools, the GAO found 463 federal employees at all GS levels, at least 14 percent of them paid for by the agency (and, thus, by the taxpayers).

In connection with those three California and Wyoming schools, the GAO uncovered another widespread scam. Since the federal government will pay for courses (but not degree programs) from unrecognized schools, representatives of every school contacted by undercover investigators offered to bill for individual courses (even though no courses were actually offered), and then to apply the federal payment for these nonexistent courses to the degree program and award the degree.

Some responses to the GAO findings suggest that the numbers were small enough not to be alarming. Consider, however, the following.

The GAO audit looked at only eight agencies, fewer than 5 percent of the total number. The GAO looked only at people with a GS-15 rating or higher, fewer than 5 percent of the total number of people. And the GAO looked for a limited number of dubious schools, again probably fewer than 5 percent.

These three "fewer than 5 percent" categories suggest that if the GAO had looked at the full categories, it would have found at least twenty times twenty times twenty—or eight thousand times as many people with unrecognized degrees.

And even that very large number does not take into account the very large number of people who have bought counterfeit diplomas with the names of real schools or who have simply lied on their resumes.

The tax-paying American people might well benefit from more action by the GAO. If the Department of Education itself could be duped by a not-too-elaborate fake school, then how many other government agencies have inadequate defenses against this sort of thing? More "sting" operations would help us learn.

And since the very modest degree audit turned up all those "time bombs," how many others might there be among the more than four million federal employees, civilian and military? Wouldn't it be extraordinary if those four million resumes were matched against the names of the one hundred largest mills?

A concerned or angry enough Congress could order the GAO not only to find out but also to tell us what it learned.

Department of Education

The US Department of Education is in an awkward and ambivalent place when it comes to degree mills. On one hand, the department is the place that many people, businesses, and organizations think first of telephoning, writing, or e-mailing to find out more about mills and to learn whether any given school is legal.

On the other hand, as Secretary of Education Rod Paige wrote in

October 2003, "the Department of Education has no oversight or regulatory authority over institutions that do not participate in the programs included in the Higher Education Act. Thus we have no independent authority or ability to determine if such a school is a diploma mill."

Paige continues that the decision as to whether any given school is a mill "is best made by appropriate regulators in the State in which the school is located."

The huge problem with this suggestion is that we are talking about fifty very different sets of state laws here and, in the world of distance education, people in one state regularly dealing with a school in another state. Therefore, we have the common situation in which a school may be completely legal in one state (for instance, California approved, Alabama approved, or Wyoming licensed) and yet be regarded as illegal and, indeed, a cause for prosecution in another state.

This said, the good news is that some very useful information on degree mills can be found, with only a bit of difficulty, online. An "advanced search" for the phrase "diploma mill" or "degree mill" takes one to a very helpful location (http://www.ed.gov/about/offices/list/ous/international/usnei/us/edlite-accred-fraud.html), with valuable information, strong warnings, and, significantly, links and references to some even more helpful nonfederal sites, such as the excellent State of Oregon one (see page 225), as well as John Bear's publisher's informational site at www.degree.net.

Here, then, are four suggestions for the Department of Education:

1. An official federal response to the problem. Secretary Paige has written (October 2003) that "this problem is serious and requires careful consideration by the Department [of Education] as to whether a federal response is appropriate."

   We suggest that it is. In 1960, for the first and only time, the then Office of Education published what was called an "Official List of Diploma Mills." There is no reason this could not be done again, avoiding the problem of state differences by including only those places that were beyond any reasonable doubt phony—perhaps, for instance, those chosen unanimously by a committee of experts in the field.
2. A more user-friendly Web site (although the current one is quite good). On the opening page, there is a "quick click" menu for major topics, such as accountability, charter schools, and tech-

nology. Adding "degree mills" there would be a good choice. And when one types "degree mill" or "diploma mill" into the regular search box, it comes up with more than five hundred "hits," the vast majority of them either minimally relevant or not at all relevant. It would be nice if the searchers were taken just to the few directly relevant places.

3. A consumer information site, directly linked to the opening page, and supported with in-print and telephone services. The extremely concerned and helpful Office of Accreditation and State Liaison within the Department of Education has been considering actions in this direction, and we think this should be encouraged, supported, and financed.

4. An ombudsman office. The Department of Education already has such an office to deal with mediating and resolving problems related to financial aid. Such an office could also deal with school and degree matters, including problems of acceptance of degrees by employers and schools, problems of schools misrepresenting themselves, and so on.

The US Congress

Because our country's founders chose not to give any control over education to the federal government, the subject has been largely a matter dealt with by the states, with the major exception of federal loan issues.

Every five or six years, when the nation's Higher Education Act is rewritten, and every special interest group, from school bus safety to naturopathic physician licensing, is focused on Washington, there are those who hope that Congress will address the matter of fake schools and degrees.

There are laws that could be passed that would address these matters. The most obvious is a federal law comparable to some of the state laws that make the *use* of a fake degree a crime.

And Congress *does* control the budgets for other federal agencies and thus could exert some influence on the FTC, the FBI, the OPM, the GAO, and others, suggesting politely that it might be good for all concerned if they helped us get rid of degree mills.

The recent degree-mill interest of elected officials such as Sen. Susan Collins and Rep. Tom Davis, and of appointed officials such as Education Secretary Rod Paige, suggest there may the best hope of congressional action in these matters since Congressman Pepper's Subcommittee on Fraud stirred everyone up more than twenty years ago.

US State Department

The Apostille is one of the most common tools used by degree mills to fool people, especially in other countries, into thinking that the US Department of State has somehow approved its school.

An Apostille is nothing more than a kind of notarized document, but at the national level, instead of the local (county) or state level.

You can take any kind of a document to a local notary, pay the small fee, and get it stamped and sealed, *no matter what the content may be.* The notary neither reads nor confirms in any way the content of the document. You can type out a declaration that General Motors owes you a million dollars and get it notarized. You can type out a document stating that you've won the Nobel Prize and get it notarized. All notaries generally do is confirm, usually by looking at a driver's license or passport, that you are the person the document says you are.

Next, you can send your local notarized statement to your state and get state notarization (typically called *authentication*). And then you can send it on to the US Department of State and get federal notarization (called *apostille*). At no point in this process is the content of the document of relevance.

So the degree mills dutifully type up a statement that they are accredited, licensed, approved, accepted, whatever, and get it notarized through the Apostille level. And then they claim that the US State Department has granted an Apostille approval to the school's charter. Very clever, if totally fraudulent. (Some mills even cheerfully point out that their Apostille is signed by Colin Powell, thereby ensuring, they say, worldwide acceptability. The same claim was earlier made about Henry Kissinger. In fact, the secretaries *never* sign Apostilles. As is made clear on the document itself, they designate a clerk to sign for them.)

The only hope for change here is that the authentications office of the Department of State is mandated to "ensure . . . that the requested information will serve in the interest of justice and is not contrary to US policy."

It may well be somewhere between an invasion of privacy and a can of worms to suggest that the various notaries public, especially at the federal level, pay attention to the content of what they are notarizing. Surely the way the Apostille process is misused cannot serve the interest of justice.

United States of America

DEPARTMENT OF STATE

To all to whom these presents shall come, Greetings:

I Certify That the document hereunto annexed is under the Seal of the State of
California, and that such Seal is entitled
to full faith and credit.*

In testimony whereof, I, Colin L.
Powell, Secretary of State, have
hereunto caused the seal of the Department of State to be affixed and
my name subscribed by the Assistant
Authentication Officer, of the said
Department, at the city of Washington, in the District of Columbia,
this 30th day of September, 2004.

Colin Powell's Signature
Secretary of State
Someone Else's Signature
Assistant Authentication Offier

* For the contents of the
annexed document, the
Department
responsibili

*** For the contents of the
annexed document, the
Department assumes no
responsibility.**

ANNEXED DOCUMENT

Allen Ezell
and John Bear
have been
awarded the
Nobel Prize
for Physics.
Dr. Ezell
earned his
Ph.D. from
Harvard Uni-
versity. Mr.
Bear has been
elected
Governor of
Nebraska.

How the Apostille is Misused by Degree Mills. An Apostille consists of a state-
notarized "Annexed Document" and a certificate from the Department of
State acknowledging that the state notarization is authentic. It can say anything
you want.

WHAT INTERNATIONAL ORGANIZATIONS COULD BE DOING

Interpol

Interpol is not a police force itself, but it facilitates the police of each of its 181 member nations working and cooperating with the police of other countries in crimes that involve two or more countries. In other words, it is a communication service, which can smooth the progress of interaction between any of the twenty thousand federal, state, and local law enforcement agencies and their counterparts in other parts of the world.

The Interpol office typically can be found inside an existing agency. In the United States, the US National Central Bureau for Interpol can be found in the Department of Justice in Washington and has, not unexpectedly, a connection with the Department of Homeland Security.

Like so many agencies, Interpol operates in a triage mode and must decide, for any given case, if it has staff, budget, knowledge, and interest in helping. It seems logical that Interpol should have interest in international degree fraud, since it fits in Interpol's priority areas of interest: money laundering, financial and high-tech crime, and public safety.

In reality, degree matters seem not to be a priority. We have heard from people who came to us for information that said they were unable to obtain through ordinary Interpol channels. For instance, a US attorney in New York tried without success to get information on the big Romanian degree seller because a local psychotherapist was using one of those degrees. And a county weights-and-measures investigator, asked to learn more about a local mailbox service that was receiving mail for a Belgian degree mill, ran into a dead end when he asked Interpol for help in communicating with Belgian authorities.

We wish Interpol would at least take international degree fraud more seriously and provide information on its Web site (www.interpol .int). Now one can find useful material on things from counterfeiting to football hooliganism, but a search for the words *degree, school, diploma,* or *certificate* came up empty.

International Organization for Standardization (ISO)

The International Organization for Standardization (abbreviated ISO in the United States) was established to develop an international system of standards so that, for instance, a Norwegian flange (made to ISO standards) would fit onto a Malaysian furnace, or a South African chemical compound could be used in a Bolivian laboratory.

Within ISO is a subdivision, ISO 9002, to cover organizations that produce, install, and service products. One of these "products" is education, leading to degrees.

Nearly twenty years ago, an unaccredited school in California began marketing the fact that they had "achieved" ISO 9002 certification. When we asked its founder, Theron Dalton, how this had happened, he was unusually candid. "The first one through the door gets to write the standards," he said in a personal communication to John Bear. "You could write standards for a cement life preserver, and as long as you make them to that standard, you'll get your ISO certification."

The encouraging news is that there was no flood—indeed, barely a trickle—of other schools following this approach. In 1999, Eastern Michigan University announced it was "the only accredited university in the northern hemisphere to be ISO 9002 certified."

It might be appropriate for the International Organization for Standardization to revisit the matter of certifying degree-granting universities, both to weed out the less-than-wonderful ones and as a boon to transnational acceptance of schools and degrees.

The United Nations

Bad and fake schools love to claim that they are in some way affiliated with or approved by the United Nations. The UN is so huge and complex and bureaucratic that there is often no one there who knows or frets about the flea who claims to have captured the elephant on which it lives. Nor does it seem practical to expect the UN to notice when a degree mill claims to be UN-approved because it made a small donation to a charter school sponsored by large corporation that was a private-sector partner of UNESCO.

There are, however, two things the UN might address.

Foremost is the matter of the International Association of Universities, self-described on its Web site (www.unesco.org/iau) as "the UNESCO-based worldwide association of universities." The IAU maintains a list of schools it calls the World Higher Education Database (WHED), and it publishes a huge book called the *International Handbook of Universities*.

While rules for being listed in the WHED must have seemed straightforward when originally formulated, they become much less clear in a world where, for instance, complications like the following can occur.

- One UN member nation can accredit a university not recognized in its own country (for instance, St. Kitts and Nevis for a university that at the time was run from New Hampshire and the Republic of Malawi for a university based in Wyoming).
- A US company can make a deal with an accredited university in another country to offer doctoral degrees in the US with little oversight from the home university. (For instance, a doctorate-granting institute that was run briefly from Florida, ostensibly linked to a traditional Mexican university that seemed to have no idea what was being done in its name.)
- People claiming to represent a UN member nation can sell the accreditation of that country to schools in another country (for instance the recent offer to sell Liberian accreditation for fees that grew quickly from $1,000 to $50,000).

In each of the above cases, and others, the schools in question either were listed in the *International Handbook* or made the claim that they would be.

It would be good if IAU's UNESCO Centre on Higher Education, based at UNESCO House in Paris, were crystal clear on the rules for inclusion and exclusion from the *International Handbook*. Some of the above-mentioned cases dragged on for a year or more, causing much public confusion.

It would also be nice to have relevant information readily available, perhaps on the IAU's Web site at www.unesco.org/iau/. At one point in 2003, for instance, a dubious school with Liberian accreditation emphatically claimed that it had been approved for inclusion in the next *International Handbook*. It took a colleague's telephone call to the director of the IAU/UNESCO Information Centre in Paris to learn that this was a lie.

Finally, the estimable United Nations University, based in Tokyo, is an international community of scholars serving as a "think tank" on matters of global concern. It is presumptuous to think that international degree fraud should be on the same page with issues of poverty, war, human rights, famine, security, and AIDS. But among the hundreds of conferences, seminars, and workshops that UNU holds or sponsors each year, perhaps one might look at (and help increase awareness of) the degree-fraud problem.

STATE AGENCIES

Every state has one or more state agencies that deal with approving or licensing new schools in the state and regulating schools that already operate in the state. A few have laws specifically relating to the use of degrees by people in the state.

With fifty sets of state laws, and with enforcement attitudes and policies ranging from strict to negligible, the situation is complex and often unclear. There are many anomalies, which making trying to "get a handle" on the state situation even harder. Here, as an example, are half a dozen.

- Montana had a decent school-licensing law but intentionally chose not to enforce it.
- California has reasonable school-licensing laws but chooses to ignore the many unaccredited schools that are really run from California although they have a token office or just a mailbox in another state or country.
- Louisiana exempted religious schools from the need for state licensing but then agreed that religious schools could offer degrees in nonreligious subjects, since God created everything.
- Wyoming also fails to regulate religious schools and allows them to offer nonreligious degrees. And Wyoming's nearly automatic licensing of unaccredited nonreligious schools has made that state a haven for the "bad guys."
- New Mexico enacted a reasonable school licensing law but then grandfathered in all the unaccredited schools that could never have qualified under the new law.
- Idaho properly regulates most schools but intentionally ignores some dreadful Idaho-based schools as long as they do not enroll students living in that state.

The Eight Questions a State Should Ask

We are not going to get into detailed recommendations for each state; that could fill an entire book.[4] These are eight questions that any state might well ask on the occasion of considering new laws or revisiting old laws relating to schools and degrees, with some short comments on each.

1. *Academic quality and/or consumer issues.* Some states look closely at curriculum. The state of New York is actually a recognized accrediting agency. Some states have little or no interest, as long as the public isn't defrauded. Indeed, in the late 1990s, California took the unusual step of moving school licensing from the Department of Education to the Department of Consumer Affairs. For schools in our state, are we concerned with the academic quality of schools, the consumer issues (not making misleading claims or taking money under false pretenses), or both?

2. *Actual presence in the state.* Are we concerned about schools that have token offices (or mailboxes) outside the state but which really are run from within our state? This is, for instance, a significant issue in California, where some very large unaccredited schools are almost entirely run from offices in California, despite claiming their authority to operate from Wyoming, Hawaii, New Mexico, and elsewhere.

3. *Out-of-state schools.* Are we concerned with schools that have no connection with our state but offer programs and degrees to state residents? Some states, such as Minnesota, have made the claim that they have the right to restrict out-of-state schools that do not meet their standards from offering correspondence or online programs to people in their state. Schools that were notified that they were in violation simply changed their rules by saying that all diplomas would be awarded only in the state where they were located and that graduates would have to travel there, or make private shipping arrangements, to receive their diplomas. A California school that received the Minnesota warning hired a constitutional lawyer, who told them she felt Minnesota was on shaky ground based on precedents for interstate commerce.

4. *Procedures for starting a new school.* Do we want to encourage people to start new and innovative schools in our state? A few states encourage this, a few tolerate it, and many discourage it. California and Indiana, for instance, encourage innovation through a meaningful but not excessively rigorous procedure of state licensing called State Approval in California and State Accreditation in Indiana. Other states, such as Louisiana and South Dakota, have adopted what is called the

"up or out" approach. New schools are permitted to operate for a fixed period of time with little oversight (two years is typical), but if they have not achieved recognized accreditation, or cannot show they are close to it, then they can no longer operate.

5. *Regulating degree use.* Are we concerned about the degrees used publicly by citizens of our state or visitors to our state, regardless of where the degrees were issued? In the 1990s, Florida enacted a law making the use of unaccredited degrees illegal. The law was badly written—not taking into account non-US schools, for instance—and was found to be unconstitutional, although the *state* Supreme Court said it had good intent and could be rewritten. Since that time, there has been a small trend toward regulating degree *use* rather than degree *granting.* Oregon, Illinois, New Jersey, Nevada, and North Dakota have passed such laws. The challenge is to be extremely clear in defining what is illegal and to have enforcement procedures in place. Oregon's detailed model regulation and North Dakota's much shorter one are included in appendix D. In these states, the use of a prohibited degree is a misdemeanor subject to fine and imprisonment. Whether passage of such laws is a trend or not remains to be seen.

6. *Clarity of the law.* Are our laws (or proposed laws) clear, unambiguous, and sensible? Florida's law badly defined eligible schools. Iowa's "up or out" law had no time provisions. Other states have suffered from intentional ambiguity—something happening "when it is felt that" certain circumstances have occurred. And a few have referred to "accredited colleges and universities" without taking note of the fact that there are many unrecognized accreditors. Hawaii has a law that makes it extremely easy to be a legal school there: in effect, having little more than one employee in the state and a small number of Hawaii residents enrolled. But even that is more than many fake schools do, and Hawaii has been aggressive in pursuing violators.

7. *Fairness and uniformity.* Are the laws enforced fairly, uniformly, and strictly, or *would* they be? We hear from regulators and enforcers that because of budget cuts, staff shortages, and lack of direction from management, they are limited—and frustrated—in their pursuit of bad schools. Hawaii, as just mentioned, has been the most aggressive in bringing legal actions against violators—more than fifty to date— largely due to the efforts of one attorney in the Department of Consumer Affairs, who operates in triage mode, due to the number of possible cases.

8. *Nature of penalties.* Are the penalties meaningful, or are wrists being slapped? Large fines are common, imprisonment is increasingly rare, and enforcement is a real problem. The state of Kansas won a million-dollar-plus judgment against degree-mill operator Les Snell, but he moved to Colorado and was not pursued. Hawaii has won numerous million-dollar judgments, but mostly against perpetrators living elsewhere, and collections are rare. Is prison a deterrent? Sometimes. Some major perpetrators (Geruntino, the Fowler brothers) never went back into the business after prison. Some (Sinclair, Kirk) actually ran their next phonies from within prison. And others (Reddeck, Pellar) went back into business as soon as they were freed.

Each of these questions is worthy of lengthy analysis and discussion, and indeed such discussions have gone on in many states over many years, sometimes harmoniously (or at least collegially), and sometimes acrimoniously.

Other Government Agencies

Noneducational or consumer-related agencies at the state, county, and city level have, from time to time, been relevant in the fight against degree mills, in matters as ordinary as sales tax (fake schools may not be collecting and paying it), zoning violations (doing business from a home), business and insurance violations (employees not being paid minimum wage or provided with workers' compensation insurance), as well as health and safety violations. (Columbia State University had sixteen people, many of them undocumented aliens, working in a small, poorly ventilated, and generally unsafe building, with no business license and numerous other violations, ignored, sadly, by the city of San Clemente, Orange County, and indeed the state of California.)

PRIVATE AGENCIES

There are hundreds of organizations and agencies that are concerned with one or more aspects of colleges and universities, accreditation, degrees, and credentials. And the issues that occur with these organizations are twofold.

First, many of them have open membership. Anyone can join. And so degree mills often say (correctly but irrelevantly) in their literature that "We are members of the American Council on Education, the International Council on Education, the Society for University Planning," and so on.

Our recommendation here is that these organizations restrict their institutional memberships to schools with recognized accreditation (or its counterpart in other nations) and that they pay attention to the use of their name by both members and nonmembers.

The second issue is that of improving public awareness of bad and fake schools. Of the myriad acronymic groups out there (AACSB, AAACE, AAHE, AAPICU, AAUA, ACBA, and so on, and that's just a small portion of the As), almost none has any public awareness or information on these matters. One exception is the Council on Higher Education Accreditation (CHEA), which *does* have several pages of useful degree-mill information, but no search engine, on its Web site (www.chea.org). Users must click down several levels into "How does accreditation work" to find those pages.

An example from a few years ago shows how valuable such organizations *could* be. There was an interesting phony university operating from Miami, using the name of a legitimate university in Peru (Villarreal) and claiming to be its "international office." Nonresident PhD degrees were offered through aggressive advertising. As many as a thousand US academics signed up, at $10,000 each, thus a $10 million business. As things began to shred (phone calls unanswered, mail returned), more and more people began writing and calling the American Council on Education, which told us at the time that it was concerned and looking into the matter. But to the best of our knowledge, the ACE never said or did anything publicly, either in the way of a warning, or advice to victims. The fake Villarreal simply faded away, and no refunds were ever made. Today, if one searches the ACE Web site (www.acenet.edu) for "diploma mill," the only "hits" are a few trivial mentions—but no useful information.

Human Resource Policies

Shortly before the FBI "raid" on the phony LaSalle University in Louisiana, LaSalle's literature listed hundreds of large companies that they said accepted and, in most cases, paid for their degrees. When we started checking on that claim, by calling the companies listed, we discovered that LaSalle's claim was correct but for the wrong reasons. Based on ten completed phone calls, we learned that four of the companies had confused the fake Louisiana LaSalle with the real Pennsylvania LaSalle. And the other six said that their policy was to accept and often pay for *all* accredited schools. They didn't know that there was such a thing as unrecognized or fake accreditation.

The lack of knowledge and skill among many corporate human resources and personnel officers was clearly determined by a comprehensive survey of them, done as part of Richard Douglas's 2003 doctoral dissertation research through the Union Institute and University.[5]

Douglas had more than 250 HR executives with major companies fill out a long and detailed questionnaire, in which they were asked to rate the acceptability of various schools when considering employees for hire, promotion, and tuition reimbursement purposes. The list of schools included everything from traditional regionally accredited institutions to out-and-out degree mills.

Douglas determined that human resource professionals often do not understand the differences between real and fake schools, and they often do not check. Many of these professionals responded that they accepted, for hiring, promotion, and tuition reimbursement, degrees from schools they did not know were degree mills.

Further, a significant subset of them ranked completely phony schools (e.g., Columbia State University) ahead of regionally accredited schools (e.g., Capella University).

In his dissertation, Douglas concluded that "human resources professionals require training regarding degree acceptance and recognition."

We concur and suggest that the problem is immense and one of great urgency.

Online Resume Services

One of the major marketing phenomena of the Internet era is the growth of online resume services. People looking for jobs, or thinking about changing jobs, put their resumes or C.V.s online, where they can be read by potential employers. Typically, there is no charge to make your resume available, and then companies and other potential employers pay a monthly fee for the privilege of searching through these resumes.

One company, Monster.com, has, through internal growth and through acquisitions, grown phenomenally to dominate this field. In 2004, it had more than 20 million resumes online, representing more than 10 percent of the entire American workforce. Using its fast and efficient search engine, employers can quickly find job seekers sorted by location, by skills, by salary . . . and by degrees claimed.

Monster.com and its two major competitors (Yahoo's HotJobs.com and CareerBuilder.com) do not investigate or verify any of the statements or claims made on these resumes. It is the case that many thousands of people list degrees from degree mills.

In 2000, at the request of ABC's *Good Morning America*, John Bear conducted a detailed search of the Monster.com database. Since ABC was looking for only a handful of people to interview, the searching was stopped after five thousand people with responsible positions *and* fake degrees had been found. Clearly, there could have been a great many more. And goodness only knows how many others—a far larger number, we suspect—list degrees from legitimate schools that they did not happen to earn or for which they had purchased a counterfeit diploma.

Of course, people should not list fake degrees on their resumes. But many do. And of course employers should use due diligence to check on these degrees. But many don't.

And so Monster.com (and the others) could perform a very helpful service simply by declining to post resumes that list degrees from bad, fake, or simply unaccredited schools. How would they choose which ones? They could either develop their own list or they could use a publicly available list, such as that produced and put online by the states of Oregon or Michigan.[6]

Sadly, this is not done, and it seems unlikely to be done. A colleague of ours, who believed he had a good personal relationship with one of the founders of Monster.com, approached that person with ample evidence of some of the dangerous fakes with resumes on Monster (the doctors, lawyers, sex therapists, teachers, nuclear engineers, and so on), with the idea that Monster could not only do a lot of good in the world but also gain an edge on its competition by weeding out these thousands of imposters.

Despite several follow-up inquiries, he never got an answer. But a few months later, the press reported that the CEO of Monster.com himself had been falsely claiming to have an MBA.

The Media

The media (newspapers, magazines, radio, and television) have played the role of both hero and villain in the fight against degree mills. On one hand, a superb four-day page-one series on degree mills in Arizona's largest daily paper was instrumental in the passage of tough new state laws and the closing or departure of dozens of fake schools operating there.[7] On the other hand, virtually every weekly issue of the prestigious *Economist* magazine has several, sometimes many, advertisements for totally fake schools. The good and the bad were ironically juxtaposed when *USA Today* ran a long and good degree-mill warning front-of-section article . . . and five pages further along were advertisements for some of the bad and fake schools at which the article warned.[8] The Internet version of the article was accompanied by paid banners for some of the worst offenders.

The message to these media is simply this: Stop running ads for unrecognized and fake schools. It is doing a terrible disservice to your readers, as well as giving added credibility to the phonies. Often we hear from an aggrieved victim, "But I saw the ad in *The Economist*. Surely *The Economist* wouldn't accept ads from fake schools." Yes, it would, and it has been doing it for years, including the notorious "PhD in 27 Days" ads and others of its ilk.

We estimate that the more than a thousand bad and fake school ads that have run in *The Economist* have cost readers many millions of dollars, as well as planted time bombs in countless resumes.

The "hall of shame" of major media that routinely run such ads include *The Economist*, *USA Today*, *Psychology Today*, *Utne Reader*, *Army Times*, and *Navy Times* (think how many servicemen and -women are being fleeced by their own trade publication), the *International Herald Tribune*, many of the airline in-flight magazines, *Investors Business Daily*, non-US editions of *Time* and *Newsweek*, and all too many more.

Frequent Publicity

The media generally have little interest in the fake schools, but they do pay erratic attention to people caught using fake degrees. While the case of the past executive director of Moral Majority, identified during Congressional hearings as holder of a degree from a diploma mill, got a lot of coverage, the 2003 discovery of questionable degree held by an undersecretary of defense got almost no media attention.

Of course, we wish there were more substantial coverage, as this is one of the few ways to discourage people from buying fake degrees. But we've gotten quite discouraged tugging on sleeves in the hope that the media will pay attention. Ezell and Bear were both involved in the federal trial of a flamboyant and colorful family from Chicago, the Fowler brothers, on trial in Charlotte, North Carolina, for running a string of a dozen or more fake schools and accrediting agencies. Ezell describes this case in chapter 1.

As it happened, the trial of Jim and Tammy Fae Bakker and Jessica Hahn was going on in the same building, so the lobby was awash in reporters and photographers. We could not interest a single one of them in the multi-million-dollar degree-fraud case that went on there for three and a half weeks. To the best of our knowledge, not a word about the Fowler brothers ever appeared in a newspaper or magazine.

As long as we are addressing the media, there is one more issue. Quite a few of the consumerist articles that do appear regarding degree mills caution the readers to deal only with accredited schools. But they often fail to go the crucial next step and warn the readers that there is such a thing as fake accreditation; that there are nearly as many fake accrediting agencies as there are fake schools. And we get the sad letters from victims saying, "But they were accredited; I checked it out."

Registrars and Admissions Officers

College registrars are faced every day with the need to make decisions on which degrees and transcripts to accept, which to question, and which to reject.

Their professional association, the American Association of Collegiate Registrars and Admissions Officers (AACRAO, www.aacrao.org), has been on the front lines of the fake-degree battle for a long time.

- They frequently have workshops on degree fraud at their national and regional conventions, conducted by Allen Ezell and other experts.
- They have an Internet forum where professionals can ask questions and exchange information.
- They sell two helpful publications dealing with these matters: a twenty-five-cent brochure and a $25 workbook, both listed in the bibliography.
- They offer, for a fee, the service of evaluating academic credentials. While the service is comparable to that performed by independent credential evaluation firms (discussed in this section), AACRAO's opinion tends to have more "clout" because it is who

it is. As a result, it could be more proactive and perhaps a bit faster in identifying and evaluating degree mills.

At the time, in 2003, when a dozen American-run unrecognized schools paid up to a $50,000 fee and made the claim of Liberian accreditation, many eyes turned to AACRAO to see what it would have to say. Many months passed because AACRAO was apparently waiting for someone formally to request and pay for an evaluation of one of these Liberian accreditees. Finally this happened, and AACRAO issued a policy statement saying that recent Liberian accreditation did not meet its standards. Prompter action might have impeded the growth of some of the dreadful schools in question.

Guidebook Publishers

The public tends to rely on the information found in published directories and guidebooks, especially when they come from large and well-known publishers. Unfortunately, in the world of college guides, this confidence is problematic. Dreadful and fake schools have been listed in major directories, either because of simple errors or, far worse, because of company policy.

In the former category, for instance, the once-preeminent *Lovejoy's College Guide* used to list the fake Edison College (Florida and Arkansas) instead of the real one (New Jersey).

In the latter category, the *now*-preeminent Peterson's not only sells space in its books to schools, where they can write whatever they want about themselves, but also the company has entered into a partnership with some "schools" whose degrees are illegal in some US states. On its Web site, www.petersons.com, the company states that "Peterson's partners with the following schools and service providers. Visit their content centers and fill out an instant inquiry to receive more information." The pull-down list, on September 1, 2004, listed thirteen schools, two of them (15 percent) in the "illegal in Illinois and elsewhere" category.

We believe these "partnerships" and these listings are misleading.

Educause

Educause is a large nonprofit association "whose mission is to advance higher education by promoting the intelligent use of information technology." In November 2001, the US Department of Commerce gave Educause the sole authority to dispense the ".edu" Internet suffix, which is widely (but incorrectly) regarded as a measure of legitimacy.

The problem is that more than fifty bad and fake schools have already been given, and regularly use, the ".edu" suffix. This was done through a combination of clerical error and lack of clear policy, mostly by the company called Verisign, which used to be in charge. Verisign mistakenly gave out more than four hundred ".edu" suffixes during its tenure.

The problem now, as reported by Alan Contreras of the Oregon Office of Degree Authorization on the official Oregon Web site at http://www.osac.state.or.us/oda/diploma_mill.html, is that "Educause has decided that because there are so many hundreds of unaccredited users, they don't want to deal with purging, so there will be *no* effort made to limit use of the .edu suffix to legitimate schools."

Contreras goes on to say that he has "already posted a formal warning on the Oregon Web site stating that the extension '.edu' is in essence a random, meaningless arrangement of letters that does not confer any kind of legitimacy on any entity, nor is it ever likely to do so."

This regrettable situation could be solved if Educause were to make the current rules retroactive and also were to apply them accurately to new applicants. They are *still* giving the .edu extension to bad and fake schools.

If Educause continues to stonewall in this matter, perhaps some of their eighteen hundred institutional members, virtually all of them properly using their ".edu," might have something to say to them.

Another solution lies in the fact that the US Department of Commerce, even though it gave the "franchise" to Educause, still retains final say on the way Educause handles .edu matters. That responsibility lies within the National Telecommunications and Information Administration within the Department of Commerce, which could invite Educause to shape up.

Colleges and Universities

A few years ago, John Bear wrote an article for *University Business*, a magazine for university presidents and financial officers. The title was "Diploma Mills: The $200-Million-a-Year Competitor You Didn't Know You Had" (http://www.degree.net/html/diploma_mills.html). The main point was that the huge phonies were not only demeaning the whole world of higher education but diverting students who might have attended the legitimate school.

The article encouraged universities to speak out actively on the problem; aggressively protect their own good name, when a fake school used the same or a comparable one; and refuse to advertise in publications where their own ad would run alongside ads for fake schools.

After the article ran, there were perhaps a dozen letters to the editor received from university presidents, all of them of the *"They* should do something!" variety.

There have been rare exceptions. The real Washington University in St. Louis got an injunction against the dubious Washington University in Pennsylvania—but the dubious one simply changed its name to Washington International. The real Thomas Edison State in New Jersey got an injunction requiring the fake Edison (run from a prison cell in Texas) to give up its name. And then there was the fake Western Washington State University, complete with its own ".edu" suffix (www .wwsu.edu), run from Norcross, Georgia. The real WWSU, in Bellingham, Washington, got an injunction, but the Georgia-run phony merely changed its name slightly to Western Washington International University, did not change its Web site, and rolled merrily along. More recently, the real American University won a domain registration dispute with the less-real Americus University, which simply disappeared.

For the most part, universities do not protect their own good name. There is a charming display at the Coca-Cola museum in Atlanta showing all the would-be competitors the company was able to stop: Boca-Cola, Roca-Cola, Koka-Cola, and so on. Would that some of that same attitude carried over to Berkeley, Cambridge University, and the University of Wyoming, for instance, who have been told about the dubious University of Berkley (a shed in Pennsylvania), Cambridge State University (a mailbox service in Hawaii), and the fake University of Wyoming (run from Switzerland), but they have done nothing.

Even worse are the counterfeiting services, routinely selling well-made copies of the diplomas and transcripts of hundreds of legitimate schools. In addition to the fraud perpetrated by the sellers and buyers of these products, and the degrading of the real school's good name, there is also the matter of both trademark and copyright violation.

Credential Evaluation Services

One of the very complex issues in higher education is the matter of international equivalencies. Is a British "honours" degree equivalent to

VNIVERSITAS
HARVARDIANA

CANTABRIGIAE IN REPVBLICA MASSACHVSETTENSIVM

QVONIAM

IOANNES BEAR

studio diligentiore et specimine erudeirionis idoneo adhibias
Professoribus Artium et Scientarium
persuasit se penitus pernoscere

CHIRURGIA CEREBRUM

Praeses et Socii Collegii Harvardiani Ordine Professorum
illorum commendante atque consentientibus honorandis et
reverendis Inspectoribus dederunt et concesserunt ei gradum

DOCTOR MEDICINUM

et omnia insignia et iura quae ad hunc gradum pertinent.

IN cuius rei testimonium nos Praeses et Decani auctoritate
rite commissa de Domini 14 Martius 1989
Collegiique Harvardiani
Vniversitatis sigillo muntis nomina subscriptsimus.

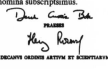

PRAESES

DECANVS ORDINIS ARTIVM ET SCIENTIARVM

DECANVS ACADEMIAE SVPERIORIS

John Bear's Harvard medical degree, with a specialty in brain surgery, came from the Alumni Arts counterfeiting service. The microscopic type at the bottom says, "This is a reproduction. No school, credit, or degree status is granted or implied."

an American bachelor's, master's, or in between? What about a Mexican "Bachilerato" or a Japanese "Gakushi"? To help resolve these questions, the US Office of Education used to offer a credential evaluation service. But this was discontinued in 1974, giving rise to the growth of independent and unregulated evaluation services—more than thirty at this time.

About half of these services belong to a trade association, the National Association of Credential Evaluation Services (www.naces.org), and while they may differ somewhat in some of their evaluations, they are unlikely to report that a degree mill or unrecognized school is equivalent to a properly accredited American university.

However, because the field is unregulated and unlicensed, anyone can hang out a shingle as a credential evaluator, including people who also run degree mills. Indeed, this has already happened.

As educational philosopher Bill Dayson wrote on DegreeInfo.com in 2003,

> Credential evaluation could very easily become the next new frontier of "degree-mill-science." Perhaps it already has. We have had phony universities, then spurious accreditation, so why not some corrupt evaluators? Unlike universities and accreditors, evaluators are faceless

and work in the shadows. You can search for schools and accreditors, but evaluators remain mysterious and hidden.

Since anyone can open a spurious credential service on the Internet, there is no way this practice can be stopped. Short of the Department of Education returning to the business of credential evaluation (extremely unlikely), we can only wish that NACES will do its best to be militant in policing its members and applicants and that registrars and HR professionals will give extra care to scrutinizing reports from evaluators with which they are not familiar.

In 2004, eleven teachers in Georgia lost their jobs after buying masters' and doctoral degrees from the spurious St. Regis University, ostensibly in Liberia.

As the *Atlanta Journal-Constitution* (March 13, 2004) reported,

> Georgia recognized degrees from St. Regis, because it was affiliated with the American Association of Collegiate Registrars and Admissions Officers, a nonprofit voluntary organization that includes a foreign education credential service. But officials with [AACRAO] said they offer membership to anyone who pays. . . . Dale Gough, the organization's director of international education services said if Georgia officials had called his association about St. Regis, he would have told them, as he has told other states, that St. Regis was a diploma mill.

Georgia was also duped by a bogus credential evaluation agency, apparently financed by St. Regis, and run by a woman in Florida (using an assumed name) who had been involved with fake schools in the past.

Better Business Bureau

In the mid-1990s, Columbia State University was the biggest degree mill in the United States. It was also a member in good standing of the Better Business Bureau, which reassured many people who went on to buy a fake degree. When experts complained about this policy, the BBB response was to say that it could not adjudicate differences of opinion.

The BBB is a place that a great many consumers turn to check out a company or organization. But they do a considerable disservice to the public by accepting as members in good standing quite an array of unrecognized schools that may operate legally in their own jurisdictions (Idaho, Mississippi, Alabama, Wyoming, etc.) but whose degrees would subject the holders to criminal action in various other states.

To their credit, the BBB does offer a one-page warning about degree mills, although a search of its site for "degree mills," "degree fraud," "fake degrees," or "credential fraud" will not find it. But under "diploma mills," the BBB does warn consumers to be careful in choosing an unaccredited school, but it makes the major error of not pointing out that there are a great many unrecognized accrediting agencies—such as the ones used by schools that are BBB members in good standing.

We'd like to see the BBB restrict membership to schools with recognized accreditation.

Headhunters

More than a few executives and administrators with fake degrees have been recruited and recommended by executive search firms, commonly known as headhunters. When this happens, not only are the headhunters doing a major disservice to their clients, but also they may be putting their own firms in jeopardy.

In 2002, there was a major page-one scandal in New Zealand when the newly hired head of one of the two national television services, Maori TV, was found to have a degree from the degree mill called Denver State University. John Davy, a Canadian, was fired, then arrested, convicted, and imprisoned, all within a few months. A great deal of the wrath of the press and the politicians fell on the headhunter firm that found and recruited him, Millennium People.

While a Millennium People director claimed that "extensive reference checks" had been done, and they were "defeated by a sophisticated international fraudster," the simple fact is that three minutes of Internet research or a call to the registrar of any New Zealand university would have produced the information that the school in question was a fake.

Millennium People went out of business as a result of the loss in business following this event. Other recruitment firms have survived, albeit with a diminished reputation, in comparable situations, as in the case of the superintendent of schools for California's second-largest school district whose headhunting firm failed to discover his fake doctorate claim.

The best advice here is, simply, that one should perform due diligence and not rely on earlier results. The California superintendent's spurious doctorate had been missed in each of his three previous top jobs, with each headhunting firm possibly assuming that earlier searches had verified the degree.

Internet Service Providers and Search Engines

This may be a little bit like making a wish that there that would be no more war, famine, or floods on our planet. We have four wishes here. The first may be on its way to coming true; the second at least is a possibility, but we hold little hope for numbers three and four.

1. *Regulate spam.* It would be nice if the big companies that offer e-mail services could do something about the millions of spam messages sent every week to their customers by the degree mills and other bad schools.

In 2004, four major suppliers of e-mail services (Microsoft, America Online, EarthLink, and Yahoo!) jointly announced that they filed the first major industry lawsuits under the new federal antispam law, the so-called CAN-SPAM act, which went into effect at the start of 2004.[10]

The complaints charge the defendants with sending a combined total of hundreds of millions of bulk spam e-mail messages to customers of the four networks on topics that include get-rich-quick schemes, prescription drugs, pornography, banned CDs, mortgage loans, cable descramblers, and university diplomas.

2. *Responsibility for site content.* The second wish has a chance of coming true, albeit probably not through the industry developing a conscience (some providers may, but there will always be rogues) or through government regulation (there will always be rogue nations as well).

As of 2004, the matter of the responsibility of Internet service providers for information appearing on their services is very much unresolved in US courts. While pre-2003 decisions followed the wish of the Congress to preserve the "vibrant and competitive market" of Internet speech by protecting ISPs from litigation, a late-2003 ruling by a California appellate court held unanimously that ISPs *can* be held legally responsible for content if they were aware of the illegality of that content.[11]

It is likely this matter will be in the courts for years to come.

3. *Offering Web sites to fake schools.* It would be so nice if Internet service providers stopped providing services to fake schools.

4. *Search engine issues.* It would be so nice if the major Internet search engines (Google, Yahoo!, Lycos, etc.) did not produce the names

of fakes intermingled with legitimate schools, when people search for degree programs.

It would be so nice if these services did not sell banner and pop-up advertising to fake schools and counterfeiting services.

Academic Research

Given the importance of degree mills in the academic world, as well as in the public arena where the fake degrees are used, it is surprising how little research has been done on the topic. Indeed, we could find only two doctoral dissertations (out of over a million done since 1861) specifically on the topic: a 1959 historical look at the subject and a 2001 experimental study of the factors people take into account in choosing a degree mill. One other, in 2003, included degree mills in research on how HR executives evaluate schools.[12]

Frustrated by the lack of information on how college registrars deal with unaccredited and fake degrees, John Bear spent several thousand dollars of his own money to send a detailed questionnaire to a large number of registrars. The findings, reported at the registrars' national convention in 2000, suggested that while they are much more knowledgeable and vigilant than the typical corporate HR person, many of them still have a lot to learn.

With thousands of graduate students each year casting about for topics for term papers, masters' theses, and doctoral dissertations, we would hope that degree-mill-related issues will be increasingly addressed.

The Public

It goes without saying that if people did not buy fake and useless degrees, the huge number of degree mills would be out of business overnight. But, realistically, that is like saying that if no one drank and drove, the number of traffic deaths would be dramatically reduced. If no one wanted to buy sex, prostitution would be eliminated. If no one gambled or used drugs, organized crime would be in big trouble. If no one fudged on their taxes, the federal budget would be balanced in a year.

So-called victimless crime has, of course, its victims.

It seems to us, however, that the crime of degree fraud can have much broader, far-reaching effects than many other crimes. Of course, we do not wish to diminish the terribleness of armed robbery, physical assault, kidnapping, and murder. But the perpetrators of these crimes typically have a relatively small number of victims. Contrast this with, for instance:

- the viewers who followed the advice of a popular TV advice giver with a fake doctorate
- the victims of a man with a fake dental degree employed at a New York clinic
- the more than a hundred thousand students affected by the policies of a public school superintendent with a fake doctorate
- the readers who followed the financial advice of a popular business columnist for a major magazine who had a fake business degree
- even the listeners who got caught in the rain following the forecasts of a popular network weatherman with a fake meteorology degree.

Our best advice to the public in general can be expressed in these two words: be careful. Or in these two words: due diligence. Or these two: be skeptical.

Do due diligence before dealing with a doctor, lawyer, accountant, therapist, and so forth. Where did they get their degrees? The diploma on the wall is not enough evidence; there are so many degree-counterfeiting services.

And do due diligence before choosing a school for yourself. Ask whether the degree you will earn will meet not only your immediate needs but also those in the future, as best you can predict. People move. People change jobs. Employers change policies with regard to degrees. Something that seemed reasonable now (or a risk worth taking) might prove to be a problem later on.

As reported in chapter 3, John Bear once testified in the trial of a state psychologist who had purchased a degree-mill doctorate and had been earning doctoral pay for six years. The man claimed he didn't know the school was illegal and that he was not troubled by their lack of a telephone, their mailing service address, or their willingness to grant the degree based on life experience and to backdate the diploma.

During his closing argument, the prosecutor turned to the jury and said, "There sits a man who clearly spent more time deciding which candy bar to buy from the vending machine than he did in choosing his university."

In summation, we suggest that the proliferation of degree mills can only be stopped (or slowed down) by a concerted effort in these five categories:

- *Demand.* Devalue the degrees purchased by prosecuting the users and publicizing the prosecution. Embarrass the "graduates."
- *Supply.* Outlaw degree mills in the states where they operate and all locations where they maintain their offices.
- *Prosecution.* Prosecute the operators under state or federal statutes.
- *Pressure.* Increase pressure on publications to refuse to accept their advertising.
- *Awareness.* Increase public awareness of degree mills and the harm done to society.

And at all times, those three two-word mottoes: Be careful. Be skeptical. Due diligence.

NOTES

1. Mike Lambert, executive director of the Distance Education and Training Council (a recognized accreditor), was instrumental in getting this Rule on the books. He, too, has been frustrated that it hasn't been enforced.

2. Some of the biggest degree mills send their diplomas and other materials by Federal Express. By virtue of going to a FedEx office, paying in cash, and putting a false return address on the envelope, the packages seem to be untraceable. Other mills use overnight delivery services in the mistaken belief that this exempts them from mail fraud charges. However, in 1989, Congress recodified the mail fraud statutes, adding private or commercial interstate carriers (title 18, section 1341, USC).

3. Late in 2003, ABC made the discovery, as reported on *Good Morning America* on November 24, that the undersecretary of defense, with responsibility for personnel policies throughout the Department of Defense, himself had a master's degree from an extremely dubious unaccredited "university" run from Louisiana (where it is illegal) and using a convenience address in Mississippi. As ABC pointed out, this senior government official was using a degree the use of which is a criminal offense in at least four states.

4. We are, however, pleased to consult with state representatives, either formally or informally, on these matters, as we have for quite a few years.

5. John Bear was one of five members of Douglas's doctoral guidance committee.

6. The Oregon list is at http://www.osac.state.or.us/oda/diploma_mill .html. The Michigan list is at http://www.michigan.gov/documents/ Non-accreditedSchools_78090_7.pdf.

7. "Diploma Mills: A Festering Sore on the State of Arizona," *Arizona Republic*, March 6–9, 1983.

8. In *USA Today*, September 28, 2003, p. 1 of the Money section.

9. Several publishers of college directories—including Peterson's and Princeton Review, two of the largest—"sell space in their books to admissions offices that want to add their own messages. . . . Critics call such tactics highly misleading to students and parents." *Chronicle of Higher Education*, June 6, 2000.

10. Acronymics at its finest: CAN-SPAM = Controlling the Assault of Non-Solicited Pornography and Marketing.

11. Bob Egelko, "Internet Providers Face Risk of Libel, Court Rules," *San Francisco Chronicle*, November 13, 2003.

12. Robert H. Reid, "Degree Mills in the United States," (PhD diss., Columbia University, 1963); Robyn Calote, "Diploma Mills: What's the Attraction?" (Ed.D. diss., University of LaVerne, 2002); Richard Douglas, "The Accreditation of Degree-Granting Institutions and Its Role in the Utility of College Degrees in the Workplace" (PhD diss., Union Institute and University, 2003).

Appendixes

Appendix A

The Ethics of Using Fake Degrees

Marina Bear, PhD, wife of coauthor John Bear, has been employed as an ethi-cist to help clients work through issues related to the use of fake degrees. This is a summary of her report in the case of a schoolteacher who bought a master's degree from an online degree mill in order to meet the job requirement for school principal. When another person who had been in line for the job of prin-cipal, a person with a legitimate master's degree, learned of the fake degree, she brought suit. The attorney for the plaintiff was troubled by the fact that the principal with the fake degree was well liked and, by all accounts, was doing a good job. What harm had been done? He asked Marina Bear for her analysis. This is an abridged version of the report, with personal references removed.

WHO DID WHAT TO WHOM: AN ETHICIST LOOKS AT A CASE OF FAKE DEGREES
by Marina Bear, PhD

It is appropriate to begin by clarifying just what it is an ethicist does. Unlike a lawyer who works with facts of the case and such elements of the law as are, or might turn out to be, relevant, and whose aim is to bring about a successful outcome for his or her client, an ethicist brings together the facts of the case and the morals of the relevant society. By examining those, an ethicist aims to bring about as clear as possible a view of where things went wrong and what might be done both to rec-tify the situation and to make it less likely that things will go wrong in the same way in the future. In addition, the hope is to leave all parties concerned with an understanding of the consequences that have resulted, or most probably will result, from the case.

Our ethics are an expression of the society in which we live. Diverse as that society is, there are basic ethical principles that we hold in common, although how those principles are applied may vary.

Societies are divided into subgroups based on ethnicity, profession, special interests, and so forth. There are codes of ethics that guide the participants of those subgroups in their common activities. They identify what is expected of us and what we may reasonably expect of others, and they identify how breaches in the moral fabric may be mended. Sometimes those codes are written down.

Professional societies often publish them and their members display them as information whose very presence proclaims the moral character of the professional.

But many areas of human endeavor are not covered by such codes. Nonetheless, by appealing to more general principles widely held to be important for the health of our society, we can usually figure out the right thing to do using reason and common sense.

In the case of the principal, it is clear that there was some wrong-doing, but it is worthwhile to take a moment to figure out exactly what the wrong was and to whom the wrong was done.

As parents and citizens, we know that we want teachers of good character working with our children. Although many of us are unaware of the exact process by which teachers are hired, we place a certain amount of trust in those administrative bodies, which often include elected school boards, to see that teachers support the highest ethical standards in their classrooms, promoting such values as honesty and fairness, in addition to fostering a love of learning and conveying specific information.

We even expect that school administrators will behave with personal discretion, if not exemplary ethical behavior, in all aspects of their lives that may come into public view. And we have all heard of the high school counselor with unfortunate bouts of occasional kleptomania or the school superintendent whose personal life challenges community standards. Often they are simply strongly encouraged to leave public service and find employment in less sensitive areas, and that is the end of it.

One of the most basic of ethical principles is justice. That means that the rules apply to all concerned and that there is a dependable regularity to their application. It means that you and I are to be treated the same unless there is a clear and relevant difference between us that justifies differential treatment.

The school system had published clear qualifications for the job of principal. To meet that basic definition of justice, those qualifications should have been asked of *anyone* applying for the position. Meeting those requirements would have been a necessary, although not sufficient, criterion for further consideration. Choosing someone to lead an enterprise always involves judging the candidates' personal talents and skills and trying to predict the dynamic of the new working unit.

There is ample evidence that the principal had a good working relationship with members of the staff. If the selection committee had been free to hire without considering the master's degree, the principal may well have been the obvious choice based on experience and the already-present support of a number of her coworkers and, presumably, some satisfied parents of children in her classes.

But the requirement of an accredited master's degree *was* there, and it was ignored. By doing so, the school board was unjust, not only to all other candidates for the position who presented the technically minimum requirements for the job but also to other potentially interested members of the public who also did not hold accredited master's degrees but might have wished to be considered.

One of the most blatant and damaging forms of discrimination occurs when those responsible for hiring come to the process with unstated criteria that will narrow the field in ways the applicants for the job cannot predict and address. The most obvious example of this is the "foregone conclusion" interview process, where the main criterion for the position is that the candidate be the one the group has already agreed, openly or tacitly, will get the job.

It is usually impossible to determine whether this has gone on, since people often discover their consciences *after* committing an ethical blunder, and rarely does such behavior issue from groups with a strong moral fiber running through them that would lead to public confessions of inappropriate action.

What we do know in this situation is that the schools and the administrators' association set the standards, but somewhere along the line they were not followed.

How were these standards compromised, and what did this come to mean?

Here comes some of the common sense mentioned earlier. A job listing appears. If it looks interesting to me, I read the fine print. What do they say they want done? How much does it pay? What are the listed qualifications?

Since the principal had served as acting principal of the school, she probably had a better idea than most applicants of the tasks the job entailed.

The second question is not as simple as it looks at first glance. The principal was well aware of the fact that salaries in school positions are based on a formula that usually includes experience and level of certification, including the highest degree completed. Two teachers may instruct the same subject at the same grade level but receive widely different salaries for so doing if one has a master's degree in the relevant field and the other does not.

In fact, the second and third questions are interlinking in this case. To get the job, the candidate was supposed to present a master's degree from an accredited college or university; the salary was keyed to the presumption of that degree. It was not wrong of the principal to aspire to hold such a position, but it *was* wrong for her to claim it without holding the degree, unless some special accommodation had been made on her behalf. We'll get to that in the "What could they have done?" portion of this report.

If the principal is to be seen as innocent of any wrongdoing, she is guilty of a surprising level of ignorance regarding academic matters. That ignorance alone might bring one to question her fitness to operate as a school administrator, except that it is hard to imagine the situation in which damage could be done to students by her ignorance of how the world of higher education really works. An elementary school principal probably has little call to counsel people concerning university life. On the other hand, by presenting a degree-mill credential, she may well jeopardize the accreditation of her school in the eyes of whatever larger body is charged with reviewing its policies and procedures.

I have visited the Web site of the "university" from which [the principal] received her master's degree. One line was sufficient to throw into doubt the validity of the institution. It claims "a proprietary method of awarding equivalencies of work experience as substitutions for formal education requirements."

This is like suggesting that one can set up a private, proprietary way of issuing change for your hundred-dollar bills. Send in a hundred-dollar bill and you'll get back eleven homemade ten-dollar bills—$110 for a $100 bill. It sounds like a good deal, but the chance that you could use them in the marketplace is small, and even if you did, you'd be setting yourself up for serious trouble.

The only way equivalencies make sense, whether of money or academic credits, is if most other relevant institutions will accept them as equivalent: that banks will accept the currency and reputable universities will accept the academic credits.

The principal simply e-mailed the "university" a short form that gave details of her experience and was immediately notified that she qualified for the master's degree.

First of all, anyone who believes that everything done on the Internet is legitimate and above-board suffers from that surprising level of ignorance mentioned above. Anyone who reads a newspaper or listens to the evening news has heard stories of scams involving the offer of items for sale that are never delivered or, if they are, turn out to be other than promised. Why do scams work? Because they seem to offer a good deal. The ["university"] degree sounds a lot like the "brand-name merchandise" for sale at bargain rates on street corners in many major cities. Vuitton suitcase for $20? No problem.

Let us invoke another basic principle, common to every system of ethical thought: Do no harm. To be good people, we are expected to keep in mind the idea that in the light of the seeming capriciousness of fate, the power of nature, and the undependability of strangers, each one of us still has the capacity for advancing the good by, at the very least, not initiating harmful actions wherever possible.

Each time we further an unjust cause by colluding with it to our temporary advantage, we do wrong. The principal would probably not buy a shiny new car from someone who approached her in a parking lot and offered it to her for $2,000, no questions asked. Even if the car came with a legitimate-seeming bill of sale and registration, the very fact of its price and the way it was presented would suggest "hot car" and all the potential trouble that implies. And she'd probably agree that buying stolen merchandise put the buyer in the position of supporting the business of thievery.

The principal's situation is all too common, even if her search for a "good deal" may have less to do with money than with two other valuable commodities: time and pride. She needed the degree in a timely manner to appear to have the basic qualifications for the position of principal. No legitimate college or university can work as fast as the degree mills. The "university" didn't even need to examine her transcript. Why should she spend months applying to universities, having her qualifications evaluated by them, engaging in lengthy negotiations to get the most credit recognized for the courses she had already taken? The degree mill just takes your word for it.

Did a red flag go up in the principal's mind over this detail? Apparently not. Consider if she had walked into a shopping mall after refusing to buy that new-looking car from the man in the parking lot and had been confronted by a man in an academic robe who said to her, "Madam, you look like somebody in need of a master's degree. I can help." After she briefly recited her qualifications, he announced that she could have a master's degree as soon as her credit card was approved. The principal did the exact equivalent, and her Internet degree is worth as much as the shopping-mall degree.

There's a reason why pride was the first of the seven deadly sins.

Many people who fall into the hands of the proprietors of degree mills know that they *deserve* that degree. They've done the equivalent work. They may have more practical experience doing the very job for which the degree is a basic requirement than some young kid just out of college. They don't feel a need to present themselves to somebody in a university and ask for the rights and privileges that accrue from having that degree because they've already done the work.

The advertisements on the Internet and in the print media feed right into that syndrome. "You may have already earned your degree. Isn't it time you reaped the benefits?" "Your hard work and life experience deserve recognition."

But there's another basic ethical truth by which we operate in this society: We have a responsibility to learn the laws and rules under which we live and a duty to follow them. We have a responsibility to know the basic laws of nature if we're going to take on the care of another living thing. And if we're going to present ourselves as ready to work in a particular environment, we have a responsibility to understand the rules of that organization and a duty to follow them.

A cab driver needs to know the rules of the road and the policies of his company regarding fares, care of his vehicle, treatment of customers, and the basic licensing he has to have to be a driver. He doesn't need to understand how getting a college degree works. And the principal didn't need to know how one becomes licensed to drive a vehicle that transports people.

But we all know there are standard ways to get what you think you need and there are often under-the-table ways to get the same thing, and it's a good idea to know which is the right one and which is the one that may get you into more trouble than it's worth.

Someone operating in the field of education has a responsibility to know how it works at any level in which she's likely to become involved and to have the common sense to distinguish the real coin of her realm.

Did the principal do wrong in "falling for" the diploma mill scam on the Internet? Yes. She is *not* an innocent victim because she had a responsibility to know how the world of higher education operates. She's not an innocent patient handing a prescription slip into a pharmacy and falling victim to the pharmacist's inattention or ignorance when she gets and takes the wrong medication. She surely would have heard the word *accreditation* during her tenure as a teacher. Most public schools, and many private ones as well, are subject to scrutiny by independent agencies to determine the standard of their operation from the cleanliness of their facility through the quality of their library as well as the evidence of learning that their students can demonstrate. Schools that fail such scrutiny may end up closing. Those who pass display their resulting certification proudly. To be unaware of the importance of accreditation is to have slipped up in responsibility to know.

There is, however, an all-too-human tendency to hope that details will work themselves out. It's a degree. It's not an accredited degree. Maybe it doesn't matter. So we use the dairy products that drifted to back of the fridge and are long past their expiration date and hope that nothing happens. We make that U-turn when there's no endangering traffic, even if there's a little sign that suggests it's not legal. We pay attention to the big stuff and hope that our overall goodness will count. Sometimes it works that way, sometimes it doesn't.

But what if the rule is wrong? If there's no traffic for blocks, shouldn't I be able to make that U-turn? Some cities try to accommodate variations: "No left turn between 7 and 9 AM." But when there's no accommodation, you don't turn left unless you enjoy meeting your local law enforcement officers in adversarial situations.

Here we should take a moment to consider what a real school does that a diploma mill doesn't—a distinction that the principal did not consider in her deposition, although she uses the word *program* to describe what preceded the awarding of the degree. A master's program involves an array of learning experiences that are designed to produce in the student "mastery" of a body of knowledge.

Virtually all legitimate schools claim a right to administer a portion of that knowledge, since they believe that in awarding their degree they are giving the student the benefit of the school's prestige and reputation for the rest of that student's career, and that reputation, in part, rests, in turn, on their turning out students whose competence in their chosen field will bespeak the high standards of the school's instructional program. In fact, many schools insist on providing *all* the education at the graduate level.

In such cases, a student who applies with a significant amount of graduate credit is awarded equivalency in credits, but not in classes, so that when the student arrives at a final project, a thesis, dissertation, or other demonstration of achievement, the student can continue working independently without paying additional school fees until submitting the final work. Thus, the school retains the right to educate the student but allows the student some credit for time and work already accomplished.

Even when classes are accepted for transfer, most schools attempt to do so by finding actual equivalencies in their own program, since a graduate program is not just an accumulation of classes taken at random but an array of related studies within a discipline designed to produce just that mastery of the field. And the primary criterion for transfer of credits to an accredited college or university is that the credits presented, in turn, were done at an accredited institution. This implies some scrutiny by an impartial body of the quality of educational programs offered by the institution.

There is no sense whatever in which the degree mill offered a "program" to the principal.

Nonetheless, she may still feel that her qualifications should have been recognized under the rules of the schools and the administrators' association.

If a rule is wrong, obviously, we can try to change it. Here we come to the "What could we have done differently?" section of this report.

The school district seems to have some flexibility. While they require their administrators to earn three units of graduate credit every three years, their rules say that requirement may be waived or extended. What if the principal or a supporter proposed a plan whereby she might meet the degree requirement in an honorable and acceptable way?

Perhaps the school board was also suffering from "ignore the details and hope they will go away" syndrome. If so, that is unfortunate.

Or it may be the case that the current rules are set in stone, and changing them is impossibly difficult. In that situation, we may be facing an unjust law. If it is, indeed, an example of an ideal candidate who cannot be hired because the regulations prohibit it and the regulations cannot be changed, then a kind of courage not usually found in school boards and similar bodies is required.

We have no better teacher in the appropriate meeting of that situation than the late Dr. Martin Luther King Jr., whose "Letter from a Birmingham Jail" stands as a model for the intelligent person of good conscience who confronts an impossible law. He said, "One who breaks an unjust law must do so openly, lovingly, and with a willingness to accept the penalty." He wrote those words while suffering the penalty of imprisonment for breaking the segregation laws of the state of Alabama in 1963.

In our case, the fact that the principal may well have been the best candidate for the position implies that the law is inappropriate—even unjust to her and to those who would benefit from her service as principal. But the fact that the breach of that law had to be called to public attention by someone who felt wronged in that breach means it was *not* done openly. And there is no evidence that the principal even accepts the fact of her participation in the breaking of the rule, so she does not have the dignity of Dr. King's position.

Wrong was done by the hiring of this person to the position of principal.

The selection committee acted unjustly in not applying the stated criteria, thus wronging the applicants and probably some members of the public. The principal failed to exercise sufficient responsibility in determining the details of the requirements for the position and the appropriate way to meet the requirement for the master's degree. Presenting herself as holding a degree to which she is not entitled may endanger the reputation, and possibly the accreditation, of the institution that she leads.

It is often difficult to determine how to right ethical wrongs. It would be a shame if the principal's successful career as a teacher, mentor of teachers, and acting administrator were to end in embarrassment and result in her quietly disappearing like the kleptomaniac counselor.

It is entirely possible that she was the best candidate for the job, and her possession of an embarrassing master's degree is an obstacle that might be overcome by the school board granting her a period of time to research the acquisition of a legitimate, honorable degree in her field so that she may end her career in the way she, and her supporters, would prefer.

This presumes the capacity for recognition of her part in the wrong-doing and her willingness to take further action toward legitimizing her employment. It is probably too much to address the question of repaying the school district for the increment in salary retained during the time she served without appropriate credential, although that may come up.

It is to be hoped that the basic values of honesty, responsibility, and justice will be upheld in the ultimate resolution of this case. By doing so, we do the best we can as individuals to maintain the moral strength of our communities.

Appendix B

The "University Degree Program"
— The Biggest Degree Mill Ever

The biggest degree business the world has ever known was started by an American living in Bucharest, Romania. The business is the one described at the beginning of the introduction. Insiders estimate that total sales, since the mid-1990s, have been more than $400 million, representing sales of more than two hundred thousand diplomas, mostly to Americans and Canadians.

In 2002, we entered into communication with an unhappy employee of University Degree Program (UDP), working at the main offices in Romania. He supplied us with a great deal of information relating to the business and how it operated

Virtually everything is done by using the Internet. The Program begins by sending out "spam" messages by the millions. While the wording varies slightly, the messages nearly all begin, "Obtain a prosperous future, money-earning power, and the admiration of all." Recipients are invited to call a US telephone number, which is an answering service. More than one hundred different numbers in a dozen or more states have been used. The recorded message invites callers to leave their name and number. Within two or three days, they receive a telephone call.

While the caller suggests or says that he is calling from England (or wherever the school currently featured is supposed to be), the calls are in fact made either from Bucharest, Romania, or from Jerusalem, typically either by natives of those countries or by South African immigrants living there.

The telemarketing call is extremely well orchestrated, with a detailed script, which is reproduced at the end of this section. Approximately one person in three ends up buying a degree during the phone call. A smaller "sideline" business involves selling counterfeit international drivers' licenses.

The school name is changed regularly; more than twenty names have been used so far. Sometimes names are changed when an earlier name gets some bad publicity; sometimes just for the sake of variety. The "degree package," as it is called, typically includes the diploma (date of one's choice), the transcript (courses and grades of one's choice), information on a degree verification service employers can call, and two extremely favorable letters of recommendation in which, for instance, Professor Bideman writes that this is one of the finest students he has ever had, and he cannot recommend her or him too highly.

Names used so far include:

Ashford University	Parkwood University
Bedford University	Ravenhurst University
Brentwick University	University of San Moritz
Carrington University	Shelbourne University
Devon University	Shepperton University
Devonshire University	Stafford University
Dorchester University	Strassford University
Dunham University	Suffield University
Glencullen University	Thornewood University
Hampshire University	University of Switzerland
Harrington University	Walsh University
Kingsfield University	Westbourne University
Lafayette University	Western Ohio University
Landford University	Westhampton University
Northfield University	Wexford University
University of Palmers Green	Xavier University
Parkhurst University	

It is more than likely that there will be other names by the time this book is in print. There is persuasive evidence, as well, that some former employees of the University Degree Program have left and started comparable businesses of their own, from Israel and elsewhere.

Authorities in the United States, England, and Ireland (where the program uses mail-forwarding services); Israel (where the diplomas are

Brentwick University on the Internet (left) and in real life (below)

printed); and Cyprus (where much of their banking is done) are certainly well aware of the business, as, of course, are the Romanians, but they seem either unwilling or unable to do anything about it, with rare exceptions.

In late 2003, the Federal Trade Commission announced that it had "settled charges" against three companies and three individuals who appear to be the ones associated with this business. They agreed to pay $57,000 in penalties (or roughly eight hours of their revenues) and to refrain from selling diplomas. Intriguingly, the order says that "if they are found to have misrepresented their financial condition, a $5 million avalanche clause would become effective."

Three months after the order went into effect, we did not notice a decline in the number of "spam" messages offering the recipient the opportunity to buy a "prestigious university degree." It is conceivable these offers are coming from other sources, but it seems more than likely that they have just moved to Internet service providers in other places.

•   •   •

Here is the telemarketing script used by University Degree Program. As you read through it, you may come to appreciate how one-third of the callers could end up buying a degree. Note that the caller is instructed to say that the school is a "nonaccredited diploma mill," but this is to be said quickly and softly. Not all callers say this. And, in our experience, if the person being called notices and says, "What did you just say?" then the caller hangs up. The boldface type, in brackets, are the instructions to the caller.

THE REGENTS OF

University of Ravenhurst

ON THE NOMINATION OF THE COUNCIL OF THE UNDERGRADUATE DIVISION
HAVE CONFERRED UPON

HAVING DEMONSTRATED ABILITY
BY GENERAL SCHOLARSHIP SUMMA CUM LAUDE -- WITH GREATEST DISTINCTION
THE DEGREE

Bachelor of Arts in Journalism

WITH ALL THE RIGHTS AND PRIVILEGES THERETO PERTAINING

GIVEN THIS THIRTEENTH DAY OF SEPTEMBER IN THE YEAR
TWO THOUSAND AND TWO

PRESIDENT OF THE REGENTS

PRESIDENT OF THE UNIVERSITY

DEAN OF THE UNDERGRADUATE DIVISION

CHANCELLOR

The University of Ravenhurst is one of the names used by the huge University Degree Program. Their very professional-looking product consists of four elements: the diploma . . .

... the transcript ...

... an effusive faculty letter of recommendation ...

From the Desk of

Frederick Bideman

12 June 2003

Dear Sir or Madam:

was enrolled in several of my correspondence classes, in fulfillment of the core requirements for his major.

As proven by his work,   was diligent, well prepared, and absorbed new material quickly. Needless to say, his high marks in my courses reflect his outstanding performance on tests and written assignments.

I am confident that   has a bright future and will succeed in all his future endeavors.

Sincerely,

Dr. Frederick Bideman
Professor, University of Ravenhurst
Correspondence Address: Prinsengr 64
Amsterdam 1015DX Netherlands

UNIVERSITY OF RAVENHURST
CORRESPONDENCE ADDRESS: PRINSENGR 64
AMSTERDAM 1015DX NETHERLANDS

... and a letter attesting to the student's graduation with honors.

June 13, 2003

To Whom It May Concern:

graduated from our University with departmental honors.

As an honors student,   was responsible for supervising undergraduates through our distance learning tutorial program. Within a short time, he proved to be such a bright, astute, and accomplished student that we utilized his talents in many aspects of our academic program.

While with our University,   maintained constant contact with faculty members. His correspondence demonstrated knowledge, sensitivity, and intelligence in dealing with complex issues, earning him the accolades of our entire academic staff.

In sum, I unreservedly recommend   for any position suitable to his outstanding background, qualifications, academic achievement, and experience. He will be a valuable asset to any organization.

Very truly yours,

Professor Henry Clausdale, PhD

Hi, this is [say your name].

I'm a registrar with the University Degree Program. I apologize for my European accent. We just wanted to contact you to tell you that, because we have some spaces left in our program, we reduced our registration fee by more than $2,000. What I am going to tell you is very important, so if you don't understand everything I say, just let me know. If now is a good time for you, I'll explain our new program and answer any questions that you might have.

[Wait—Continue only if you are not interrupting and he is not in a rush!]

That's great! The name of our institution is Thornewood University. We have no central campus. Our campus is the homes and offices of our students. We are not affiliated with or located in any country, but we do have a mailing address in the United Kingdom. We are fully recognized members of distance-learning organizations in Europe. Our original founders got together in 1983 and now we are part of a multinational group.

First of all, let me be honest with you. If you're looking for an accredited university, I suggest that you register at Harvard or Yale, pay the several hundred thousand dollars tuition, and study the many years required. Is this what you want?

[Wait—If "Yes," hang up!]

Or, would you rather have the benefits of an Ivy League education immediately with very little cost? [Wait!] Of course you would, so listen carefully! We don't give a damn about other universities, employers, professors, or anyone else. We only care about *YOU!* We will do anything legal, moral, and reasonable on your behalf. As your [speak softly and fast] nonaccredited "diploma mill," [normal speech] our job is to take care of *your* needs and wants by backing up *your* credentials. For example, we supply you with documents because of your work, private study, and life experience. Are we what you're looking for?

[Wait—If "No," hang up!]

Before I tell you more about our program, I want to tell you that I'm on your side 100 percent, and I am listening to everything you tell me. So that I can recommend the best program for you, please tell me, career wise, what you want out of your future.

[Wait!—listen closely to him, showing interest.]

In which field of study do you want your degrees?

[Wait!—You can recommend a field of study here if needed.]

Good choice! Now, let me ask two brief questions. Do you feel that you have the potential to be a qualified professional in your field? [Wait!]

Do you feel that you only lack documentation of your accomplishments. [Wait!] With your background, I feel that you can take advantage of a PhD in [state the name of his field] or an MBA—the price is the same so, which do you prefer, a PhD, MBA, or both? [Wait!]

Of course, we'll give you a bachelor's and master's for background, right, [say his name.]? [Wait!] You can comfortably use these diplomas to supply the documentation that you lack.

These nonaccredited diplomas should reflect your credentials so that you can use them for business, employment, and personal purposes. However, this program will be successful only if the degrees are in a field in which you are qualified.

In fact, the initial diplomas and transcripts that you receive are sample documents that we tailor make according to your instructions. These documents are free when you pay to register for the program. Of course, you cannot use sample diplomas for licensing or for transferring credits.

Now, before I tell you the low price of registration in our program, let's custom design your diplomas so that you know exactly what you are getting. Your diplomas will look exactly like those diplomas you've seen many times hanging on the walls of doctors, lawyers, and other professionals. Actually, most university diplomas look very much alike, but let's select a university and make your diplomas look like theirs. Of course, the diplomas will bear our university's name. What's your favorite university. [Wait!]

[If they can't think of one, suggest UCLA, if you must!]

That's a good choice because they have a very impressive diploma. What name do you want printed on the diplomas? [Wait!] Can we put on your diplomas that you graduated with top honors? [Wait!] As to the graduation dates, we want them to correspond to your age. What year were you born? [Wait!] We'll date the diplomas to (dates—bachelor's, 2 years after DOS; master's, 4; MBA and PhD, 6.)

You can assume any titles that come with your diplomas. For instance, when you get the PhD, or MBA, you can legally call yourself doctor or put "PhD" after your name. Do you plan to call yourself doctor? [Wait!]

In addition, to show what good students receive, there are custom-made transcripts and recommendation letters from professors at the university. Isn't this a great idea? [Wait!] We'll also issue laminated wallet-sized replicas of your diplomas so you can carry your credentials in your wallet to impress your friends. Do you understand? [Wait!]

Along with your materials, you'll receive our e-mail address, our UK mailing address, and our fax number for you to give to prospective employers or anyone checking your credentials. Naturally, when we receive an inquiry concerning your qualifications, we verify that you received your diplomas. We even send certified copies of transcripts when requested. You do want us to back you up when someone checks, don't you? [Wait!]

You have one full year to make any changes on your diplomas free of charge. The rest is up to you. You receive optional correspondence course lists and evaluation examinations so you can take the courses and get recognized degrees whenever you have time. Once your diplomas arrive along with their supporting materials, you're set for life. That's all there is to it. Isn't this perfect—[use his name]? [Wait!]

Excellent! Where do you want your diplomas and materials shipped? [Wait!] What is your daytime phone number? [Wait!] What is your evening/weekend phone number? [Wait!] What is your fax number? [Wait!] What is your e-mail address? [Wait!]

Now, [use his name], our program is perfect because you designed it yourself but, if I were you, I'd only be concerned about one thing.

[Wait for him to say "What's that?"] Will your friends and relatives be jealous of your newfound success? [Wait!]

Let me ask you this—If I were to give you $250,000 in cash right now, would you give me $10,000? [Wait!] Of course you would. Do you know that a person with a college degree can earn $25,000 more per year? [Wait!] That means over ten years, a degree can be worth more than $250,000 in extra earnings. In other words, I'm offering you the equivalent of maybe a quarter of a million dollars, right, [use his name]? [Wait!]

Moreover, we both know that I'm not going to ask you for $10,000. So now, how much are you willing to pay for $250,000 in cash? [Wait!]

<If he says $3,400 or more> Well, [his name], I have an additional surprise for you. If you can invest just [the price he said minus $500] in your future for the program—for signing up right now, on this call— I'll mark your account "Paid in Full." It can't get any better than that. Which is easiest way for you to pay—cash, check, or credit card? [Wait!]

<Go to "Wire," "Check," or "Credit Card">

<If "Negative">

I'm a little confused, [his name]. you told me that you are willing to pay [the price he said], and I say the registration fee is only **(the price he said minus $500.)** What would you suggest? **[Wait!]**

<If anything else>

Well, I'll tell you what. If you can invest just twenty-nine hundred dollars ($2,900) in your future for the program—for signing up right now, on this call—I'll mark your account "Paid in Full." It can't get any better than that. Which is easiest. way for you to pay—cash, check, or credit card? **[Wait!]**

<Go to "Wire," "Check," or "Credit Card">

<If "Negative" go to "Price">

<Western Union>

I'm not going to ask for your credit card information—but to best advise you on how to pay, I need to know if you have your MasterCard, Visa, or Discover credit card with you right now.

<Not have credit card>

Great! The reason I asked is that I have a way for you to invest in your future without leaving your seat. All you need is a telephone. Your investment goes to our agent in London. This is the easiest way for you to make investment. But, if you don't mind taking a few minutes to go to your local bank you can make your investment there. Which do you prefer—do you want to make your investment by telephone or do you want to go to your local bank. **[Wait!]**

<Bank—go to "bank wire">

<Telephone>

As you know, Western Union is the biggest money transfer company in the world. Western Union will take your investment by phone using your credit card. You don't even have to leave your seat. Just follow these simple instructions. **[Read the numbers also.]**

1. Dial Western Union at 1-800-225-5227.
2. Ignore the recording.
3. Do *not* press any phone buttons.
4. Wait about 15 seconds until the recording stops.
5. When the recording stops a person will answer the phone.
6. Tell the person that answers that you want to use your credit card to send **[Amount]** to London, England.

7. Send the money to our agent in London:

> His name is—David Neilson
> The company name is—Wheelie International Ltd
> The city is—London, England

8. Western Union will charge you **[say $ from chart]**, but if you call and make your investment right now as soon as we hang up, we'll pay the Western Union fee for you. You can subtract the **[$ in box]** from your payment. That means that if you only have to send us **[amount minus $ in box]**. If you pay any other time, you will have to pay the full **[amount]**.

[chart, showing fees of $25 for sending up to $100, up to $240 for sending $4,000]

Please repeat those eight steps back to me?

[Wait!—Go slowly here—Make sure that he can read back to you all eight steps, including spelling the names "David Neilson" and "Wheelie" correctly. Be sure they understand the process 100 percent.]

If you ignore the recording and do NOT press any numbers on the phone, you shouldn't have any problems. But sometimes you have to be patient with Western Union. I want to tell you that Western Union is very strict on credit card orders. They frequently double-check everything and call you back or may even ask for your social security number or date of birth. This is for your protection, but it can be annoying. If you have any problems at all with Western Union—do *not* be discouraged. Just start over. That's all there is to it. If Western Union won't take the full payment, just pay whatever they allow you to. The next time we talk, I'll tell you how to pay the balance.

Western Union can take your order right now, so as soon as we hang up, I'll get you registered and have your diploma and materials engraved and shipped international overnight. Of course, this will cost us a small fortune, but I trust your word. As you now know, **[his name]**, the university will spend a great deal of effort and expense to get you your diploma and materials immediately—all at a fraction of the cost of other institutions. Do I have your word that all the information that you have given me is correct? **[Wait!]** Do I also have your word that you'll call Western union right now and pay? **[Wait!]**

I'll call you back in about ten minutes to get the receipt number.

<Will not promise to pay>

I'm sorry, but I can't commit the university to spend all the money necessary to get your diploma package produced, and shipped overseas, unless I have your word that you will pay for the materials. You can understand this, can't you, [his name]? [Wait!]

<If still balks>

I'm sorry that we can't help you today, but give me a call if you change your mind. . . .

<If stalls by saying he'll pay later.>

You can pay whenever you like, but let's face it, you'll never get to it, and you'll lose out. I can't let you blow your only chance to secure your future. Call Western Union right now!

<If he still will not pay right now—do not press>

No problem. When will you pay? [Wait!] Great! I'll call you then.

After you give me the receipt number, you'll have your diploma and materials in less than ten business days. Do you have any questions? [Wait and answer all questions] Remember, if you do not receive your materials exactly as promised—you pay nothing. Again, the name of the institution is the Thornewood University. My name is [your name]. My phone number is 713-866-6590. If you have any questions please call twenty-four hours a day. Thank you very much. [Wait for him to hang up.]

Do you have your business or personal checkbook with you? [Wait!]

<Not have checkbook with him>

Can you call home or your office to have someone read you the name of the bank and numbers on a check?

<Yes!>

Great! All you need are the name and address of the bank and the long computer number at the bottom of a check.

<No!—Go to "Bank wire">

Great—I'll wait while you get it! [When he gets the checkbook] Read me the name, address, and telephone number if any on the top of the check? [Wait!]

<Not give check info—go to "Bank wire">

Read me the name, address, and telephone number of the bank that is written on the check. [WAIT!]

<If no address written on check—ask for city and state of his branch]

Tell me the check number. [Wait!] Read me all the computer numbers that are written on the bottom of your check. [Wait!]

To make it easy for you to invest in your future, we have our students make their payments through "University Systems." University Systems is a company that specializes in educational financing. University Systems will pay us, and you will pay them. Unless you are financing, we pay any charges that are incurred, so you only pay your registration fee.

University Systems has a very simple procedure that allows you to pay by check. Their bank has an agreement with all American banks to honor each other's procedures, so you do not have to send them a check for payments. A signed receipt will come with your bank statement. Obviously, you have to be sure that the money is in your account when it is due.

That's all there is to it. I'll take care of the rest. I'm going to prepare your package right now; your materials will arrive in less than ten business days after the check clears your bank. This means that you will receive your materials in two to four weeks. [If he says this is too long—go to "Bank wire!"] Now, as you know, [his name], the university will spend a great deal of effort and expense to get you your diploma and materials immediately—all at a fraction of the cost of other institutions. Do I have your word that all the information that you have given me is correct? [Wait!] Do I also have your word that you will make this investment in your future as promised? [Wait!]

<Will not promise to pay>

I'm sorry, but I can't commit the university to spend all the money necessary to get your diploma package produced, and shipped overseas, unless I have your word that you will pay for the materials. You can understand this, can't you, [his name]? [Wait!]

<If still not promise>

I'm sorry that we can't help you today, but give me a call if you change your mind.

Do you have any questions? [Wait and answer all questions.] Again, the name of the institution is Thornewood University. My name is [your name]. If you have any additional questions, please call twenty-four hours a day. My number in the United States is 713-866-6590.

Now, [his name], if the university contacts you, please be sure to mention that [your name] registered you. Thank you very much. [Wait for him to hang up.]

<Bank wire>

Great! Now, [his name], I want to explain something to you. As a reputable institution, we have to verify your identity. Your bank knows you, so we will ask you, as we do all our students, to go to your local bank and make your investment there. You can understand this, can't you, [his name]? [Wait!]

Besides being convenient, there are several advantages to making your investment at your local bank. You can certainly trust your own bank. In addition, your local bank will accept cash, credit card, or check. They may even loan you money if you have good credit with them.

Banks do this procedure all the time, so this will be real easy for you. And don't worry! If you have any problems whatsoever, I promise that I'll take care of them for you. Before I give you the simple bank instructions, what is the name of your bank? [Wait!—Don't push.] What is the telephone number of your bank? [Wait!—Don't push.]

Got it! Now, here's all you do to secure your future. It's better to use your regular bank because they already know you, but you can go to any bank. At the bank, explain to the teller that you want to wire money. Tell them that you want to send [price agreed upon] by an international wire to:

Chase Manhattan Bank
1 Chase Manhattan Plaza
New York, USA
SWIFT CODE: CHASUS33
Account Holder (or Beneficiary): Singer & Friedlander
Account Number: 001-1-949-245

<Important>—All wire transfer forms have a field for additional information. This field is usually called "Message," "Additional Information," "Reference," "Special Instructions," "Extra Instructions," or something like that. This field is not part of the wiring instructions per se. However, to make sure that you get credit for your wire, be sure that they write your code in this special field. Your code is: "Wheelie Number 16044."

[Have him repeat back the instructions exactly—then,] Super! As long as you give the bank all this information correctly, and your special code "Wheelie Number 16044" in the "special instructions" field on the wire form—that's all there is to it. We'll take care of everything else. As soon as we hang up, I'll get you registered immediately and have your diploma and materials made to your specifications and shipped international, because I trust your word that you will go to the bank right away. Will you be able to get to the bank today/tomorrow, [his name]? [Wait!]

I also want to caution you that some banks will only allow you to wire up to a certain amount on your credit card. But don't worry about this or any other problem—just pay as much as they allow by cash, check, or credit card. If there's a problem, I'll take care of it.

As soon as you finish at the bank, please fax me a copy of the wire transfer receipt, [his name]. Our fax number is 501-325-3844. If we don't receive the fax, I'll call you back immediately. As soon as we receive your fax, we'll assume that you've paid, and you'll have your diploma and materials in less than ten business days.

Now, as you know, [his name], the university will spend a great deal of effort and expense to get you your diploma and materials immediately. This is all at a fraction of the cost of other institutions. Do I have your word that all the information that you have given me is correct? [Wait!] Do I also have your word that you will go to the bank immediately and make this investment in your future as promised? [Wait!]

<Will not promise to pay>

I'm sorry, but I can't commit the university to spend all the money necessary to get your diploma package produced, and shipped overseas, unless I have your word that you will pay for the materials. You can understand this, can't you, [his name]? [Wait!]

<If still won't promise>

I'm sorry that we can't help you today, but give me a call if you change your mind. . . .

Do you have any questions? [Wait and answer all questions.] Again, the name of the institution is Thornewood University. My name is [your name]. If you have any additional questions, please call 24 hours a day. My number in the United States is 713-866-6590. Now, [his name], if the university contacts you, please be sure to mention that [your name] registered you. Thank you very much. [Wait for him to hang up.]

<Credit card>

<You should only be here if the client can only pay by credit card>

If you have a MasterCard or Visa, we'll be more than happy to accept your credit card. Unfortunately, because I have no way of seeing your credit card and identification over the phone, you will have to fill out an application to pay by credit card. So that we understand each other clearly, the application will state everything we talked about today. Obviously, the application will require you to fax copies of your credit card and identification. I will send you the application by e-mail immediately.

The e-mail will arrive shortly. When it arrives, print it out. I will call you back in about ten minutes to help you fill out the application and answer any questions that you might have. What is your e-mail address?

<When you get the e-mail address, send him the single payment or the multi-payment credit card app—then call him back ten minutes later and help him fill out the app.>

<NOTE: If he refuses to complete the credit card application—he didn't buy the product!>

<Western Union Cash>

If you would like to make your investment in cash, you can go to your local Western Union. Paying by Western Union is simple and of course, you get our unconditional guarantee. After I give you instructions, I'll call you back and give you the address of the closest Western Union Office. Just go down there and tell them you want to send [amount] to London, England. Make certain that you tell them that this is a "will call." Saying it is a "will call" tells Western Union that they do not have to deliver your money. Our accountant will come and pick it up. Our accountant's name is:

His name is—David Neilson
The company name is—Wheelie International Ltd.
The city is—London, England

To make certain you have all the information, could you please repeat those steps back to me? **[Wait!] [Go slowly here—Make sure that he can read back to you all the steps, including spelling the address out.]**

Western Union will charge you **[$ in box]**, but if you go there and make your investment right now as soon as we hang up, we'll pay the Western Union fee for you. You can subtract the **[$ in box]** from your payment. That means that if you only have to send us **[amount minus $ in box.]** If you pay any other time, you will have to pay the full **[amount.]**

Please remember to tell them to send the money as a "will call," and you shouldn't have any problems.

Western Union can take your order right now, so as soon as we hang up, I'll get you registered and have your diploma and materials engraved and shipped international overnight. Of course, this will cost us a small fortune, but I trust your word. The university will go to a great deal of effort and expense to get you your diploma and materials immediately at a fraction of the cost of other institutions. Do I have your word that all the information that you have given me is correct? **[Wait!]** Do I also have your word that you will make this investment in your future as promised? **[Wait!]** When do you intend to go to Western Union? **[Wait!—write down whenever he says he is going to pay!]**

I'll call you back **[whenever he said above]** to get the receipt number so that you can be sure to get enrolled immediately, **[his name]**. As soon as you give me this receipt number, you'll have your diploma and materials in less than ten business days by private overseas carrier.

Do you have any questions? **[Wait and answer all questions.]** Remember, if you do not receive your materials exactly as promised— you pay nothing. Again, the name of the institution is the Thornewood University. My name is **[your name]**. My phone number is 713-866-6590. If you have any questions please call 24 hours a day. Thank you very much. **[Wait for him to hang up.]**
<Price>

I can understand that, **[his name]**. But, let me ask you this, if I were to give you the entire four degree programs for thirty-six hundred dollars ($3,600) would you be angry at me? **[Wait!]**
<Positive response—go to "Western Union">
<Negative response>

I can appreciate that too, **[his name]**. So, how about this? I'll give you the entire four-degree program for the minimum basic program investment of twenty-four hundred dollars ($2,400.) Now, **[his name]**, I don't know your financial status, so you have to be truthful with me: Can you afford to pay the twenty-four hundred dollars today? **[Wait!]**
<Negative response—go to "Down payment">
<Positive response—go to "Western Union">
<Down payment>

If you don't have the money on hand—no problem! You can pay a deposit of **[50 percent of total amount]** now, and you can pay the other **[50 percent of total amount]** later. How does this sound? **[Wait!]**

<Negative response>

If 50 percent is a little too much for you right now, how about this! You can pay a deposit of [20 percent of total amount] now, and you can pay the other [80 percent of total amount] over the next two years. This means that we trust you for 80 percent of the cost. How does this sound?

[Wait!]

<Positive response—go to "Western Union">

<Negative response>

Look, [his name], I just don't understand. I'm giving you everything that you need to secure your future. I'm even giving you the entire four-degree program for a fraction of the cost of any other university. I'm not asking you to trust me. I'm the person doing the trusting! All I ask is that you invest 20 percent down. I trust your word for the 80 percent balance over the next two years. I'm willing to do anything that you ask as long as it's reasonable. So tell me—what do you want to do? [Wait!] <If "Too much money" continue—if anything else go to "Western Union"!>

Well, [his name], I can understand that. But let me ask you this. If the entire diploma program were free, would you register right now? [Wait!]

<If "no"> I'm sorry that we can't help you, but give me a call if you change your mind. You have my number.

<If "yes"> Of course you would register because it's something that you need right now, don't you agree? [Wait!] Therefore, it's just a matter of how important your future is to you. Obviously, I can't give you the entire diploma package for free. But I can give you the next-best thing. If you can invest [20 percent of total amount] in your future, I'm willing to accept it and forget about the [80 percent of total amount] balance. I'll mark your account "Paid in Full." You will receive the entire program in less than ten business days. How does this sound? [Wait]

<If "yes">

Great, [his name], I'm marking you down right now as "Paid in full." <Go to "Western Union">

<If "no">

I'm sorry that we can't help you, but give me a call if you change your mind. You have my number.

•   •   •

As we were winding up work on this manuscript, the University Degree Program was making big news in California, where a reporter discovered that the man whom Governor Schwarzenegger appointed to "clean things up" as deputy director of the state Department of Motor Vehicles himself had only two college degrees, both of them purchased (and backdated) from the fake University of Palmers Green in Romania.

Appendix C

The Media Professional's Guide to Finding People with Fake Degrees

We are often asked by media professionals—newspaper, magazine, radio, and television reporters, editors, and producers—if we know of any people using fake degrees in their geographical area or in their area of special interest (military, teachers, clergy, etc.).

While the answer sometimes is yes, our more common response is to give advice on how to find such people on their own. Often it is all too easy. Here are the three ways that regularly work for us and for many others. Asking us is still an option, via our Web site at http://www .degreemills.com.

INTERNET SEARCH OR LEXISNEXIS/GOOGLE NEWS SEARCH

The search needs to be made for a specific degree-mill name and, typically, either a geographic area and/or a job specialty. Such a search will find articles that have already appeared regarding people and those degrees. In addition to articles about "time bombs" that have already exploded, there will also be articles in which a person's bogus degree is referred to in either a positive context ("Local Principal Completes PhD at Columbia State University") or simply as a routine mention in an article about another aspect of the person's life entirely, or as just a listing in a school's catalog, a church's board of directors, a company's annual report, and so on.

The next question, of course, is for which schools to search. There is not a simple answer, since even a smaller or older school with only a few findable alumni may still produce the politician, sheriff, principal, or business leader one hopes to find.

A good starting place often are some of the larger and more enduring names such as Columbia State University, LaSalle University (Louisiana), each of the twenty-or-more schools in the University Degree Program (see appendix B), and the Sussex College of Technology.

Many other school names can be found on the official list that is available from the state of Oregon as well as other sources, all described in appendix H.

While LexisNexis is almost always the best media search, Google, which searches forty-five hundred publications, works well, although only for recent stories.

RESUME SERVICES

There are three very large online services in which people in the job market can post their resume at no cost, and then employers pay a fee in order to search through those resumes. Because all three services have fast and accurate search capabilities, it is possible, for instance, to search for the name of a degree mill and either a geographical area or specific set of ZIP codes, various job categories, or both. For instance, it is possible to search for "Harrington University" and "US Army" and a given set of ZIP codes.

Monster (www.monster.com) is the industry leader, with well over 20 million resumes online.

CareerBuilder (www.careerbuilder.com) and HotJobs (http://hotjobs .yahoo.com) each are approaching 10 million resumes online. The three services each claim that there is no more than 20 to 25 percent overlap between names. In other words, they suggest that only one person out of four or five will post his or her resume on more than one service.

There are many different pricing plans offered, ranging from a subscription of a few weeks, with a limited number of "views" to annual subscriptions with unlimited numbers of views. A "view" means actual inspection, and printing, of a resume. Often, however, it is possible to search for a certain school and other criteria and read brief overviews of the resumes found, without being charged for a view.

Costs run from $400 or $500 for a subscription of several weeks to $5,000 and up for an annual full-service subscription. Pricing plans seem to vary often, and each service has its own unique set of plans.

Monster.com, for instance, offers geographical searches, covering only those clients living within a certain radius, for instance, a hundred miles, of any given ZIP code.

What can one expect to find in such a search? We recently had the opportunity for a very short "test drive" at one of the two smaller services. In the time available, we did a search for five "schools" that we regard as degree mills and found 170 "hits" for the least popular, on up to 754 for the most.

Bear in mind that these resume services represent only a tiny fraction of American workers, and, of course, only include those people who choose to mention their "alma mater" on their resume; many people don't. They also tend to be people in lower-paying and less responsible jobs, although many media people tell us they have readily found teachers, sheriffs, clergy, therapists, and so on.

WHO'S WHO SEARCH

Marquis, the publisher of twenty Who's Who biographical directories, offers a searchable database of, as the publisher describes it, "over 1 million of the most accomplished individuals from all fields of endeavor including: government, business, science and technology, the arts, entertainment and sports." The flagship volumes are Who's Who in America and Who's Who in the World. The rest are either geographical (such as Who's Who in the East) or demographic (law, medicine, finance).

Most biographies include information on academic degrees earned. While the cost of a year's subscription (there are no shorter ones available) is $1,600, more than a few newspapers and magazines already have subscriptions to facilitate research on breaking news stories, obituaries, and such (www.marquiswhoswho.com). When we expressed interest in doing research with the database, we were given a free five-day, one-hundred-search trial run.[1]

ASK ON A NEWS FORUM

There is one very active Internet news forum where some members are eager to help locate both fake schools and the people who use their degrees. When a major network was seeking people using the degree of just one particular fake school, a request at www.degreeinfo.com led to reports on several dozen people using that degree. Six of these people, including a college professor, a popular television personality, a man with a responsible job at a nuclear power plant, and an inspector at a controversial tire plant, were interviewed on the air.

While most replies one gets at DegreeInfo are reliable, it is a lightly moderated forum, and there are some spokespeople for some of the dubious schools that may respond, defending their school, typically without revealing their affiliation.

REFINING ONE'S SEARCH

While there are well over a thousand degree-granting schools that have been called degree mills, we suspect that the twenty or thirty that are most active at any given time probably account for well over half the degrees, although there have been two very large ones—LaSalle University and Columbia State University, with at least fifteen thousand "graduates" each—that were closed in the late 1990s.

LaSalle exemplifies one of the problems that can occur. There is a very real and traditional LaSalle University in Philadelphia, as well as the fake in Louisiana. In chapter 3, we offer advice on how to refine one's search in the section on how to check out a school. (In this instance, in order to find the *fake* LaSalle, one might search for ["LaSalle University" + Louisiana - Philadelphia]: the school name as a single phrase, plus the word *Louisiana*, and *not* including the word *Philadelphia*.) The fact that the real LaSalle has very few doctoral programs, while the fake LaSalle specialized in PhDs, can be helpful in a search.

Columbia State University, while a rich source of fake degree buyers (our Monster.com and other database searches found about a thousand), also has its challenges. There are, of course, many legitimate entities using the word *Columbia*, but even putting the full name in quotation marks, as good search protocol suggests, can have errors. For instance, we found that about 5 percent of "hits" in a "Columbia State

University" search were, in fact, really for the legitimate "Columbus State University" but had been mistyped in the original source documents.

That kind of problem, plus the fact that people do change their names, whether on marriage or at other times, is just a reminder to use all appropriate due diligence before "going public" with a degree-mill accusation.

Appendix D

The Oregon and North Dakota Statutes

T he states of Oregon and North Dakota have model legislation for any state, nation, or indeed school or business considering a policy on the use of degrees.

Oregon has the most comprehensive law in the United States. It focuses primarily on the *use* of academic degrees. The North Dakota law is much shorter and addresses both the *issuing* and *use* of degrees. Both were enacted in their present form in 2004. We have left out the detailed references to statutes that are, of course, available in the original.

OREGON

OREGON STUDENT ASSISTANCE COMMISSION, OFFICE OF DEGREE AUTHORIZATION

VALIDATION OR INVALIDATION OF CLAIM TO POSSESS AN ACADEMIC DEGREE

Purpose and Scope

(1) This rule implements Oregon Revised Statutes (ORS) 348.594 to 348.615 and 348.992 insofar as each section therein relates to ORS 348.609, intended to protect postsecondary institutions, businesses and other employers, professional licensing boards, patients and clients of degree holders, and all citizens from any person claiming to possess

a valid academic degree that in fact was issued by a fraudulent or sub-standard school or by some entity posing as a school.

(2) In order to be valid in Oregon as a public credential usable for general academic or professional purposes, under ORS 348.609 a claimed degree must have been awarded by a school that:

a) Has accreditation recognized by the US Department of Education or has the foreign equivalent of such accreditation; or

b) Has been approved through the Office of Degree Authorization (ODA) to offer and confer degrees in Oregon; or

c) Is located in the United States and has been found by the commission acting through the Office of Degree Authorization to meet standards of academic quality comparable to those of an institution located in the United States that has accreditation, recognized by the US Department of Education, to offer degrees of the type and level claimed by the person.

(3) This rule applies to any claim to possess an academic degree made by any person acting within the state, acting outside the state while domiciled within the state, or acting outside the state on behalf of an organization that is located within the state.

Stat. Auth.: ORS 348.609
Stats. Implemented: ORS 348.603 & ORS 348.609
Hist.: ODA 2-1998, f. & cert. ef. 8-12-98; ODA 1-2001, f. & cert. ef. 6-27-01; ODA 3-2003, f. 10-29-03, cert. ef. 11-1-03

Definitions of Terms

(1) "Office" means Office of Degree Authorization, as represented by the administrator or designated agent.

(2)(a) "Degree" means any academic or honorary title, rank, or status designated by a symbol or by a series of letters or words-such as, but not limited to, associate, bachelor, master, doctor, and forms or abbreviations thereof, that signifies, purports, or may generally be taken to signify:

A) Completion of a course of instruction at the college or university level; or

B) Demonstration of achievement or proficiency comparable to such completion; or
C) Recognition for non-academic learning, public service,
or other reason of distinction comparable to such completion.

(b) "Degree" does not refer to a certificate or diploma signified
by a series of letters or words unlikely to be confused with
a degree, clearly intended not to be mistaken for a degree,
and represented to the public so as to prevent such confusion or error.

(3) "Confer a degree" means give, grant, award, bestow, or present
orally or in writing any symbol or series of letters or words that would
lead the recipient to believe it was a degree that had been received.

(4) "Claim a degree" means to present orally, or in writing or in
electronic form any symbol or series of letters or words that would lead
the listener or reader to believe a degree had been received and is possessed by the person speaking or writing, for purposes related to
employment, application for employment, professional advancement,
qualification for public office, teaching, offering professional services or
any other use as a public credential, whether or not such use results in
monetary gain.

(5) "School" means any person or persons, whether incorporated
or not, engaging or appearing to engage in the activities of a school, college, university, institute, academy, seminary, conservatory, or any other
such educational entity, or of any organized group of such entities. The
activities attributable to a school include instruction, measurement of
achievement or proficiency, or recognition of educational attainment or
comparable public distinction.

(6) "Accredited" means accredited and approved to offer degrees at
the specified level by an agency or association recognized as an accreditor
by the US Secretary of Education, under the 1965 Higher Education Act
as amended at the time of recognition, or having candidacy status with
such an accrediting agency or association whose pre-accreditation is also
recognized specifically for HEA purposes by the Secretary of Education.

(7) "Foreign equivalent of such accreditation" means authorization
by a non-US government found by ODA to have standards at least as
stringent as those required by US approved accrediting agencies at the

same degree level. This determination may be made through one or more of the following methods at ODA's discretion:

a) Direct investigation of foreign standards;
b) Reliance on an evaluation and determination made by the National Association of Collegiate Registrars and Admissions Officers; or
c) Evaluation of the transferability of courses and degrees earned in the foreign country to accredited Oregon institutions at similar degree levels.

(8) "Academic Standards" means those standards in 583-030-0035 or the equivalent standards of an accrediting body that relate to admission requirements, length of program, content of curriculum, award of credit and faculty qualifications.

(9) "Standard School" means a school that is accredited by a federally recognized US-based accreditor, has ODA approval to issue degrees in Oregon, has ODA approval as a non-Oregon US based school under ORS 348.609(d) or has ODA approval as a foreign school under ORS 348.609(a).

(10) "Substandard School" means an unaccredited entity that offers credentials purported to be degrees without requiring the type and level of academic work typically needed to earn a degree. An unaccredited entity is a substandard school if it has any one of the following characteristics:

a) issues degrees without requiring any substantial student academic work.
b) Issues degrees based solely on the student's life experience or portfolio without requiring any college-level work submitted to and evaluated by faculty with appropriate academic degrees from accredited institutions.
c) Issues degrees without requiring that at least 80 percent of student work for which credit is given be college level work appropriate for the degree.
d) Issues degrees using more than 20 percent of required credits based on the student's life experience.
e) Issues degrees using more than 20 percent of credits transferred from an unaccredited school, unless the transferring school is approved by ODA.

f) Issues degrees without at least 80 percent of student work for credit being evaluated by faculty with accredited degrees or degrees from an ODA-approved school one level above the level of degree issued to the student, or holding an appropriate professional degree or doctorate.

g) Issues degrees without requiring at least 30 hours of student work (combined cumulative in and out of class, including labs and practica) per quarter credit hour (45 hours per semester credit hour) awarded. Award of credit for achieving appropriate scores on ODA-approved nationally normed college-level examinations such as CLEP, Advanced Placement or New York Regents meets this standard.

(11) "Diploma mill" or "degree mill" means an unaccredited school that meets any one of the following conditions.

a) Issues degrees without requiring any student academic work.

b) Issues degrees based solely on the student's life experience or portfolio without requiring any college-level work submitted to and evaluated by faculty with appropriate academic degrees from standard institutions.

c) Issues degrees using more than 50 percent of required credits based on the student's life experience or portfolio.

(12) "College level work" required for a degree means academic or technical work at a level demonstrably higher than that required in the final year of high school and demonstrably higher than work required for degrees at a lower level than the degree in question. From lowest to highest, degree levels are associate, bachelor's, master's and doctoral. Professional degree levels may vary. College level work is characterized by analysis, synthesis and application in which students demonstrate an integration of knowledge, skills and critical thinking.

[Publications: Publications referenced are available from the agency.]
    Stat. Auth.: ORS 348.609
    Stats. Implemented: ORS 348.603 & ORS 348.609
    Hist.: ODA 2-1998, f. & cert. ef. 8-12-98; ODA 3-2000, f. & cert. ef. 8-8-00; ODA 1-2001, f. & cert. ef. 6-27-01; ODA 3-2003, f. 10-29-03, cert. ef. 11-1-03

Validation of a Secular Degree

(1) Any person claiming in Oregon to possess an academic degree shall, upon request from the Office of Degree Authorization, have an official transcript of the degree sent directly to the Office from the registrar or other appropriate official of the conferring school.

(2) Where validation of a degree by telephone or electronic means seems readily obtainable from a school, the Office at its discretion may postpone with option of waiver the requirement for a transcript upon receiving from the degree claimant the name, address, and telephone number of the conferring school. Requirement of one or more transcripts may be reinstated at any time if other methods of validation are not sufficient for a conclusive determination.

(3) Upon receipt of evidence of a valid degree, the Office shall inform the degree claimant that a validation has been entered into the record, which shall specify any title and abbreviation that may be used to claim the degree.

Stat. Auth.: ORS 348.609

Stats. Implemented: ORS 348.603 & ORS 348.609

Hist.: ODA 2-1998, f. & cert. ef. 8-12-98; ODA 1-2001, f. & cert. ef. 6-27-01; ODA 3-2003, f. 10-29-03, cert. ef. 11-1-03

Invalidation of a Degree, Warning, Enforcement

(1) A person who may not have known that his or her claimed degree is invalid is given the benefit of the doubt as to intent, so as to reflect consideration for the apparent victims of diploma mills, and will be referred to listings of appropriate degree providers.

(2) Failure to provide when requested a transcript or other information needed for validation of a degree is prima facie evidence under statute that the claim to such degree is invalid.

(3) Failure or inability to produce conclusive evidence of a valid degree or of entitlement to a religious exemption results in a warning from the Office that the claimant must thereafter cease and desist from making the invalidated claim.

(4) Subsequent to such warning and in violation thereof, any renewed claim of an invalid degree exposes the violator to penalties as set forth in statute and under OAR 583-050-0026(5).

(5) Any violation of ORS 348.603 or 348.609 may result in any or all of the following sanctions.

a) Prosecution for a Class B misdemeanor under ORS 348.992.
b) Injunction against further use of the claimed degree.
c) Civil suit for violation of the Unlawful Trade Practices Act, if applicable.
d) A civil penalty not to exceed $1,000 per violation.

Stat. Auth.: ORS 348.609
Stats. Implemented: ORS 348.603, ORS 348.609 & ORS 348.992
Hist.: ODA 2-1998, f. & cert. ef. 8-12-98; ODA 1-2001, f. & cert. ef. 6-27-01; ODA 2-2002, f. & cert. ef. 10-10-02

Disciplinary Action; Civil Penalty Considerations

(1) A violation of any provision of OAR 583, division 050 is cause for levy of a civil penalty by the Commission under ORS 348.609.

(2) In establishing the amount of the penalty for each violation, the Commission shall consider, but not be limited to the following factors:

a) The gravity and magnitude of the violation;
b) The person's previous record of compliance with the provisions of ORS 348.594 to 348.615 or with the rules adopted thereunder;
c) The person's history in taking all feasible steps or in following all procedures necessary or appropriate to correct the violation; and
d) Such other considerations as the Commission may consider appropriate.

(3) An "incident" for purposes of the penalty schedule means a single use of the invalid degree in a specific venue in a specific time period.

a) Examples of specific venues include but are not limited to publications, job applications, web sites, spoken presentations, mailings, e-mails, flyers, posters, advertisements and handouts.
b) Examples of specific time periods include one-time uses and

serial uses, e.g., monthly advertisements, annual publications such as college catalogs and the like. In the case of continued usage during a period of employment, each regular pay period (e.g., one month) in which the invalid degree is used is considered a specific time period and therefore a separate incident.

(4) The Commission may impose a civil penalty, provided that it first gives the person an opportunity for a hearing as outlined in ORS Chapter 183.

Stat. Auth.: ORS 348.609
Stats. Implemented: ORS 348.609
Hist.: ODA 2-2002, f. & cert. ef. 10-10-02

Schedule of Civil Penalties for Violations of Laws and Rules

In assessing civil penalties, the Commission desires to be both consistent and equitable and to consider and evaluate each case on an individual basis. The actual civil penalty which the Commission imposes shall be based on the Commission's consideration of the factors in OAR 583-050-0027. The Commission shall impose a penalty per incident based on only one of the invalid degree activities listed below, i.e. a single incident cannot result in a penalty from more than one category. Civil penalties shall be imposed according to the following schedule for use after warning by ODA of a degree found invalid by ODA:

(1) When such use is related to a position in any employment sector, paid or unpaid, involving public health or safety for which a degree of the type found invalid is required for employment or licensure: $1000 per incident.

(2) When such use is intended to induce or encourage payment of money by students, clients, customers or others for whom the degree may serve as an attractant or legitimizer related to a service provided in the business or not-for-profit sector: $1000 per incident.

(3) When such use is in public employment not related to public health or safety for which a valid degree of the type claimed is required or is necessary based on the conditions of employment: $500 per incident.

(4) By a teacher at any level, including K-12 and postsecondary education: $500 per incident.

(5) When such use is likely to deceive the public as to the user's qualifications but no money is sought or received by the user as a consequence in whole or in part of the invalid use: $300 per incident.

(6) When in violation of any other provision of OAR 583, division 050: $300 per incident.

(7) Repeated violations of any kind may result in a penalty of $1,000 for each repetition occurring after a penalty is imposed by the Commission or an injunction against the usage is issued by a court.

Stat. Auth.: ORS 348.609
Stats. Implemented: ORS 348.609
Hist.: ODA 2-2002, f. & cert. ef. 10-10-02

Unaccredited Degree Claims

(1) A claimant of an unaccredited US degree may submit to the Office information indicating that the school conferring the degree is operating legally in another state and could reasonably be considered for approval in Oregon under OAR 583-030.

a) A reasonable possibility of approval can be demonstrated by submitting to ODA the appropriate review fee and sufficient evidence that the unaccredited institution could meet ODA academic standards under OAR 583-030 for authorization to operate in Oregon if it chose to make such an application.

b) ODA may, upon its own motion, evaluate an unaccredited institution and determine whether it has a reasonable chance to meet Oregon authorization standards without a degree user making such a request.

c) If a request for evaluation under this section is not made to ODA within 30 days of notification that an unaccredited degree is being used contrary to Oregon law, the degree user's right to such a review is waived and ODA may pursue appropriate enforcement action. Degree users may, within the first 30 days, request up to 30 additional days for the purpose of gathering material necessary to apply for an evaluation.

(2) A claimant of a non-US degree issued by a degree supplier not accredited by a US accreditor may submit to the Office informa-

tion proving that the supplier issuing the degree has the following characteristics.

a) The supplier is operating legally in its host country.
b) The host country has a postsecondary approval system equivalent to US accreditation.
c) The supplier has been approved through the demonstrable application of appropriate standards by the host country's accreditor equivalent.
d) All degrees issued by the supplier are legally valid for use within the host country.

[Publications: Publications referenced are available from the agency.]
Stat. Auth.: ORS 348.609
Stats. Implemented: ORS 348.603, ORS 348.609 & ORS 348.992
Hist.: ODA 2-1998, f. & cert. ef. 8-12-98; ODA 1-2001, f. & cert. ef. 6-27-01; ODA 3-2003, f. 10-29-03, cert. ef. 11-1-03; ODA 4-2004, f. & cert. ef. 5-14-04

Inquiries and Complaints

(1) Monitoring and validating degree claims will be done by the Office in the course of routine activities such as approving faculty members of schools seeking authorization to offer degrees in Oregon, advising employers or professional licensing boards on applicant credentials, examining backgrounds listed by candidates for public election, and reviewing telephone directories or other publications for advertisements that list degrees.

(2) Any citizen as a matter of general information may ask the Office to discuss whether a degree encountered sounds questionable, and any citizen as a matter of public protection may ask the Office to validate a degree claimed by an identified individual. It is entirely optional for an inquirer unsure about a degree to make a formal complaint, because an inquiry alone does not imply that the inquiring citizen has accused the degree claimant of any deception.

Stat. Auth.: ORS 348.609
Stats. Implemented: ORS 348.603 & ORS 348.609
Hist.: ODA 2-1998, f. & cert. ef. 8-12-98

Fees for Validation Services

(1) ODA charges a fee for some services provided under OAR 583-050. The fee schedule is as follows: [Table not included. See ED. NOTE.]

- a) Agencies or organizations that have contracted for basic degree validation services with ODA do not pay a per-request fee. Contract rates are as follows: [Table not included. See ED. NOTE.]
- b) Fees for all inquiries, including contracted rates, must be paid in advance by bank check, money order or interagency fund transfer to: State of Oregon—ODA Oregon Student Assistance Commission, 1500 Valley River Dr. Suite 100, Eugene OR 97401.

(2) ODA may require reimbursement of costs for other requests at the discretion of the agency, depending on the nature of the request and available staff resources. Such fees may not exceed the actual cost to the agency to provide the service, based on staff rates and related costs.

(3) ODA may waive validation and evaluation fees:

- a) If the request for information is for purposes of criminal investigation; or
- b) If the consumer protection benefits of ODA action warrant a waiver, provided that sufficient staff time is available.

[ED. NOTE: Tables referenced are available from the agency.]
Stat. Auth.: ORS 348.609
Stats. Implemented: ORS 348.603 & ORS 348.609
Hist.: ODA 3-2003, f. 10-29-03, cert. ef. 11-1-03

NORTH DAKOTA

H.B. 1068 synopsis

An act to create and enact three new sections to chapter 15–20.4 of the North Dakota Century Code, relating to the issuance, manufacture, and use of false academic degrees or certificates, and to provide a penalty.

SECTION I

A new section to chapter 15-20.4 of the North Dakota Century Code is created and enacted as follows:

Unlawful to issue, manufacture, or use false academic degrees—penalty.
1. It is unlawful for a person to knowingly issue or manufacture a false academic degree. A person who violates this subsection is guilty of a class C felony.
2. a. It is unlawful for an individual to knowingly use or claim to have a false academic degree:
      (1) To obtain employment,
      (2) To obtain a promotion of higher compensation in employment,
      (3) To obtain admission to an institution of higher learning, or
      (4) In connection with any business, trade, profession, or occupation.
   b. An individual who violates this subsection is guilty of a class A misdemeanor.
3. As used in this section, "false academic degree" means a document such as a degree or certification of completion of a degree, course work, or degree credit, including a transcript, that provides evidence or demonstrates completion of a course of instruction or course work that results in the attainment of a rank or level of associate or higher that is issued by a person that is not a duly authorized institution of higher learning.
4. As used in this section, "duly authorized institution of higher learning" means an institution that:
   a. has accreditation recognized by the United States secretary of education or has the foreign equivalent of such accreditation;
   b. has an authorization to operate under this chapter;
   c. operates in this state and is exempt from this chapter under section 15–20.4–02;
   d. does not operate in this state and is
      (1) licensed by the appropriate state agency, and
      (2) an active applicant for accreditation by an accrediting body recognized by the United States secretary of education; or

e. Has been found by the state board for career and technical education to meet standards of academic quality comparable to those of an institution located in the United States that has accreditation recognized by the United States secretary of education to offer degrees of the type and level claimed.

SECTION 2

A new section to chapter 15–20.4 of the North Dakota Century Code is created and enacted as follows:

Unlawful to use degree or certificate when coursework not completed—penalty.

1. An individual may not knowingly use a degree, certificate, diploma, transcript, or other document purporting to indicate that the individual has completed an organized program of study or completed courses when the individual has not completed the organized program of study or the courses as indicated on the degree, certificate, diploma, transcript, or document:
   a. to obtain employment;
   b. to obtain a promotion or higher compensation in employment;
   c. to obtain admission to an institution of higher learning, or
   d. in connection with any business, trade, profession, or occupation.
2. An individual who violates this section is guilty of a class A misdemeanor.

SECTION 3

A new section to chapter 15-20.4 of the North Dakota Century Code is created and enacted as follows:

Consumer protection—false academic degrees. The state board for career and technical education, in collaboration with the North Dakota university system, shall provide via Internet Web sites information to protect students, businesses, and others from persons that issue, manufacture, or use false academic degrees.

Appendix E

Accreditation

In most countries, degree-granting institutions are either run by or approved by the national government, so there is no need for a separate, independent agency to say that a given school is OK.

But the US Constitution does not mention the concept of education, and things have evolved so that school evaluating and licensing is done by the states and by private entities called accrediting agencies. The main federal role is to ensure that the accrediting agencies deal properly with federal matters such as guaranteed student loans.

Accreditation in America, then, is a process in which an accrediting agency, comprising persons who are, theoretically, impartial experts in higher education, looks at a given school, or department within a school, and determines whether it is worthy of approval.

There are six regional accreditors (representing six regions of the country), as well as professional accreditors (representing specific areas of study: chemistry, music, psychology, etc.), and national ones (for distance learning, continuing education, etc.). And there are a great many accrediting agencies that were set up by less-than-wonderful schools or groups of schools for the purpose of accrediting themselves and thus fooling well-meaning potential students, who know enough to *want* accreditation but don't realize there can be *useless* accreditation.

Who "accredits" the accreditors? In the United States, there are two sources: the US Department of Education, which recognizes accreditors who follow the guidelines for federal loans, and the Council on Higher Education Accreditation (CHEA), a private agency with more than three thousand schools as members. It is safe to say that every accreditor whose accreditation principles and procedures are generally accepted in the academic, government, and business world are recognized by one or, in nearly all cases, both of these. About sixty recognized accreditors are listed on the CHEA Web site (www.chea.org).

Among the more than two hundred unrecognized accrediting agencies, there are a very small number that are either too new or too untraditional to be recognized. But many of the other agencies, even those that operate quite legally (very few jurisdictions have laws regulating accreditors), will typically accredit a new school within days, even minutes, of its coming into existence. Indeed, many unrecognized accrediting agencies are just another button on the telephone of the school that set them up.

Many of these unrecognized agencies exist only on the Internet. Some use mailing service addresses. Some have been formed in or by other countries generally to accredit schools either in the United States or controlled by Americans that would be unlikely to qualify for generally accepted accreditation.

Some accreditors use the ploy of accrediting Harvard, Yale, and Princeton (without their knowledge) along with a bunch bad or fake schools.

Some unrecognized accrediting agencies have some acceptance in certain situations; many do not.

Here is a list of more than two hundred accrediting agencies that, as of late 2004, are *not* recognized either by CHEA or by the US Department of Education. Inclusion on this list does not mean that the accreditor is good or bad, real or fake, but *only* that it not recognized by either of those two entities. As always, people will need to make their own decisions as to where to draw a line on their own continuum.

By "unfindable" on the following list, we mean that despite our best efforts at Internet and other searches, we were not able to locate the accreditor or any independent reference to it. And by "Oregon law," we mean that the schools mentioned are on Oregon's official list of schools whose degrees are illegal in that state. (Five or six other states have laws comparable to Oregon's.)

•   •   •

Academy for Contemporary Research. Accreditor claimed by various now-defunct schools.

Academy for the Promotion of International Cultural and Scientific Exchange (www.apics.com). Switzerland, Hawaii. Associated with people who were a part of La Jolla University in California and Louisiana, Irish International University, and others. Has accredited the fake Monticello University.

Accreditation Agency for European Non-Traditional Universities (http://aentu.tripod.com). Its slogan is "Knolwedge [sic] is Power." Registration is claimed in Republic of Ireland, the only telephone number listed is in New York. Has accredited the possibly defunct Ballmore Irish University.

Accreditation Association of Ametrican [sic] College [sic] and Universities. Has accredited American University of Hawaii.

Accreditation Association of Christian Colleges and Seminaries. Had been in Morgantown, Kentucky, and now cannot be located.

Accreditation Commission International. See Accrediting Commission International.

Accreditation Governing Commission of the United States of America (www.agc-usa.org). The chief accrediting commissioner is associated with schools that claim Liberian accreditation and others. Has accredited American Coastline, Breyer State, University of Northern Washington, and others.

Accrediting Association of Christian Colleges and Seminaries. Sarasota, Florida.

Accrediting Commission for Colleges and Universities. Cannot locate. Claimed by Intercultural Open University.

Accrediting Commission for Specialized Colleges. Gas City, Indiana. Established by George Reuter and "Bishop" Gordon DaCosta on DaCosta's dairy farm. The only requirement for candidacy was a check for $110. Reuter went on to start the International Accrediting Commission (qv).

Accrediting Commission International (ACI) for Schools Colleges and Theological Seminaries (www.accreditnow.com). Beebe, Arkansas. The International Accrediting Commission was closed down by the Missouri attorney general following a clever sting operation. ACI arose shortly after and (despite the written denial of founder Dr. John Scheel) offered immediate and automatic accreditation to IAC members. (We have Scheel's letter making the offer.) ACI does not make a list of accreditees public, but more than 150 schools have been identified that claim their accreditation, more than two-thirds of them religious.

Accrediting Commission of Independent Colleges and Schools (http:// accrediting.virtualave.net/accreditation.html). Bald Knob, Arkansas. This religious accreditor has a name almost exactly like the recognized Accrediting Council for Independent Colleges and Schools, and both use the "ACICS" acronym.

Accrediting Council for Colleges and Schools. Unfindable accreditor of Intercultural Open University.

Advanced Online Business Education Society (www.online-business-education.org). The only schools they accredit are associated with the American Management and Business Administration Institute, such as AMBAI University.

AF Sep. The unfindable accreditor claimed by Beta International University.

Akademie fuer Internationale Kultur und Wissenschaftsfoerderung. See Academy for Promotion of International Cultural and Scientific Exchange.

Alternative Institution Accrediting Association. Washington, DC. Has accredited several fake schools.

American Accrediting Association of Theological Institutions (http:// www.christianbiblecollege.org/index.htm). Rocky Mount, North Carolina. The Christian Bible College is at the same address. Used to charge $100 for accreditation.

American Alternative Medical Association. See American Association of Drugless Practitioners.

American Association of Accredited Colleges and Universities. Unfindable accreditor claimed by Ben Franklin Academy.

American Association of Drugless Practitioners (www.aadp.net). Accreditor of Clayton College of Natural Health, Southern College of Naturopathy, and so forth. Had been at same residential address as the American Alternative Medical Association.

American Association of Independent Collegiate Schools of Business. Unfindable accreditor once claimed by Rushmore University.

American Association of Nontraditional Colleges and Universities. Accreditor claimed by short-lived Southeastern Internet University.

American Association of Nontraditional Collegiate Business Schools. Unfindable accreditor once claimed by Rushmore University.

American Association of Nontraditional Private Postsecondary Education. Listed as a "suspect accreditor" by the New Brunswick Department of Education.

American Association of Schools (www.a-aos.org). Temple City, California. It maintains a list of "recommended institutions" composed mainly of legitimate schools plus one unrecognized school, which has shared an ISP with the accreditor.

American Council for Freedom and Excellence in Higher Education. Unfindable accreditor claimed by the fake Regency University.

American Council of Home Study Colleges. Swartz Creek, Michigan. Apparently nonexistent accreditor claimed by the short-lived Prescott College of Business.

American Council of Private Colleges and Universities. Unfindable accreditor set up by Hamilton University, Wyoming.

American Education Association for the Accreditation of Schools, Colleges and Universities. Unfindable accreditor claimed by the University of America.

American Educational Accrediting Association of Christian Schools. Dothan, Alabama.

American Educational Association of Non-Traditional Christian Schools. Dothan, Alabama.

American Federation of Christian Colleges and Schools. Lakeland, Florida.

American Institute of Healthcare Professionals. See Central States Consortium of Colleges and Schools.

American International Commission for Excellence in Higher Education. Fake accreditor used by Les Snell's fake Amherst University.

American International Council for Assessment Universities, Colleges and Schools. Unfindable accreditor claimed by Wittfield University.

American Naprapathic Association. Unfindable accreditor claimed by Chicago National College of Naprapathy.

American Naturopathic Medical Certification and Accreditation Board. Accreditor claimed by Westbrook University. Its accreditation letter is identical to that written by the National Board of Naturopathic Examiners.

American Notable Universities and Colleges Association (www.anuca .org). Washington, DC. It accredited legitimate schools (without their consent or knowledge) as well as spurious ones.

American Psycotherapy [sic] Association. Katy, Florida.

APIX Institute. Unfindable accreditor claimed by Horizon University, France.

Arizona Commission of Non-Traditional Private Postsecondary Education. The accreditor set up by Southland University when it moved from California to Arizona. After a protest from the real Arizona Commission, the name was changed to the Western Council.

Assessment and Qualifications Convention. Established by a school operator to offer accreditation.

Association for Online Academic Accreditation (www.aoaa.org). It accredits MacArther University, Ratchford University, and many others. It claims that it has tried to become recognized but that US laws prohibit this.

Association for Online Academic Excellence. Its list of accredited members is not too different from the State of Oregon's list of schools whose degrees are illegal there. http://216.36.213.212.

Association for Online Distance Learning (www.afodl.com). The single-page Web site for this unrecognized accreditor lists among its accredited members Almeda College and University and Bond College and University. At another site (www.geocities.com/tafodl), the association also accredits Chase University, which has the same domain registration details.

Association Internationale des Educateurs pour la Paix Mondiale. At least three universities on the Oregon list have claimed this accreditation.

Association of Accredited Private Schools. Unfindable accreditor claimed by City University Los Angeles and others.

Association of Career Training Schools. its literature said, "Have your school accredited with the Association. Why? [It] could be worth many $$$ to you."

Association of Christian Colleges and Theological Schools (www.accts .cc). Paducah, Kentucky. It says that it is an accreditor for Christian schools that do not wish to deal with a professional accreditor.

Association of Christian Schools and Colleges. Unfindable accreditor claimed by Pickering University.

Association of Christian Schools International. Colorado Springs, Colorado. Seems to have some acceptance in the world of religious schools.

Association of Distance Learning Programs (http://www.nahighered .org/accreditation.htm). The accreditor of schools that have also claimed Liberian and/or Russian accreditation, including the International College of Homeland Security, International University of Fundamental Studies, Irish International University, and others.

Association of Distance Learning Programs. See National Academy of Higher Education.

Association of Fundamental Institutes of Religious Education. AFIRE was active in the '80s; now it cannot be located.

Association of International Colleges and Universities. Unfindable accreditor claimed by Wittfield University.

Association of Open and Distance Education (www.aode.org). Accreditor claimed by Burkes University.

Association of Private Colleges and Universities. Established by a founder of Trinity College and University. It originally said it was a nonprofit entity but changed that claim when challenged. It says that it is set up to "annihilate illegal degree mills."

Association of Virtual Universities, Colleges, and Schools. Unfindable accreditor claimed by Julius Caesar University.

Association of World Universities and Colleges. Apparently established in Switzerland by the president of the University of Asia. Accredits the University of Asia.

Australian Universities Association. Accreditor previously claimed by the University of Asia. Web site registered to proprietor of the University of Asia.

Board of Online Universities Accreditation (www.boua.org). New Orleans, Louisiana. Claimed by Rochville University and Ashwood University.

British Public University System (www.ac-edu.org). It claims to be licensed by the British Honduras Higher Education Policy Commission (British Honduras changed its name to Belize in 1981). It seems to act as an umbrella organization for a group of schools (Croxley Heritage University, London Sanford University, Victoria Brooke University, etc.) that claim accreditation from Euro American Accreditation Council for Higher Education.

Central Orthodox Synod. Unfindable accreditor claimed by International Reform University.

Central States Consortium of Colleges and Schools (http://www.aihcp .org/csccs.htm). Warren, Ohio. Affiliated with the American Institute of Healthcare Professionals, which accredits some schools on the Oregon list.

Christhomas Consortium London (www.ccledu.ac). Accreditor claimed by International University (Missouri), which calls it "the recognized official body of accreditation in the U.K."

College for Professional Assessment. Unfindable accreditor claimed by Thomas Jefferson Education Foundation and others.

Commission for the Accreditation of European Non-Traditional Universities. Accreditor claimed by the University de la Romande.

Commonwealth Universities Association (www.cwlthuniversitiesassoc .org.uk). Accreditor claimed by the University of Asia. Site is registered by the president of the University of Asia.

Congress for the Accreditation of Educational and Training Organization (www.accred.ip3.com). Accredits Dublin Metropolitan and Calamus International universities. Formerly Non-Traditional Course Accreditation Board.

Correspondence Accreditation Association. Accreditor created by and claimed by Trinity College and University in the United Kingdom.

Council for International Education Accreditation (www.ciea.org). Accreditor for Almeda University, American University, Ashworth College, and dozens of others.

Council for National Academic Accreditation. Cheyenne, Wyoming. It wrote to schools offering accreditation for $1,850.

Council for the Accreditation of Correspondence Colleges. Louisiana. Accreditation claimed by several otherwise unrecognized schools.

Council on Post Secondary Accreditation. Unfindable accreditor claimed by South Atlantic University.

Council on Postsecondary Alternative Accreditation. Unfindable accreditor claimed by Western States University.

Council on Postsecondary Christian Education. Nonexistent accreditor claimed by the owners of LaSalle University and Kent College in Louisiana.

Distance Education Council of America. Delaware. Clearly designed to be confused with the recognized Distance Education and Training Council. Sold accreditation for $200, $150 extra for an "excellent" rating.

Distance Graduation Accrediting Association (http://accredit.t2u.com). Accreditor claimed by St. Regis University, Capitol University, Orienta College and University, and others.

Distance Learning Council of Europe. Accreditor claimed by Wexford University; its site is almost identical to that of the European Council for Distance and Open Learning.

Eastern Christian Accrediting Association of Colleges, Universities and Seminaries. Claimed by several schools; it now cannot be located.

Educational Quality Accrediting Commission (www.eqac.org). Created by Bircham International University; accredits American Coastline, Irish International, and many others.

Euro American Accreditation Council for Higher Education (www.euro-america.uni.cc). Accredits schools affiliated with the misleadingly named British Public University System (located in Belize): (Croxley Heritage University, London Sanford University, Victoria Brooke University, etc.).

Euro-American Accreditation Agency. Cyprus. Formed by an accreditor of Northwestern International University.

European Committee for Home and Online Education (http://www .echoe.org.uk/about.htm). Accreditor of University of Dorchester, University of Dunham, Strassford University, Shaftesbury University, Stafford University, and so forth.

European Council for Distance and Open Learning. For a long time, the world's largest degree-mill scam—the University Degree Program based in Romania—avoided any mention of accreditation when pitching the phony degrees from the University San Moritz, University of Palmers Green, Harrington University, and dozens of others. In 2001, the program established the Web site for this accreditor and began mentioning it in its sales pitches.

European Council for Home and Online Education. Unfindable accreditor claimed by Renshaw's College.

Global Accreditation Commission. Unfindable accreditor once claimed by Adam Smith University and others.

Global Accreditation for Christian Schools. Unfindable accreditor claimed by Dayspring University.

Global Accreditation Organization for Life Experience and Education (www.gaolee.co.za). South Africa. Accreditor for Cambridge International University, the fake University of Palmers Green, and others.

Government Accreditation Association of Delaware. Unfindable accreditor claimed by Yorker International University and Albert University.

Higher Education Accrediting Commission (www.heac.org). Their mission is to accredit other accrediting agencies: the Board of Online Universities Accreditation, the Universal Council for Online Education Accreditation, the International Accreditation Agency for Online Universities, and the World Online Education Accrediting

Commission which are all affiliated with the same schools—Ashwood, Belford, and Rocheville universities.

Higher Education Services Association (http://hesa-edu.org). The accreditor for a group of schools including Ellington University, Garfield Technical College, Lexington University, Stanton University, and others. It will accredit only schools "sponsored" by its members.

Integra Accreditation Association. It sent out a mailing in 2000 inviting schools to apply; it's now unfindable.

Inter-Collegiate Joint Committee on Academic Standards (www.jointcommittee.org). Controlled by affiliates of College Services Corporation, it accredits Vernell University and Alexandria University, as well as names that appear on the diplomas sold by the your-degreenow.com and degrees-r-us.com Web sites.

InterAmerican Association of Postsecondary Colleges and Schools. Unfindable accreditor of Universitas Sancti Martin.

Interfaith Education Ministries Association of Academic Excellence. Washington, DC. Accreditor of St. Regis University, Dorcas University, Bircham International, Advanced University, and others. It also does foreign credential evaluation.

International Academic Accrediting Commission (www.iaac.us.tt). No clues as to where this is, other than a fax number in the Tacoma, Washington, area. No mention of people or schools, but it apparently accredits "Mave University."

International Accreditation Agency for Online Universities (www.iaaou.org). Accreditor claimed by Belford University.

International Accreditation and Recognition Council (www.iarcedu.com). Nerang, Australia. Accredits Warnborough, Southern Pacific, and Queens University of Brighton (which has a Berkeley, California, address), among others.

International Accreditation and Registration Institute (www.i-a-r-i.org). Accreditor claimed by the apparently defunct Nation University.

International Accreditation Association. Claimed accreditor of University of North America; now it cannot be located.

International Accreditation Association of Nontraditional Colleges and Universities (www.iaancu.nu). Claimed to be in British West Indies, it has a nonfunctioning Web site in Niue.

International Accreditation Commission for Post Secondary Education Institutions. Claimed accreditor of University of the United States and Nasson University, both operated from a convenience address in Mobile, Alabama.

International Accreditation for Universities, Colleges, Institutes, Organizations and Professionals. Had been listed as accreditor for Trinity International University, University of Honolulu USA, and Chase University. Address is in Houston, Texas; domain registration was in Bellevue, Washington.

International Accreditation Society (www.usias.org). Its list of accredited schools includes lots of real ones (Harvard, Stanford) as well as many on the Oregon list.

International Accrediting Agency for Private and Post Secondary Institutes. Accreditor claimed by CliffPort and Glanmount universities, apparently in Pakistan.

International Accrediting Association (http://www.ulc.net/shop/default .bak). Accreditor for the Universal Life Church and its $100 PhDs.

International Accrediting Association of Ministerial Education. Accreditor claimed by Valley International Christian Seminary; now it cannot be located.

International Accrediting Association of Nontraditional Colleges and Universities. British West Indies. Accreditor claimed by Postsecondary Education Institute. Now it cannot be located.

International Accrediting Commission for Postsecondary Institutions. Accreditor once claimed by Adam Smith University; now it cannot be located.

International Accrediting Commission for Schools, Colleges and Theological Seminaries. Holden, Missouri. More than 150 schools, many of them Bible schools, were accredited by this organization. The story of the Missouri attorney general's clever "sting" operation, setting up a fake schools that it instantly accredited, is told on page 102. See Accrediting Commission International for Schools, Colleges and Theological Seminaries.

International Association of Colleges and Universities. Accreditor claimed by the dubious University of America.

International Association of Educators for World Peace (http://www .earthportals.com/Portal_Messenger/mercieca.html). Fairfax, California. Accreditor claimed by European Union University.

International Association of Fake Universities (http://www.boxfreeconcepts .com/iafu/gc/gcd001.html). It says that it is a fake accreditor, but some of the fake schools it accredits have realistic names; also, it will print a diploma with the university name of your choice.

International Association of Monotheistic Schools. Accreditor claimed by Alan Mitchell School of Psychology. It cannot be located.

International Association of Non-Traditional Schools. Accreditor claimed by some British degree mills, now it cannot be located.

International Association of Schools, Colleges and Universities (www .iascu.org). Antwerp, Belgium. Accredited at least four schools on the Oregon list. URL is not operational.

International Association of Universities and Schools (www.angelfire .com/ia/iaus). Geneva, Switzerland. Incorporated by Robert K. Bettinger, President of Barrington University, it accredited Barrington for three years, but no longer.

International College and School Accreditation Association. Listed many legitimate schools plus Pennington University. It cannot be located.

International Commission for Excellence in Higher Education. Accreditor established by and claimed by the fake Monticello University.

International Commission for the Accreditation of Colleges and Universities. Gaithersburg, Maryland. Accreditor established and claimed by the United States University of America.

International Commission on Academic Accreditation. Unfindable accreditor claimed by Freedom Bible College.

International Commission on Distance Education (http://www .intcode.org/english/english.html). Madrid, Spain.

International Council for Accreditation and Academic Standards (www .icaas.us). It cannot be located. Accreditor of Adams University, Kendall University, MacArther University, Ratchford University, and Ross College, among others.

International Council of Assessment Universities. Accreditor claimed by Wittfield University and Darton University. It cannot be located.

International Council of Colleges and Universities. Was in Lebanon, Tennessee. It cannot be located.

International Council of Higher Education (www.iche-online.org). Switzerland. Accreditor claimed by Trident University of Technology.

International Council on Education (www.webnow.com/educouncil). Elmhurst, New York. Many links don't work, and bits are cut and pasted from other sites, but it asks $5,500 for an application. Inter-American University claims accreditation from ICE.

International Distance Education and Training Council (www.idetc .org). No connection with the recognized Distance Education and

Training Council. It lists all the DETC schools as ones it accredits and one more, American Central University.

International Distance Learning Accreditation Council. Accredits many legitimate schools, also Americus University (which shares a phone with the council), South Pacific University, International University for Professional Studies, and others.

International University Accreditation Foundation. Apparently established by Chief Alexander Swift Eagle Justice of the Cherokee Western Federation. It has accredited Swift Eagle's International Theological University, and others.

Internet University Accreditation Association (www.internetaccreditation .biz). Although it claims to accredit fifty-six Internet universities world wide, only three are listed—Alcott University, University of the Islands, and Western Ohio University, the last being the only one we can find.

Korean Royal Association of Professors. Accredits the nonexistent Aardvark University, apparently created by pranksters to get a school listed first in some directory.

Life Experience Accreditation Association. Accreditor claimed by Earlscroft University, now it cannot be located.

Louisiana Capital Education Foundation. Accreditor claimed by Louisiana Capital College, now it cannot be located.

Mid States Accrediting Agency. Listed as a "suspect accreditor" by the new Brunswick Department of Education, Canada.

Middle States Accrediting Board. Accreditor claimed by Thomas University, now it cannot be located.

Midwestern States Accreditation Agency. Claimed accreditor for Tony Geruntino's schools in the 1980s: American Western, National College of Arts and Sciences, and so forth.

National Academy of Higher Education (http://www.nahighered.org/ accreditation.htm). Accredits many schools on the Oregon list.

National Accreditation Association. Riverdale, Maryland. Associated with the fake American International University, it offered accreditation to many schools with no visits required.

National Association for Prior Learning Assessment Colleges (www .naplac.org). Run by, and accredits only, Trinity Southern University.

National Association for Private Post Secondary Education. Washington, DC. Listed as a "suspect accreditor" by the New Brunswick (Canada) Department of Education.

National Association for Schools and Colleges. See National Association of Private Nontraditional Schools and Colleges.

National Association of Alternative Schools and Colleges. Accreditor claimed by Western States University, now it cannot be located.

National Association of Open Campus Colleges. Springfield, Missouri. Claimed as accreditor by the fake Southwestern University.

National Association of Private Nontraditional Schools and Colleges. Established in Grand Junction, Colorado, in the 1970s by people associated with Western Colorado University. It has seemed to make sincere efforts but has been repeatedly rejected by the US Department of Education. At its peak it had several dozen accreditees, now only four.

National Association of Private Theological Institutions (www.weaccredit.org). New Albany, Indiana. While it once accredited a University of Indiana that was not the real U of I, it now accredits five Bible schools and a Christian martial arts university.

National Board of Education. For several years, the claim was made that this was an official Liberian organization, and its accreditation was offered for $50,000. The address was a mailbox rental service in Washington. After many unfavorable newspaper articles showing the connection with individuals associated with various schools on the Oregon list, NBOE began to be phased out on various Web sites.

National Board of Naturopathic Examiners. Shares its address with Matt's Health Foods, whose owner is a faculty member of a school it accredits and is chair of the accrediting agency.

National Council for the Accreditation of Private Universities and Schools of Law. Accreditor claimed by the fake Monticello University.

National Council of Schools and Colleges. Accreditor claimed by International University in Louisiana and California, now it cannot be located.

National Diet and Nutrition Association. Accreditor claimed by Universitas Sancti Martin, now it cannot be located.

National Distance Learning Accreditation Council (www.n-d-l-a-c.com). Accreditor claimed only by Suffield College and University and Redding University.

National Educational Accrediting Association. Mentioned in some school literature, now it cannot be located.

National Federal Accreditation Assembly. Accreditor claimed by Laureate University and others.

National Private Schools Association Group (www.npsag.com). We chose not to pay the $750 or more it charges to see its database of 130,000 schools, so we are not sure what it does, but it seems to involve accreditation.

New Millennium Accrediting Partnership For Educators Worldwide (www.napfew.com). Founded by "the enlightened staff" of the University of Berkeley, which is the only school it accredits.

Nontraditional Course Accreditation Board. Former name of Congress for the Accreditation of Educational and Training Organisation. Accreditor claimed by Calamus University and Dublin Metropolitan University.

North American Association of Unaccredited Colleges and Universities (www.geocities.com/kl3434us). The irreverent site candidly admits that the schools it accredits are as fake as the accreditor and include Central University of Natural Therapy, Prairie Institute of Social Science, and Switzer United College of Kansas.

North American College and University Accreditation Agency (www .81x.com/nacuaa/nacuaa). Claims to currently serve fifty-five institutions throughout the region but names none. Possible connection with Western Ohio University.

North American Regional Accrediting Commission. Accreditor claimed by International University (Los Angeles, California), now it cannot be located.

Northwest Regional Accrediting Agency. Listed as a "suspect accreditor" by the New Brunswick (Canada) Department of Education.

Oxford Educational Network (www.oxfordeducationalnetwork.com). Claims to operate under a Royal Charter granted by King Charles I of England in the year 1640. Run from a post office box in Fort Worth, Texas. Affiliated with the Most Rev. Patriarch Dr. Chief Alexander Swift Eagle Justice.

Pacific Association of Schools and Colleges. Serious effort started in 1993 by a former California state education official but did not last.

Parliamento Mondiale per la Sicurezza e la Pace. Accreditor claimed by Senior University, Wyoming. It awards titles of nobility from an address in Palermo, Italy.

Professional Board of Education (www.pboe.org). West Lebanon, New Hampshire. Accreditor claimed by Concordia College and University and others.

Society of Academic Recognition. Accreditor claimed by the spurious University of Corpus Christi, now it cannot be located.

Southeast Accrediting Association of Christian Schools, Colleges and Seminaries. Milton, Florida. Accreditor claimed by Evangelical Theological Seminary and others.

Southern Accrediting Association of Bible Colleges and Seminaries. Accreditor claimed by Logos Christian College and Covenant Life Christian College, now it cannot be located.

Southern Association of Accredited Colleges and Universities. Listed as a "suspect accreditor" by the New Brunswick (Canada) Department of Education.

Southern Cross International Association of Colleges and Schools. Accreditor claimed by Cambridge Graduate School, Kelvin College, and others, now it cannot be located.

Southwestern Association of Christian Colleges. Accreditor claimed by St. Thomas Christian College, now it cannot be located.

Transworld Accrediting Commission (www.iaaou.org). Siloam Springs, Alaska. Accreditor claimed by Cumberland University.

United Colligate [*sic*] College Association. Accreditor claimed by Earlscroft University, now it cannot be located.

United Congress of Colleges. Accreditor claimed by Earlscroft University, Canterbury University, others, now it cannot be located.

United National Universities. An "accreditational organization" associated with the opoerator of an unaccredited school, apparently defunct.

United Nations Convivium for International Education (www.unitednationseducation.org). Associated with the operator of an unaccredited school, it had listed hundreds of traditional schools along with some others. The URL at is inoperative.

United States Commission of Colleges (www.uscoc.org). Claims to be an official military accreditor and accredits only Armed Forces University.

United States Distance Education and Training Council (www.usdetc.org). After a brief hiatus in 2003 when the real DETC complained, the US-DETC's Web site is back and as misleading as ever, listing a great many real schools and a few others less real.

Universal Accrediting Association. Accreditor claimed by the Universal Life Church and University.

Universal Accrediting Commission for Schools, Colleges and Universities. Athens, Greece. Accreditor claimed by Romano Byzantine College, now it cannot be located.

Universal Council for Online Education Accreditation (www.ucoea .org). Accreditor claimed by Belford University and Rochville University.

Uniworld Association Incorporated (www.uniworld.org). Accreditor claimed by University of Asia. Web site registered to the president of the University of Asia.

Virtual University Accrediting Association (http://www.accrediting .com/vuaa.htm). Accreditor claimed by International University of Fundamental Studies, University of Northwest, and others. See also International University Accrediting Association.

West European Accrediting Society. Liederbach, Germany. Established by the later-imprisoned owners of a group of degree mills including Loyola, Lafayette, and Cromwell universities.

Western Accrediting Agency. Listed as a "suspect accreditor" by the New Brunswick (Canada) Department of Education.

Western Association of Private Alternative Schools. Claimed as accreditor by Western States University, now it cannot be located.

Western Association of Schools and Colleges. This is the name of the legitimate regional accreditor. A fake one was established by the later-imprisoned operators of many degree mills (Loyola, Roosevelt, Cromwell, etc.).

Western Council on Non-Traditional Private Post Secondary Education. Established by the founder of Southland University. See also Arizona Commission of Non-Traditional Private Postsecondary Education.

World Association of Universities and Colleges (www.web-hed.com/ wauc). Established in 1992 by Dr. Maxine Asher, founder of American World University, and run from a secretarial service address in Nevada. Accredits many schools in the United States and elsewhere. When James Kirk was imprisoned for LaSalle University, he started Edison University from his Texas prison cell, and it quickly got WAUC accreditation. When the Louisiana attorney general closed down Cambridge State University as a degree mill, it moved to a mailbox service in Hawaii and has WAUC accreditation. In 1999, William Howard Taft University, formerly a WAUC accreditee (and now with recognized accreditation) brought suit against WAUC. Highlights of the action from a Taft press release: WAUC was "not able to provide any documented evidence that it had ever conducted a site visit at any member institution," and although it had "consistently promoted itself as a nonprofit corporation," it acknowledged in writing that "WAUC is a for-profit corporation."

World Council of Excellence in Higher Education. Claimed as accreditor by Intercultural Open University, now it cannot be located.

World Council of Global Education. See World Council of Postsecondary and Religious Education.

World Council of Postsecondary and Religious Education (http:// www .wnho.net/wcpre.htm). Formerly World Council of Global Education. Part of the World Natural Health Organization. Accreditor once claimed by Bernadean University. Accredits a small number of religious schools.

World Online Education Accrediting Commission (www.woeac.org). Accreditor claimed by Ashwood University.

World Organization of Institutes, Colleges and Universities (http:// www.omegauniversity.com/accreditation1.html). Accreditor claimed by Omega University.

World-Wide Accreditation Commission of Christian Educational Institutions (http://fgcfi.tripod.com/wwac.htm). Richmond, VA. It says that "in accordance with the Inspired teaching of the Bible, [we have] chosen not to seek endorsement with either the EAES or CHEA." Affiliated with the Spirit of Truth Institute, which sells honorary doctorate degrees.

Worldwide Accrediting Commission. Cannes, France. Set up by later-imprisoned owners of a group of degree mills (Loyola/Paris, DePaul, etc.) to accredit their own schools.

Appendix F

Time Bombs

We're devoting a fair amount of space to "time bombs"— instances of people with fake degrees—simply because we have learned, in our many public talks and interviews, that this is a really good way to get people's attention and to drive home the significance of the problem in ways that charts, tables, and cumulative statistics cannot do as well. It is one thing to read that there are many thousands of teachers and doctors with fake degrees; it is quite another to learn that *your* child's history teacher or *your* family doctor has a fake degree.

As you look at these examples from the hundreds of thousands, possibly millions, of cases out there, remember that these are more than impersonal statistics—every single one is a real person whose behaviors have had (or will have) significant impact on himself or herself, as well as employers, schools, churches, government agencies, and quite possibly the general public.

There are two parts to this list. The first section consists of time bombs that have *already* exploded, with nearly all the cases coming from newspaper and television news stories and from various publicly available court documents.

The second section consists of *unexploded* time bombs: those that are still ticking away, buried in peoples' resumes and in the files of their employers. These come mostly from our searches of some of the large online resume-posting Web sites, as well as from various press releases and newspaper articles where bad and fake schools are mentioned without awareness of what they are.

ALREADY-EXPLODED TIME BOMBS

Los Angeles teacher with fake doctorate. During the 2004 trial (child molestation) of a teacher hired by the Los Angeles Unified School District, it came out that he had been hired on the basis of a fake master's and doctorate and was earning higher pay because of these degrees.

Florida sheriff and fraud specialist, himself with a fake degree. It was page-one news when a veteran sheriff was found to have a degree from a fake that sells them by return mail. He insisted, when exposed, that he had spent two arduous years working on that degree.

"Doctor" with fake medical degrees faces fourteen years in prison. Gregory Caplinger had practiced for many years in North Carolina and elsewhere, with seven fake degrees, including an MD he bought for $100. Finally indicted and convicted, he escaped but was recaptured and imprisoned.

Community college professor commits suicide when his two worthless degrees are exposed. The Luzerne College faculty member also lied about being a Navy SEAL.

University of Iowa senior staff member with five fake degrees, including two doctorates. She had used the degrees professionally for ten years and received a major postdoctoral grant from the National Institutes of Health. She was sentenced to thirteen years in prison.

Fire chief with a fake degree in fire science. The fire chief of Alexandria, Kentucky, was fired when the fake degree he had bought twenty years earlier was discovered.

Congressional candidate with a fake "British" degree. Democratic candidate David LaPere in California's twenty-first district lost the election after his fake degree from Wexford University was publicized.

Governor candidate said "Regis University" (real), but the degrees were from "St. Regis University" (not real). Alicia "Chucky" Hansen, candidate for governor of the US Virgin Islands, reported the name of her alma mater incorrectly.

University president loses job over fake degree. The President of Quincy University in Illinois claimed his master's was from the traditional LaSalle University in Philadelphia, but when it came out that it was really from the fake LaSalle in Louisiana, he was invited to resign.

Five small-college coaches all in trouble for fake degrees around the same time.

The Fayetteville State men's basketball coach, the Campbell University women's soccer coach, the track and basketball coaches at Methodist College, and an assistant cross-country coach at St. Andrews all got in trouble over regrettable degrees.

College president resigns when fake degree claim is revealed. The president of Toccoa Falls College, a Georgia religious school, resigned after the student newspaper revealed he did not have the master's listed on his resume.

Michigan legislator with a fake degree. State representative Gloria Schermesser claims to have a bachelor's degree from the fake Columbia State University.

Speaker of the House "pulls a Toronto." The speaker of Nigeria's federal House of Representatives was disgraced and forced from office when it turned out that the degree he claimed from the University of Toronto was never earned. Now degree fraud in Nigeria, quite common, is known as "pulling a Toronto."

Miami superintendent resigns before starting work when fake degrees revealed. The new deputy school superintendent for facilities and construction had three degrees from the dreadful St. Regis. As a newspaper put it, "At least he spared the district the embarrassing decision of whether to lower standards for a grown-up with questionable ethics while raising them for struggling kids."

Pediatrician at university hospital with fake medical degree. A respected member of the medical staff at the Cowell Hospital on the University of California at Berkeley campus was revealed to have stolen his medical diploma from his similarly named cousin.

Allegheny College football coach resigns when degree fraud revealed. He listed a bachelor's degree that he never earned.

Million-dollar Australian executive. Glen Oakley had a six-figure government job and a professorship at the University of Newcastle's Graduate School of Business when his three fake degree claims were revealed. Now he faces ten years in prison.

City employee in Ohio with a fake and backdated degree. The inspector in Lorain explained his phony degree as a "youthful mistake" made twenty-four years earlier, but the mill in question, Shelbourne, was only two years old; however, it does offer to backdate diplomas.

College professor exposed on ABC. Two years after being *humiliated* on national TV for obtaining a college teaching job with a phony Columbia State degree, the professor in Michigan *still* lists "PhD" after his name at his new job.

Senior building inspector with two fake degrees. In 2003, a senior San Francisco city official lost a $126,000-a-year job when his resume fakery was discovered.

North Dakota state senator has a PhD illegal in his state. North Dakota law makes use of unrecognized degrees a criminal offense, presumably including the PhD claimed by state senator Tim Flakoll, a member of the state higher education committee, from a school whose "campus" was a mailbox service in Louisiana, which claimed to operate from England.

Two generals with fake degrees arrested. Two South African brigadier generals were arrested when their fake university credentials were discovered. The directorate of special investigations said these arrests were "just the tip of the iceberg," and further investigations were underway.

Bausch and Lomb CEO forfeits $1.1 million over false degree claim. Chairman and CEO Ronald Zarella forfeited a bonus of $1.1 million for falsely claiming to have completed an NYU master's degree. The fake degree claim was revealed by TheStreet.com columnist Herb Greenberg.

California's poet laureate loses job over nonexistent degree. Quincy Troupe, also a popular professor at the University of California, San Diego, decided to retire when state employees discovered he did not have the university degree he had long claimed.

Top college executive with a fake doctorate. The managing director of Sydney International College in Australia was shown on the college Web site to have his degree from the fake Harrington University. When this was exposed in a national newspaper, the Web site was immediately changed.

Michigan executive fired over Hamilton degree. The man's job description required a degree. When he brought legal action after the firing, the ruling stated in part, "The employer's determination that (employee) did not obtain a 'college degree' and thus failed to fulfill a term of his hiring agreement is based on entirely convincing evidence. . . . The so-called degree . . . he had allegedly earned on or about January 5, 2000, is, simply stated, a hoax. . . . The conclusion that follows from this record is that Hamilton fabricated a transcript to comport with the 'Degree of Bachelor of Science' it awarded to (the employee) and (the employee) was a willing partner. (The employee's) course of conduct in pursuing his so-called degree from Hamilton demonstrates an intent to deceive the Employer into accepting a degree he knew to be without merit or validity."

Medical doctor with fake degree convicted of manslaughter. In North

Carolina, Laurence Perry, who bought his MD from the fake British Virgin Islands School of Medicine, was convicted after a child he took off insulin, in favor of an untested product, died.

Texas police chief in trouble over fake bachelor's. Dickinson, Texas, chief Ron Morales was put on administrative leave after his fake degree was discovered. He had been earning an additional $5,600 a year because of the degree.

Bible school president ousted over fake credentials. Michael McCorvey, president and founder of Upstate Bible College and Theological Seminary, lost his job when it was determined that he misrepresented his credentials.

Expert witness in many burn cases had only fake degrees. Gary S. Stocco, who often testified against burn victims who were suing those they believed were responsible for their burns, pled guilty to perjury and obtaining money by false pretenses after an investigation into his credentials of this "burns analysis expert" found backdated degrees from the fake University of San Moritz.

Indian tribe administrator with two fake degrees. When the local newspaper looked into this, the paper decided to ignore it, since it doesn't "out" private citizens with fake credentials, and in any event, it said privately, "the tribe loves him and doesn't care what degrees he has or doesn't."

Testimony of top forensic pathologist disallowed because of his degree. In Trinidad, the testimony was disallowed in a court case when it became known that the "doctor" in question earned his doctorate at an unaccredited school ostensibly operating in Hawaii but really run from California.

University provost resigns after fake PhD claim revealed. The former provost of Cheyney University, Pennsylvania, was forced to resign when her claim of an Oxford doctorate was found to be false.

"Misstated" degree big news in Canada. An eight-column top-of-page headline in the *Financial Post* was about a class action lawsuit filed by investors in one of the companies of Hong Kong billionaire Richard Li, asserting, in part, that his claimed Stanford University degree in computer engineering reassured them about investing in Rediff.com. Li subsequently admitted that he had attended Stanford but had not earned a degree.

Psychiatric social worker and state employee with fake PhD. The employee at the Warren Correctional Institution lists his PhD in social work from the fake Columbia State University.

Department of Justice task force member with a fake MBA. A county sheriff who serves as a national board member of the Internet Crimes Against Children Task Force of the US Department of Justice has an MBA from a totally fake university.

Court administrator loses job because of fake degree. The administrator for the largest court in Arizona was fired after ABC revealed that he had purchased his degree from a Louisiana degree mill.

"The Love Doctor" loses her job when it turns out she's not a doctor. The popular radio and television personality who was fond of reminding callers that she was a doctor and had the answers, in fact, was exposed on *Good Morning America* as having a fake PhD.

Nuclear industry executive with two fake degrees. The consulting firm's Web site says the firm "provides superior service to clients in the nuclear power industry enabling them to become more competitive." One principal consultant bought his degrees from a degree mill whose campus is a South Dakota mailbox.

Prominent forensic counselor with three fake degrees. A principal speaker at the National Association of Forensic Counselors national convention claimed three degrees from Hamilton University and was working on a second doctorate from another unrecognized Wyoming school.

Pittsburgh school psychologist with a fake PhD accused of child molestation. Only in the publicity leading up to his molestation trial was it discovered, in 2003, that the man in question had been hired on the basis of a doctorate he bought for $3,000 from Columbia State University.

Administrator director for a US Congressman. She has an unrecognized bachelor's degree and an MBA from Hamilton University in Wyoming.

Veritas CFO forced to resign after degree claim exposed. The software executive had fabricated some credentials, including a claimed Stanford MBA.

Alabama senate candidate with a fake doctorate. The state senate candidate insisted he did not know. He told a reporter for the *Birmingham News*, "I spent a year and a half of my life on this thing. Frankly, I'm a little ticked off about it."

Lawrence Livermore Lab director resigns over a degree matter. The lab's associate director did nothing to correct being called "doctor" in official press releases.

Fake cancer doctor guilty of fraud and grand theft. He treated thousands of cancer patients before being charged and convicted.

Medical director did not have a medical degree. The head of a New Zealand regional government office did not have the Polish medical degree she claimed, and she turned out to be a man as well.

Head of public television network with fake credentials. The Canadian chosen to head New Zealand's Maori television network claimed his MBA from Denver State University, an American fake. He was fired, indicted, convicted, and imprisoned within two months.

Television computer expert with a fake doctorate. Robert X. Cringely, featured in a PBS special, claimed a PhD from Stanford and to have been a professor there. The *San Francisco Chronicle* revealed neither was true.

Athletic commissioner loses Dartmouth job over degree claim. The former commissioner of the Mid-Eastern Athletic Conference did not become athletic director at Dartmouth when his false master's degree claim became known.

United Way executive resigns amid fake degree charges. The Beaver County, Pennsylvania, executive had claimed a degree from the fake Harrington University.

Texas transit executive lists two degrees she didn't have. The $210,000-a-year president of the Houston area transit authority was revealed by the Houston *Chronicle* not to have two claimed associates' degrees.

Alabama councilman with a fake degree. The twice-elected Birmingham councilman turned out not to have the real degree he claimed, but did have one from an Arizona degree mill.

President of a radio network with a fake bachelor's degree. His "executive biography" describes his presidency of two radio groups in the west and his bachelor's degree from the spurious Northwestern International University.

Top law school administrator fired for using counterfeit law diploma. The man at the National Autonomous University of Mexico claimed his political enemies were out to get him, after he presented a counterfeit diploma. Mexico had recently implemented security measures to identify fake diplomas.

Finalist for state department head withdraws when fake degree revealed. The *Oregonian* newspaper reported that the US Coast Guard captain had been one of three finalists to head the state's Department of Environment Quality, but he withdrew when his degree from Missouri degree mill Northwestern College was revealed.

Vanderbilt basketball coach fired over resume discrepancy. The women's team coach was fired twenty-four hours after being hired, when it turned out that one of the two masters' degrees on her resume could not be confirmed.

Christa McAuliffe Academy CEO has two dubious degrees. The founder,

CEO, and principal of the state-approved K–12 institution in the state of Washington has his MEd and PhD in educational leadership from a widely publicized institution ostensibly in Liberia.

Prize-winning speaker with a fake PhD. The winner of the "Outstanding MADD Speaker of the Conference Award" lists a PhD from the fake Harrington University along with a real one from DePaul. She speaks on self-esteem.

Geffen lies about UCLA degree, then gives the school $400 million. Entertainment executive David Geffen says he lied about having a degree from UCLA in order to get a job working in the mailroom at William Morris. Years later, he gave a $400 million donation to UCLA.

Massachusetts mayor's fake degree claim. The mayor of Salem, Massachusetts, who ran for reelection, has admitted that he has lied for years about having a degree from the University of Massachusetts. As a sidelight, this man stated that the city planner he appointed has a Harvard degree, which seems not to be the case.

School board member with two fake degrees. A member of the board in Salina, Kansas, was discovered to have his only two degrees from a degree mill that was closed in South Dakota but that resurfaced in the Caribbean.

Six hundred thousand time bombs in China. *The Chronicle of Higher Education* reported that "according to government statistics, six hundred thousand fake diplomas are circulating in China, although many government officials suspect that the actual number is much higher." Apparently most of them are counterfeit diplomas of real schools. "It seems insiders at real universities are selling diplomas for hefty prices."[1]

Canadian therapist with a fake PhD. It was page-one news in St. Catharines, Ontario, when a school therapist with a doctorate from the fake LaSalle University in Louisiana was arrested for fraud.

Hollywood studio head falsely claims Yale degrees. When the head of Columbia was accused by actor Cliff Robertson of forging his signature to misappropriate funds, reporters looked closely at the man and discovered that his degree claims were false.

Pro football team owner's fake degree claims. The former owner of the Indianapolis Colts football team publicly claimed certain degrees and a distinguished military record. It turned out that he had neither.

Psychologist at large state hospital fired when fake doctorate revealed. The man at Alabama's Bryce Hospital bought his PhD diploma from a counterfeiter and was discovered after the FBI closed it down.

Executive director of Moral Majority with a fake degree. The Congressman Pepper hearings discovered this man, who was also in charge of ten Department of Education regional offices. He stated in the subcommittee report that his degree was "not as high a quality as I would have liked."

Engineer at Kennedy Space Center with fake electrical engineering degree. The FBI discovered him in the customer list of an Arizona degree mill.

Nuclear engineer with three fake degrees. The FBI discovered an engineer at Westinghouse Nuclear International with a fake PhD and two other fake degrees in mechanical engineering.

Joint chiefs of staff man with a fake doctorate. The officer, assigned to the Pentagon, had bought a fake PhD in history.

Fake engineering degree at Three Mile Island. The FBI discovered, after closing a degree mill, a customer who worked at the nuclear power plant, using his fake mechanical engineering degree.

Fake PhD in electrical aerospace engineering at Johnson Space Center. The man with the fake doctorate was discovered in an FBI search of his "alma mater."

Army chief medical officer with a fake degree. He went undetected until, as a staff anesthesiologist at an Army hospital, his error resulted in a patient's permanent brain damage. He was sentenced to twelve years for aggravated assault.

Pharmacist with fake medical degree sent to prison. The man in Los Angeles found a real MD with the same name and got copies of his diploma. He was sentenced to three years for mistreating a man with acute diabetes.

Bogus psychiatrist charged in death of client. He stole his roommate's credentials and was employed at a medical center. He was arrested after he had prescribed a potentially lethal medication to a woman with a history of suicide attempts who did, in fact, kill herself.

Patient of heart surgeon with fake medical degree dies. The California man stopped a patient's medication. When she died, it was discovered she had left him half a million dollars, which the family contested.

Man with bogus dental degree employed at New York clinic. He specialized in installing braces, until he was caught.

Florida psychiatrist had two counterfeit doctorates. His fake Columbia and Stanford degrees got him staff privileges at two hospitals.

Accountant in New York got work as an emergency room physician. He was caught when a nurse noticed he referred to "sewing people up" instead of "suturing."

Twelve people die on fake nurse's watch. The Illinois woman got employed as a night supervisor at a Florida nursing home using a fake degree. Following twelve deaths in two weeks, she was fired but not arrested. .

Seagate hires engineer with fake Oxford degree. He was fired from the $95,000-a-year job when discovered twelve days after his hiring.

UNEXPLODED TIME BOMBS

This is a very small sample of people currently using degrees from degree mills. These people have been discovered either by doing Internet searches for the names of the schools or by inspecting the resumes they have posted on online job hunting services.

We have chosen not to identify these people by name or company/organization affiliation because of the small possibility that the publicly available information is in error. We hope employers, enforcers, and the media will become increasingly careful in preventing, or dealing with, situations like these.

Note that all the schools involved in the following cases are beyond-any-doubt degree mills, not "borderline" or "gray area" schools.

Expert witness with three fake engineering degrees. The purchaser of a $300,000 motor home sued the manufacturer and dealer when many problems arose. The expert witness for the manufacturer testified that the vehicle was perfect, and the problems were all caused by the incompetent buyer. But that "expert" has three degrees in mechanical engineering, all from the totally fake University of San Moritz.

Senior missile electronic supervisor with fake BA. The Army man worked with the Avenger missile system.

Safety director at a large nuclear power site. He is responsible for radiological protection at a major nuclear site and has a fake bachelor's.

Man in charge of Army security clearances has fake law degree. The Airborne Ranger at a military installation has top security clearance and a fake degree from the University of San Moritz.

Faculty member at a regionally accredited university with three fake degrees. The official Franklin University site shows her with two degrees from the fake American National University and a doctorate from the equally fake Berkley University.

TQM officer for naval security with a fake BA. The total quality management officer provides guidance to thousands of military personnel worldwide.

Surgery transplant administrator with a fake PhD. She works at an Ivy League university's medical school.

Nuclear reactor engineer with three fake degrees. The manager for an industrial company has a fake BA, MA, and PhD.

Navy head of major department with a fake BA. He manages $4 billion worth of equipment.

Dot-com executive with a fake doctorate. The president and chief technology officer of sizeable "dot-com" company lists an MBA and PhD from Vernell, the fake university invented by the people at YourDegreeNow.com.

Engineer responsible for airline safety has a fake engineering degree. The Lockheed NASA employee's fake degree is in manufacturing engineering.

Sheriff with fake degree. He currently is head of operations for a good-sized sheriff's office.

Prominent stage and corporate hypnotist with a fake doctorate. His promotional literature says, "Having earned a PhD in psychology from Columbia State University, [he] is a recognized expert in the field of hypnosis . . . presenting quantum stress management workshops at corporate events and universities around the country."

Manager of navy personnel with fake MA. He heads personnel for a large navy base.

Army troop school manager with fake bachelor's He manages the school at a large army facility.

Prominent author with a fake honorary degree. The author of an Oxford University Press book lists his fake American honorary doctorate.

Army surgical nurse with a fake bachelor's. She is with a surgical and medical intensive care unit.

Connecticut psychotherapist with a fake PhD. The man in question is still in business, specializing in anxiety, depression, and panic. His PhD was bought from the mill that specializes in twenty-seven-day (or less) doctorates.

Department of Justice task force member with fake MBA. The sheriff in charge of his county's special investigations is a national board member of the Internet Crimes Against Children Task Force.

Staff manager for federal agency with a fake degree. He managed staff for a high-profile agency and had a fake BA.

Officer for Judge Advocate with fake BA. He is head of information technology for an Office of the Staff Judge Advocate.

Army pilot with a fake bachelor's. She has flown many dignitaries and manages electronic warfare equipment.

Health-care conglomerate promotes man with two fake degrees. Its press release said the former president of a medical center will work with the chief executive officers in his new position. He has two fake degrees from Columbia State University.

Army counterdrug specialist with two fake degrees. The senior supply logistics officer has a bogus bachelor's and master's.

State information systems executive with fake bachelor's. The director of information systems in the office of the secretary of state has a bogus degree.

Disaster recovery executive for major oil company with fake master's and doctorate. The executive has a diploma-mill MA and PhD.

Nuclear deactivation engineer with a fake degree. The engineer responsible for nuclear deactivation activities at a large nuclear facility has a fake BA.

University clinical director with fake PhD in microbiology. The head of a major university's campus clinic has a diploma-mill MS and PhD in microbiology and genetics.

Police department grievances officer with fake degree. The person dealing with hardships and grievances in a large city police department has a spurious master's.

Bank security head with a fake degree. A director of security for a good-sized Florida bank has his only degree from a California mill.

Army compliance officer with a phony bachelor's. The corps of engineer officer teaches code compliance to inspection teams.

Michigan city councilman with fake bachelor's. The councilman also serves as a corrections officer at a large prison.

New Hampshire police detective with degree-mill bachelor's. The officer has a fake BA.

Polygraph expert with a fake PhD. The lie detector expert has his doctorate from LaSalle University acquired shortly before the FBI raid and the guilty pleas of its founders.

Jury screening company president with a fake doctorate. The president of a company that screens potential jurors himself has a fake PhD in psychology.

University professor with a fake British degree. The doctorate from the fake Sussex College is rationalized on the man's Web site as having been awarded prior to the Education Reform Act of 1988—in other words, before it was *officially* fraudulent.

University professor with a fake doctorate. A university Web site lists a professor of music who "earned" his degree from a fake university.

Golf pro with a fake MBA. The official biography of a member of the PGA tour lists an MBA from the fake Columbia State University.

Army operations manager with fake bachelor's. The degree of the operations manager at a large base comes from a California degree mill.

Hospital corpsman with fake bachelor's. A Navy senior chief hospital corpsman has a fake BA degree.

Texas police officer with two fake degrees. A senior police officer has a bogus BA and MA.

University trauma center head with fake master's. The "Ivy Leaguer" also lectures in the school of medicine.

Police executive with a fake PhD. The supervisor of litigation and fraud units for a big city police department lists a PhD from a degree mill.

Head of national crime organization with three fake degrees in criminal justice. The chairman a Washington-based organization has a degree-mill BA, MA, and PhD in criminal justice.

City manager with two fake degrees. The city manager of a fast-growing southern city has a bogus BA and MA.

Fire chief with fake bachelor's. The chief of a southern California city has a phony BA degree.

County air-quality engineer with fake degrees. An engineer for this county has a fake BA and MA in public administration.

Training executive for large company with two fake degrees. The head of training and education for a Fortune 500 company, responsible for more than fifty thousand employees, has a fake BA and MA.

Securities company head with two fake doctorates. The president of an investment and securities firm has two fake PhDs, including one in business ethics.

Police community affairs officer with a bogus doctorate. The officer with a big city police department claims a PhD from a California mill.

Medical instrument executive with fake health-care and MBA degrees. The CEO of a sizeable medical instrument company lists those two fake degrees.

Network health reporter with fake PhD. A health-care executive who does frequent network reports has a fake doctorate.

Quality assurance staff member with fake immunology degrees. The former beverage industry employee lists fake BS and MS degrees.

Police fraud specialist with a fake MA. The police detective specializing in sexual assault and insurance fraud has a degree-mill master's.

Property manager in charge of $6 billion in government assets with fake master's. The administrator at the major facility has a bogus MA.

Railroad engineer with two fake engineering degrees. The engineer reports having responsibility for all of his company's engineering work in a major industrial center.

State prison officer with a fake BA. The lieutenant in North Carolina's Division of Prisons has a diploma-mill bachelor's.

City's human resources executive with a fake HR degree. The director of human resources for an eastern city has a bogus master's in human resource management.

Senior drug company executive with a fake doctorate. A senior manager and former Army officer has a BA and a PhD from a degree mill.

Medical school professor with a fake doctorate in public health. The professor has a real MD and has used a fake PhD in public health from Columbia State University.

Nuclear industry consultant with two fake degrees. A senior consultant to the nuclear power industry has a fake BS and MS in this field.

College administrator with a fake master's. An Midwest community college administrator lists a fake MS from a California degree mill.

NOTE

1. "Diploma Forgery Goes Electronic in China," *Chronicle of Higher Education*, September 21, 2001.

Appendix G

The Counterfeiters

Counterfeiting services are very much a product of the Internet age and the significant advances in technology. In the ten years of the FBI's DipScam, there was only one serious counterfeiter. In the last couple of years, there have been more than a hundred. Some offer simple designs created with a page layout program, but more than a few sell quite realistic replicas of the real diplomas, complete with gold seals and signatures.

WHERE DO THEY GET THESE ORIGINALS?

It used to be a challenge to get enough original diplomas to go into the counterfeiting business. Once again, the Internet has simplified the task. These seem to be the main methods:

- Requesting replacement diplomas from real schools in the names of the people who originally earned them. Most schools will replace lost or damaged diplomas, and some are not as militant as they should be in checking out requests.
- Internet sites of naive legitimate schools that show their diploma and document-framing services that show examples of their work.
- Estate sales, yard sales, eBay, and so forth. A recent eBay search for "diploma" found 2,366 current auctions, ranging from an old

In 2004, a degree-counterfeiting service was put up for auction on eBay.

Yale diploma with a $4,500 starting price on down to numerous counterfeits in the $15 to $50 range.

- Recreated from snapshots of diplomas on people's walls, taken surreptitiously with digital cameras.
- Trade-ins: in order to get our counterfeit Harvard PhD, you must send us a copy of your legitimate Stanford BA diploma.
- Dishonest people at real schools and print shops.
- Simply stealing them from people's walls.

Once the genie is out of the bottle, it cannot be put back. If even one actual or replica Harvard diploma enters the marketplace, with the easy exchange of JPEGs and PDF files on the Internet, no more are needed.

Nowadays, very few gatekeepers (HR people, registrars, et al.) care about seeing the actual diploma, so all the security measures that have been implemented—holograms, metallic strips, microprinting, watermarks, sophisticated multicolor printing, secret code numbers, and such—seem less important. And whether necessary or not, some of the counterfeiters are matching the new technology anyway, claiming to offer most or all of these measures, including holograms.

AN INTERNATIONAL PROBLEM

The counterfeit diploma problem is clearly an international one. Internet searches have found newspaper articles from dozens of countries on every continent. Here are just a few recent stories, out of many found on the Internet.

Japan

"The trade in counterfeit degrees is uncontrollable, and people are virtually able to 'purchase' good employment. Therefore, many incompetent state officials have a job for life" (*Financial Times*, March 25, 2003).

United Arab Emirates: UAE to clamp down on fake degrees, certificates

Labor officials in the United Arab Emirates are looking at ways to curb a wave of forgeries of degrees and certificates following the introduction of tougher requirements for foreign workers. . . . Some business managers have admitted paying for forged certificates. They argue they cannot afford to hire staff who meet the requirements and fake certificates are their only option if they want their business to stay afloat. . . . They claim the only beneficiaries of the new rule are agents dealing in forged certificates" (*Al-Jazeerah*, December 28, 2003).

China: Forged authentication papers found

The Certificate Authentication Department of the Shenzhen Talent . . . was initially set up to check diplomas submitted by job applicants for authenticity, as counterfeit degrees have become more prevalent. . . . About 5 percent of the more than 44,000 diplomas and certificates sent to the department for examination in the first half of this year were found to be fake" (*China Daily*, August 25, 2003).

England

Sellers of bogus degrees appear to be thriving despite the efforts of the authorities to shut them down (BBC, January 5, 2004).

Israel: 5,500 government employees believed to have fake or forged university degrees

Israeli police are investigating a British university that issued fake degrees to 5,500 Israeli government employees. Teachers, police, army officers, and senior civil servants were among those who paid for fictitious qualifications from the University of Humberside, which has changed its name numerous times and is now known as the University of Lincoln" (*Times of London*, January 22, 2004).

The Counterfeiting Services

Well over a hundred have operated on the Internet in the last few years. They change their names, locations, and services offered even more often than the fake schools. This is a representative sample of ones in business at this time. New ones can always be found by doing an Internet search for "counterfeit diplomas" or "counterfeit degrees." Here are some that were active at the time we went to press.

A Bogus PhD (www.bogusphd.com). It claims that its degrees "look official and real" and "may even closely resemble a genuine degree from some actual college or university," but it has only one design. Diplomas are $39.95 and come with any university name, date, degree, and specialty, including medical, dental, and law.

AAAardvark University (http://www.boxfreeconcepts.com/aaardvark .html). Billing itself as the world's first fake university, it offers a wide variety of bachelors', masters' and doctoral degrees to individuals meeting the criteria of IAFU, the International Association of Fake Universities. AAAardvark issues its degree through BoxFree Concepts.

Back Alley Press (www.backalleypress.com). A part of Shun Luen Co., closed down in Ottawa, Canada, and now in China. Back Alley points out that US counterfeits are of low quality because of strict US laws, but in China the government is lenient about high-quality "novelty items," whether watches, software, or diplomas. Authentic-looking diplomas from more than one thousand universities, with transcripts, for $137 to $700.

BestFakeDiploma.com (www.bestfakediploma.com). This wording is identical to that of SuperiorFakeDegrees.com, and like it, BestFakeDiploma.com links to, and is a front for, DiplomaServices.com.

Black Market Press (www.blackmarket-press.net). Custom-designed transcripts and diplomas. It also offers a do-it-yourself option that provides customers with templates and supplies, including seals and security holograms, that allows them to create their own transcripts and degrees. Information on lock picking, identity theft, and bank fraud is also available.

BoxFreeConcepts.com (http://www.boxfreeconcepts.com/fake/ diplomas .html#). Three fake diploma design templates are sold, with others available for more schools, transcripts, and so forth. See also Magic Mill.

Closed University (www.closeduniversity.com/ecommerce). This claims to offer "safer" diplomas because they are from closed schools, but most of the hundreds of authentic designs offered are from currently operating schools, from Arizona State to Wichita State. Diplomas and authentic-looking transcripts are about $120 each. Affiliated with Replicadiploma.com.

Closedcollege.com (www.closedcollege.com). Diplomas and transcripts from several hundred genuinely closed schools, although some-

"Closed University" is one of the many Internet services selling "replacement diplomas" and authentic-looking transcripts, no questions asked.

times only a closed branch campus of a still-thriving school (such as Antioch University, San Francisco). The convenience address in Washington is also used by the bogus accreditor of Hartford University and others.

Cooldegree (www.cooldegree.com). Although it invites you to "Impress your friends and colleagues with a diploma from a well-known University, in any field of study that you desire," most of its diplomas feature the name of fictitious schools, such Denver State University. They once offered verification services for an additional fee, but no longer.

Counterfeit Library (www.counterfeitlibrary.com). This fascinating site was the discussion forum for the degree-counterfeiting industry. It closed down in July 2003, but three years of archives can still be read on the "Wayback Machine" at www.archive.org.

Degree Now (www.degree-now.com). See Degrees-R-Us.

Degrees-R-Us (www.degrees-r-us.com). This became the poster child for counterfeiting services when the Government Accountability Office (GAO), at the request of Sen. Susan Collins, bought Lexington University degrees in her name. The GAO learned that the business is run from his Las Vegas home by a disbarred attorney, and it also operates as University Services Corp. and College Services Corp. Diplomas were sold from a wide range of schools, including Chapparal Western University, Columbia Western, Cranston, Hampton, Vernell, and Lexington, through half a dozen nearly identical Web sites.

Digital Products (www.fakeid.cwc.net). This British outfit offers fake diplomas, drivers' licenses, computer certifications, and printing equipment.

Diploma Collection (www.diplomacollection.com). You can choose any high school for a diploma, but the higher degrees, including a doctorate in medical science, all come from the fake Cambridge State.

Diploma Masters (www.diplomamasters.com). This offers a long list of schools, customized transcripts, and a "third party" verification service. This claims to be "an official distributor for a third party 'Record Verification' provider," apparently affiliated with counterfeiters Fantasy Diplomas and DiplomasForLess and degree mills Lexington and Ellington universities and Global Church Theological Seminary and University, their accreditor (the Higher Education Services Association), and Verification Services.

Diploma Replacement Services (www.diplomareplacementservice

.com). Fakes sold from virtually any school for $124 to $370. It requires a notarized statement affirming you have earned the degrees you're buying, but it reminds you that notaries don't know if you're telling the truth. It claims that a competitor named DiplomaServices.com has stolen its business plan.

DiplomaMakers.com (www.diplomamakers.com). This claims to be the largest supplier of novelty online degrees in the world, with diplomas in three sizes from any university on earth, from $70 on up, "Guaranteed to fool even your professor!" It was shut down by Canadian authorities in 2001 and moved to Nevada, but there is another counterfeiter, ReplacementDiplomas.com, at the same mailbox service address in Canada.

Diplomaone.com (www.diplomaone.com). It says that its "documents will pass the test when it comes to authenticity" and "will fool the most suspecting individuals." Any school, degree, and date for $99 and $200 more for a verification service.

Diplomas and More (www.diplomasandmore.com). It markets its products extensively on eBay. The diplomas do not purport to be exact replicas of the originals, but Diplomas and More allows you to choose the degree (except medical), the name of the school, and the grades shown on the transcript.

Diplomas for Less (www.diplomasforless.com). Counterfeit diplomas for $100 ($50 more for overnight delivery) from most US high schools and universities, except the University of Phoenix, University of Houston, University of California, Syracuse University, or from any institution in Illinois or Connecticut. Affiliated with various other counterfeiters, fake schools, and verification services.

DiplomaServices.com (www.diplomaservices.com). Medical, dental, law, and all other diplomas from almost any school for $100 and up. It charmingly calls its competitors' products "garbage."

Diplomaville.com (www.diplomaville.com). It seems to specialize in "extremely detailed reproductions" of University of California diplomas, with raised seals, for $250. Stanford, Johns Hopkins, Columbia, and more than one hundred others cost a bit less. High school diplomas, GED certificates, and fake computer certifications are sold as well.

Documents and Such (www.documentsandsuch.com). For $49.95, this Web site allows you to select from four different templates, the name of the school, the type of degree, the major (no restrictions), and the graduation date.

Espionage Unlimited (http://www.espionage-store.com/cert.html).
Diplomas and everything from military credentials to drivers' licenses
for $30 and up, $10 more for Gothic lettering.

Fake Diplomas (www.fake-diplomas.com). Curiously, despite the
name, there is information only on real schools. Perhaps it is hoping to
sell space to the fakes.

Fakedegrees.com (http://fakedegrees.com). For $50 you join for six
months and use the software and templates to create your own
diplomas. Curiously, the site offers Harvard, Oxford, and Cambridge
but not Yale or Princeton. Transcript and letter of reference capabilities
are promised.

FakeDiplomas.com. (www.fakediplomas.com). Probably the same as
fakedegrees.com. If you send in a good picture of a diploma, you get
free membership.

Fantasy Diplomas (www.fantasydiplomas.com). Virtually identical
to Diplomas for Less and Diploma Masters.

Graduate Now (www.graduatenow.com). See Degrees-R-Us.

Home School Diplomas (http://members.tripod.com/~deed). This
amateurish site on a free server piously states it will not make diplomas
for accredited schools. The samples displayed are for a fictitious school
(Southern University of Theology) and a degree mill (Metropolitan
Collegiate). $50 for a diploma, more for a transcript.

I Need a Diploma.com (www.ineedadiploma.com). Diplomas for
most schools in most subjects for around $100. Extra for transcripts,
honors degrees, and "security holograms."

Ideal Studios (www.idealstudios.com). This low-tech company,
which has been around forever, sells paper, ribbon, gold seals, and a
sheet of press-on letters for $29.

Magic Mill (http://www.boxfreeconcepts.com/magicmill/index
.html). Although it offers silly diplomas from such institutions as Flat-
ulence University and Innuendo State, other names, such as Carolina
Coast University and Southern States University, lend themselves to
abuse, and you can order a diploma, including medical and dental,
with any school name you like.

Make Your Own Degree (www.myodegrees.com). Formerly an all-
purpose counterfeiter, now it provides only links to, and serves as a
front for, Fakedegrees.com.

Novelty Diploma Center (www.nd-center.com). All degrees from
almost any school for $400, $200 more for a custom seal. It claims that

it has "the most extensive list of colleges and universities in the world," and "no one will ever doubt of your degree."

Peter Leon Quinn (www.peterleonquinn.com). The self-styled designer of impressive authentic-looking certificates used to display samples, but now they must be requested by e-mail.

Phony Diplomas (www.phonydiploma.com). Document Printing Services, LLC, operating under the name Phony Diplomas, sells both customizable in-house designs and actual replicas selectable from a list of about 150 actual diplomas. No medical or dental degrees, and no sales to the state of Connecticut, even though they are located in Virginia.

Premier Degrees (www.premier-degrees.com). See Degrees-R-Us.

Real Diploma Printers (http://diplomareplication.andmuchmore .com). "100 percent Replicated and Authentic" diplomas from most US, Canadian, and British universities, "guaranteed to fool anyone." Mysteriously priced at $300 for one degree, $500 for two, and $1,200 for three.

ReplacementDiplomas.com (www.replacementdiplomas.com). Medi-

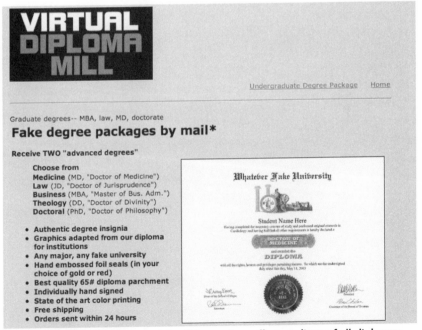

"Virtual Diploma Mill" is a counterfeit service, selling replicas of all diplomas, including medical and dental degrees, from any university.

cal, dental, law, and other degrees, both from closed schools and existing ones. Orders mailed to Laval, Quebec, Canada.

Secretknowledge.com (www.secretknowledge.com). Rather crude-looking fake from this British site for about $5, "guaranteed to work or your money back."

Superior Fake Degrees (www.superiorfakedegree.com). Apparently a front for DiplomaServices.com.

Virtual Diploma (http://www.boxfreeconcepts.com/download/degree.html). The "Virtual Diploma Mill" is another entry to the BoxFreeConcepts site.

Wall Candy Degrees (www.boxfreeconcepts.com/download/degree.html). Simple diplomas from four fake schools for about $10: Canterbury College, St. Charles University, Michigan Institute of Technology, and Southwestern Christian College.

Your Degree Now (www.yourdegreenow.com). See Degrees-R-Us.

Appendix H

How to Find Schools without Recognized Accreditation

We have made the point, again and again, that among the schools without recognized accreditation, there exists a continuum, from those that are undeniably fake to those that have various levels of acceptance.

Further, we have made clear that each person, each organization, each agency, each decision maker, and each gatekeeper must decide where to draw a line on a continuum, saying, in effect, that "those on one side meet my needs, and those on the other side do not."

In the course of constructing or devising one's own list of schools that are either acceptable or not acceptable, it can be very helpful to look at other lists and to get opinions from other people and groups. Here are some approaches to consider.

SCHOOLS THAT *DO* HAVE RECOGNIZED ACCREDITATION OR THE EQUIVALENT IN OTHER COUNTRIES

There are about fifteen thousand degree-granting institutions whose degrees are generally accepted by other schools and by most employers. Although there may be very rare exceptions, it is generally safe to say that if a school is among those fifteen thousand, the degrees are acceptable in almost any situation.

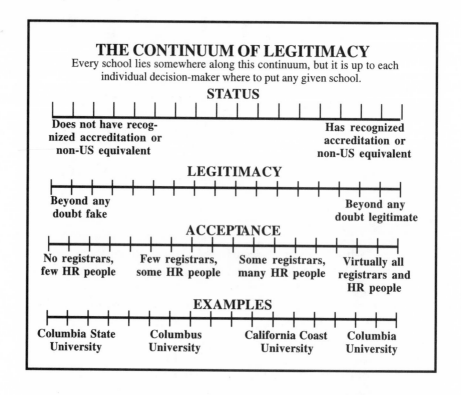

For schools in the United States and its territories

The most reliable printed source is the *Higher Education Directory*, published every November, listing and briefly describing every school with recognized accreditation and those that are candidates for accreditation (see the bibliography).

An online list can be found through the site of the Council on Higher Education Accreditation (www.chea.org).

For schools in the countries in the British Commonwealth

The Commonwealth consists of more than seventy nations, territories, and protectorates, from Australia and Canada, to nineteen African nations, to others in Asia and the Pacific. The widely or universally accepted institutions in the Commonwealth are all members of the Association of Commonwealth Universities. They are described in considerable detail in the *Commonwealth Universities Yearbook,* published every three years by Palgrave Macmillan, in two very large volumes (more than twenty-five hundred pages), one for Great Britain and one for everywhere else.

For the rest of the world

We have mentioned a few problems with the *International Handbook of Universities,* with regard to listing less-than-wonderful schools that are, nonetheless, accredited or recognized by some United Nations members, but this is a very minor problem—fewer than half a dozen schools out of more than fifteen thousand listings. And so the *International Handbook* remains the best single source of information on the degree-granting schools of nearly two hundred nations. There is considerable overlap with the directories listing US and British Commonwealth schools.

It is safe to say that if a school is in the *International Handbook,* the odds are extremely high that it is entirely legitimate. And if a school is not listed, there could well be need for further investigation.

The *International Handbook* is published approximately every three years (the seventeenth edition came out in 2003), so newer or newly qualifying schools might not be listed. The editors of the book, however, are generally willing to say whether a given school will be included in the next edition.

The book is published by Palgrave Macmillan. Details are in the bibliography.

FINDING INFORMATION ON SCHOOLS THAT DO NOT HAVE GENERALLY RECOGNIZED ACCREDITATION

The Oregon List

The state of Oregon maintains a long list of degree-granting institutions, the use of whose degrees are a criminal offense in that state. The official Oregon list can be found online at http://www.osac.state.or.us/oda/diploma_mill.html.

Some of the schools on the list are simply identified as not acceptable in Oregon, while scores of others are identified as diploma mills.

The Michigan List

The state of Michigan has an official list of about three hundred institutions whose degrees are not accepted by that state. That list is available online at http://www.michigan.gov/documents/Non-accreditedSchools _78090_7.pdf

The Australian List

Australia's main national newspaper, *The Australian*, has paid close attention to degree mills and other unrecognized schools, whether or not they have a connection with Australia. On September 2, 2002, it published a long list it called "Universities to watch out for. The A-Z lists: An extensive guide to active, emerging and recent degree mills and officially unaccredited universities, compiled from original research by the *Higher Education Supplement*" (http://www.theaustralian.news.com .au/common/story_page/0,5744,5017662%255E23004,00.html).

Bears' Guide

The book that John Bear and his daughter have written on earning degrees by distance learning lists institutions in three separate chapters: those with recognized accreditation, those that are clearly degree mills, and about two hundred that they choose to put in an "in-between" chapter. The fifteenth edition of *Bears' Guide to Earning Degrees by Distance Learning* can be found in many libraries and bookstores and is described on its publisher's site, www.degree.net.

Degreeinfo.com

Gray-area schools are routinely discussed on the active news forum at www.degreeinfo.com. It is not necessary to register in order to search more than one hundred thousand archived messages. Bear in mind this is a lightly moderated site, and there will be some advocates of various unaccredited schools offering their opinions.

TWO COMPLICATIONS IN THIS PROCESS

There are two major complications at work whenever anyone attempts to locate information on any given school. Any list of such institutions will be somewhat out of date even before the ink dries in a new book for two reasons: the field is changing so fast, and the schools often change their names. A few words on each phenomenon.

This fast-changing field

In 1850, there was one and only one school in America that might have been considered a degree mill. A century later, there were a couple of dozen active ones. By 1985, when Rep. Claude Pepper's subcommittee on fraud looked at the field—a matter described in chapter 1—there were about two hundred schools that he chose to call "fake." The 1999 edition of *Bears' Guide* listed two hundred places that the authors were willing to call "degree mills" and one hundred more "gray area" ones.

By 2003, these numbers had grown to four hundred and two hundred, respectively. Now, new degree-granting entities that do not seem to have recognized accreditation (or the equivalent in their country) are appearing at the astonishing rate of one new school name every two or three days: more than 150 in the last year alone. Some seem clearly fraudulent; some may be sincere new efforts; others may fall in between.

In other words, if you don't find a school you're looking for, it may be that it only came into existence last month—even if it claims to have been founded in 1842 and that Abraham Lincoln was a student.

Changing Names

Some of the "bad guys" change their names nearly as often as they change their socks. As soon as one of their schools gets some bad publicity, or an attorney general starts showing special interest, it's back to the drawing board, literally, for a new identity.

The $50-million-a-year phony University Degree Program described in appendix B began as the University of San Moritz and was renamed the University of Palmers Green, followed at three- or four-month intervals by additional names for the same fraudulent enterprise.

When Internet sleuths discover the internet protocol (IP) number for a degree mill (a number in this format: 66.236.24.230[1]), they sometimes find names of related fake schools along with support entities such as fake accrediting agencies and referral services. Sometimes other school names will be found that have been reserved but are not yet in use: often a dozen or more "universities in waiting" that presumably will go into business as other names are retired. Investigation of nearby IP numbers on the same hosting computer may lead to additional finds.

Finally, when researching a school, it is important to keep in mind, too, that bad schools often have names similar or identical to good schools, and people do get this wrong. An Internet search for the fake "Columbia State University" inevitably turns up some listings for the legitimate "Columbus State University"—not because of a faulty search but because someone wrote the wrong name on some document. The same thing has happened, for instance, with the fake "California Pacifica University" and the legitimate "California Pacific University."

NOTE

1. This example happens to be the IP address for a person who is associated with quite a few schools. This IP address hosts nearly one hundred domains.

Appendix I

Laura Callahan's Story

*One of the biggest degree-mill stories of 2003–2004 was that of Laura
Callahan, a senior director in the Department of Homeland Security's Office of
the Chief Information Officer. In June 2003, the* Government Computer
News *reported that Callahan had three degrees from a Wyoming school identified as a degree mill. Callahan resigned in March 2004. Homeland security said
that "it is the agency's policy not to comment on individual personnel matters."
We felt that the perspective of an articulate degree-mill victim would be relevant
to this book. We invited Callahan to tell her side of the story, which we offer
without comment. Prior to her homeland security position, she served as deputy
chief information officer for the Department of Labor, an information technology
branch chief for the Clinton White House, and numerous other information
technology positions spanning several decades during her civil service career.*

THE HUMAN TOLL OF DEGREE MILLS:
A STUDENT'S PERSPECTIVE
BY LAURA CALLAHAN

Degree mills have been around for over a century and recaptured the
headlines during the summer of 2003 when it was reported that several
high-ranking federal government officials possessed degrees from
degree mills. These government officials worked at numerous agencies,
including the Departments of Defense, Transportation, and Homeland
Security and the National Science Foundation and General Services
Administration.

Congress was swift to act and called for an investigation into all federal agencies to understand the depth and breadth of the situation. The Government Accountability Office (GAO) conducted the investigation and reported in May 2004 that almost every federal agency had employees with degrees from unaccredited colleges and universities—typically referred to as "degree mills."

It seems appropriate to look at the issue of employee motivations and behavior to answer the question why it appears that a large number of federal employees are dishonest.

One relevant issue is that, as the Council for Higher Education Accreditation puts it in its fact sheet, "Important Questions about Diploma Mills," "There appears to be no consistent definition of a diploma mill." Further, there is clearly confusion as to which educational institutions are legitimate and which are not. On May 10, 2004, Rep. Thomas M. Davis (R-VA) wrote to the director of the Office of Personnel Management, "I am most concerned that federal employees may not have access to information that would allow them to determine whether a degree represents legitimate educational achievement" (*Washington Post*, May 10, 2004). Kay Coles James, director of the Office of Personnel Management (OPM), responded by saying that the OPM is reviewing the issues Davis raised, including how to identify a diploma mill.

The media were swift to seize upon the degree-mill issue. Many newspaper, magazine, and television stories focused on the basic concept that degree mills are unaccredited schools where one can buy a degree through the mail, usually without completing any course work.

A few federal employees were singled out and relentlessly attacked by the press, and politicians alike, as being violators of trust, liars, phonies, and cheaters. One network news reporter even referred to a specific student as behaving like a terrorist. This sensationalism and condemnation of the employees was quick and easy and required little effort to manage. The results were immediate gratification for those in positions of authority and those who yielded to the power of the press.

My careful analysis of the media coverage suggests that one key element has been either overlooked or ignored: that not all students *know* they have degrees from schools that are considered "degree mills." Because of this, calling for immediate termination of *all* employees who possess degrees from unaccredited institutions is disturbing.

We have lost focus on the true criminals: the people who start and run degree mills. These criminals are scam artists who, in many cases, set up elaborate facades for the purpose of swindling people out of their money in return for degrees of little or no value.

The Internet enables these scam artists to perfect their money-making schemes by electronically weaving their bogus school information with that of legitimate educational institutions that offer distance-learning and degree-completion programs. An unsuspecting student can easily fall prey by believing the misrepresentations of illegitimate schools whose Web sites and Internet publications appear almost identical to advertisements from legitimate schools.

I have read numerous articles and Internet discussions where many students admitted they have been scammed but were afraid to raise the issue openly for fear of being fired, attacked, or publicly humiliated. The fact is that we *need* students to come forward and report questionable institutions so that authorities can move toward shutting them down and prosecuting their operators.

But this directly conflicts with the fear of demonization, and of unilateral punishment, which may well keep some innocent victims from coming forward. Stereotyping *all* holders of such degrees as people who knowingly interacted with known degree mills to commit fraud and mislead people is contrary to the very foundation of our jurisprudence system, which begins with the premise that one is innocent unless proven guilty.

In the same vein, we also need to exercise care that our charge to shut down phony institutions does not inadvertently impact legitimate schools that may be too new or too nontraditional to apply for accreditation or have chosen, for philosophical reasons, not to pursue accreditation (as with some respectable religious schools).

Senator Susan Collins of Maine wrote to Secretary of Education Ron Paige on January 15, 2004, commending the Department of Education for deciding to prepare a list of schools, both accredited and unaccredited, that are considered acceptable by US Department of Education standards. Until such a list is compiled, no single authoritative government source cites legitimate schools. Senator Collins then describes the confusing and circuitous routes citizens currently take, looping through Web pages and scanning lists to try and determine if a given school is legitimate. She suggests that both accredited and unaccredited schools may be on the list.

It will be quite a challenge for the Department of Education to develop a transparent process that explains clearly why one unaccredited school's degrees are considered acceptable and another's are not.

The demand for online distance-learning programs and the growth of the Internet has created the environment where degree mills can operate and avoid detection. The number of innocent students swindled is significant and indicative of the sophistication of degree-mill scams.

Some degree mills are simple operations where one receives a degree in exchange for money, with no further interaction required between the student and school. This simple degree-mill operation is the most commonly known and probably the easiest for informed students to recognize and avoid.

The more difficult scams to spot are degree mills with distance-learning programs that require some course work, have physical campuses and faculty, claim accreditation (or do not mention accreditation at all), and require regular interaction with students. The reasons for the interactions vary and may include discussing past academic work to determine transfer credit eligibility or award of credit for work experience.

The more sophisticated operations require students to complete courses or write papers to satisfy specific degree-completion requirements. The operational characteristics of these degree mills mimic those typically found at reputable schools, making it more difficult for students to know they are being scammed, especially if they are distance learners who are not able to physically inspect the campus.

By now the reader may be thinking it should be easy to tell a degree mill from a legitimate school, no matter how sophisticated the fake may be. Well, as a victim of a degree mill, let me share with you my experience with the hope you pass along my story to others to help people avoid falling prey to a degree mill.

First, let me provide some background information so one can understand my personal motivation behind pursuing any type of college degree. I was already employed and worked for over fifteen years in my field. None of the positions I held, including my position at homeland security, had any academic requirements. Applicants were required to demonstrate the specific knowledge, skills, and abilities to qualify for the position. After years of sweat and hard work, I reached one of the highest rungs possible on the career ladder for someone in my line of work. My salary was generous, and I truly loved my work.

My wish to obtain a degree was most definitely *not* for financial gain, to seek another job, or to ascend further with my current employer. I wanted to complete college for purely personal reasons: a task that had been left undone and required closure.

After talking with friends and colleagues and reading various articles, I found comfort knowing that I was not alone with my desire to complete college. In fact, the US Department of Education lists "personal reasons" among the factors that motivate adults to pursue college degrees.

I was raised in a typical middle-income household. While I never was left wanting for the basics, the idea of pursing a traditional college education was not an option when I graduated from high school. So I served in the military, completed my Associate in Arts degree through a regionally accredited distance-learning program, and embarked on my business career.

Over the years I accumulated many college credits by various means: traditional classrooms studies at major universities and both corporate- and military-sponsored training recognized as being equivalent to college credit by the American Council for Education. I had many credits, but I was unable to fulfill the residency or specific degree-completion requirements of a traditional school.

After working for more than fifteen years, my desire to return to the traditional classroom was of little interest. Further, I lived in a high cost-of-living area where two household incomes were necessary for subsistence, and my salary was the higher of the two. The loss of my income would have had a negative impact on my family. And so, having earned my first degree entirely through distance learning, I turned again to that approach to complete college.

In 1999, I searched for distance-learning information via the Internet and quickly entered the state of information overload. There was so much information (and disinformation) intermingled with chitchat from discussion groups. Hundreds of distance-learning programs were advertised, all claiming to help adults obtain college degrees conveniently while studying at home.

I found several warnings about degree mills, but after sifting through hundreds of articles and Web pages, I never did find an authoritative list of *known* degree mills. Information on mills varied by state, and my state was silent on the issue.

Even more confusing, some authoritative sites warned against any school offering degrees without requiring course work. But my own regionally accredited associate degree required no course work at the school, only the transfer of credits from my prior learning experiences.

Bottom line: I knew there were questionable schools out there, but how could I avoid them and find a legitimate one?

I found one checklist designed to determine if a school might be a degree mill. Four of the key points were

- there should be a physical campus, not just a post office box,
- there should be a published faculty listing to ensure the school wasn't run by just one person,
- there should be means for interaction with the faculty, and
- the school should be accredited.

Even though accreditation is optional, it was clear to me that it was desirable. And yet, as many others have written, accreditation is a complex concept, with the existence of regional, national, and professional accrediting agencies. Some are recognized only by the Department of Education, some only by the Council on Higher on Higher Education Accreditation, some by both, and some by neither.

I also learned that there are cases where unaccredited schools are considered acceptable by the federal government. For example, according to the US Office of Personnel Management's Operating Manual, Qualification Standards for General Schedule Positions, Part E.4, available via the Internet at www.opm.gov, courses taken at the unaccredited US Department of Agriculture's Graduate School would be accepted by the federal government as equivalent to courses taken at regionally accredited schools.

The recurring theme was that accredited schools and the degrees they issue appeared to be widely accepted, and one should avoid unaccredited schools since their degrees and courses may not be of any value. Since I did not intend to use my degree for my job (none was required for my position), I decided that I would find a school that had some type of accreditation, but the *type* of accreditation was not important to me nor a focus of mine. I believed that as long as the school possessed some type of third-party accreditation, I would receive a quality education.

I wanted to select an accredited distance-learning program that best fit my needs. In the course of my search, I located an education referral service that advertised that it helped students find a college or university that best fit their needs. The Academic Resource and Referral Center (ARRC) advertised its services across the Internet as well as in well-respected newspapers and magazines. ARRC offered an evaluation service to match students with prospective schools based on an examination of a student's educational background and work experience. They stated they drew from a pool of more than five hundred universities and that any university it worked with had to maintain a full-time registrar's office to ensure degrees could be confirmed.

ARRC sounded like a good place to start, especially since the registrar's office requirement would weed out phony schools operating out of post office boxes (remember the checklist).

ARRC said that the diploma awarded would not show that the degree work was done online. Some press reports have used this as a sure sign of phoniness, but it is the case that many traditional universities, such as Villanova and the University of Southern California, make comparable statements about their online programs.

After several months sifting through information available on the Internet, I was ready to submit my information to the ARRC and obtain a referral to a university. The idea of having a neutral third party refer me to a school was comforting and eased my degree-mill concerns.

I compiled my portfolio containing all the information requested for evaluation by the ARRC: prior college experience, test scores, industry certificates, military- and corporate-sponsored training, and work experience. The documentation pile for my background came to more than 250 pages, including documentation of nineteen computer science courses.

About two weeks later, the ARRC notified me that it was referring me to Hamilton University in Wyoming, nearly two thousand miles from my home.

Since I was not familiar with Hamilton University, I requested its accreditation information, student handbook, and any other distance-learning degree-completion information. This information arrived by mail about two weeks later: a complete, well-presented student package describing the university, its policies, programs, religious affiliation, accreditation, and enrollment forms. I confirmed with its accrediting agency that Hamilton University was indeed accredited and in good standing. I then applied the checklist that I had found several months earlier, and I was pleased to see that no red flags went up regarding degree mills.

Hamilton University evaluated my portfolio and advised me that my prior credits and learning experiences would be accepted and transferred into the school. Hamilton notified me I was eligible to enroll in its dual completion program, where a student could complete a bachelor's and master's simultaneously. I was told that because of my educational background, I would need to complete a required ethics course and a major thesis before receiving my degrees. The school advised me that I could take the ethics course at the campus or via distance learning. The required thesis would have to be a formal written paper addressing a topic in my field of study. A proposal would need to be approved by a faculty adviser before writing the paper.

I enrolled, paid my tuition, elected to take the ethics course via distance learning, and requested the course materials be sent to my home. I spent several weeks reading the text and completing the work assignments for the ethics course. I submitted my work package to the faculty adviser for acceptance and grading. I was subsequently notified by e-mail that I had passed the course with a grade of A.

During the time I was working on the ethics course, I wrote and submitted a thesis proposal, which was approved by my faculty adviser. After several months of research and writing, I submitted my paper that was well over twenty pages in length. The university notified me several weeks later that my thesis had been accepted and received a grade B. I was informed by my faculty adviser that I had satisfied all degree completion requirements. After I sent in the required form, I received my diplomas, my transcripts, and an order form for a school ring.

My sense of personal accomplishment was gratifying—I had finally finished college. My family was equally proud, and my mom bragged to anyone who would sit still long enough to listen how her child was one of the first in the family ever to complete college.

Several months later, I was in the process of completing some routine personnel paperwork at the office. There was a section requesting information about any schools attended. I told my human resources specialist that I completed college at Hamilton University through its distance learning program, as well as some continuing education courses at Georgetown University's Government Affairs Institute. I asked if I should include this information even though my job did not require any academic credentials, and it had not previously been provided. She advised me to record all schools attended and all degrees or certificates received. She said the Office of Personnel Management preferred to have complete education information on all federal employees.

The human resources specialist reviewed my form and sent me an e-mail message, in late June 2000, acknowledging the information was complete and accepted and that all was well. She also advised me that she was forwarding my paperwork along to OPM as required by standard practice to receive its final concurrence. Approximately six weeks later, in August 2000, my local human resources specialist advised me that my paperwork was reviewed and approved by the Office of Personnel Management.

In 2001, a year after the Department of Labor approved my bachelor's and master's, I decided to pursue the PhD from Hamilton. The process was a similar one and included writing a dissertation. Needless to say, I still believed Hamilton was legitimate. Of course, now with hindsight being 20/20, I know Hamilton is a diploma mill, and its degrees are worthless. Ironically, my Hamilton dissertation proved useful to someone. The Department of Labor used it as the framework to its E-Government Strategy, which it published two years after my work and is still using it today.

THE DEGREE MILL NIGHTMARE BEGINS

More than three years after the above-described events, I received a frantic telephone call on a Friday evening in May 2003 from my organization's public affairs office. A staff member advised me that a reporter had just published a story alleging that I lied about my academic credentials and obtained my degrees from a degree mill.

I thought this had to be a mistake, since I didn't lie about anything. Degree mills were fake, unaccredited schools that offered degrees in return for money without requiring any course work, right? My school had a campus, faculty, and full-time registrar's office; was accredited; and had a religious affiliation. And, of course, there was that third-party referral through ARRC.

Subsequently, Allen Ezell advised me that his investigation revealed the ARRC appeared to be the "front end" of an operation where all unsuspecting students were referred to the degree mill called Hamilton University. Compounding the deception was the apparent physical detachment of the ARRC from Hamilton University. ARRC's address was in Chicago, Illinois, far from Hamilton University in Wyoming.

Now I was learning that the religious organization affiliated with the university appeared to be a disguise for the purpose of claiming a religious exemption from Wyoming state oversight. The third-party accrediting body appeared to be run by the same people who operated the religious organization sponsoring the university. In other words, the accrediting body was an "accreditation mill," a term I had not heard before. So many well-meaning warnings say, "Make sure the school is accredited" but don't go the crucial next step and say, "Make sure the accrediting agency is legitimate."

Allen Ezell referred to the Hamilton University, the ARRC, and the religious entity as being "slick" and "a high-end operation" where the average citizen, who does not have access to investigative resources or possess expert knowledge in degree-mill scams, could be easily tricked into believing the school was legitimate.

Even more disturbing information was to come to the surface. Hamilton's home state of Wyoming had received more than a few complaints from unhappy students and alumni but had taken no action, not even the posting of a general warning on its state education site. Finally, following discussions with Ezell, my attorney, and me, the state looked closely at Hamilton and eventually passed a law that limits schools with religious licensing to grant only religious degrees.

To add to my dismay, I subsequently learned that the Office of Personnel Management's Adjudications and Suitability Branch, located in Boyers, Pennsylvania, which provides human resources oversight to the entire federal government, apparently maintains an internal list of "known" degree mills, including Hamilton University. To the best of my knowledge, this list has never been published. If it had, employees could easily avoid such schools.

Remember that a human resources specialist advised me to include the Hamilton information on my paperwork and that my file was reviewed several times subsequently. Is it possible none of the human resources personnel involved actually checked the OPM's internal secret degree-mill list? Did they even know such a list existed?

The simple fact is that if I had known I had been scammed and was the victim of a degree mill, of course I would not have represented the degrees as being legitimate. And I would have immediately notified law enforcement authorities.

Allen Ezell advised me that the man who established Hamilton University had earlier been in trouble with the state of Hawaii, which fined him heavily for misleading students about the legitimacy of the school and required him to cease operations. The experience gained in Hawaii enabled him to perfect his scam as he moved operations to Wyoming, with its then-negligible school-licensing laws.

What is a student who unknowingly falls prey to a degree-mill scam supposed to do? Unable to find clear information, I started my own research by asking advice from a professor at a well-known university. He advised me to write to the degree mill and have it rescind my degree. This, I felt, might have been a reasonable step but for the fact that I now knew I was dealing with a high-end scam artist who presumably had years of experience avoiding accountability and dodging the law.

My personal motivation to complete college was still there and remained unfulfilled. I was not going to let a scam artist steal my self-esteem. I may be guilty of being naive and I accept that criticism, but I am not a "fake" or "phony." From an academic perspective, I did what I thought was the most logical step—to set the degrees aside and start over.

What did my employer of several decades do? It considered me guilty right from the start, as evidenced by the fact that I was suspended, and my security clearance revoked even before my employer conducted an investigation into the matter. It was clear to me that I was not going to be treated fairly or receive any due process.

It was also clear that my employer did not review my personnel file or examine investigative records prepared by the Federal Bureau of Investigation and other authorities. Because of the relentless criticism I received in the press and from some political representatives—people who did not know the facts behind my situation—there was created an environment where it was impossible to receive a fair, objective, and unbiased review.

To this day, many reporters and politicians speak without knowing the facts and without talking to me. After nearly a year of this, faced with a no-win situation, I resigned so I could get on with my life. What comes next? How do we get to the root cause and fix the problem so other students don't have the same experience as I had? First of all, we need to focus on the criminals who own and operate the degree mills. How can phony schools establish operations under the noses of federal, state, and local law enforcement officials?

Many degree mills advertise in well-respected newspapers and magazines, such as USA Today and The Economist. Shouldn't the media research who their advertising clients are and refuse to run ads from schools that cannot demonstrate their legitimacy?

Given the federal government's own admissions of lack of clarity and guidance, how are students expected to determine the difference between degree mills and legitimate schools?

CRIME AND PUNISHMENT OR CRIME AND PROFIT?

The focus in the courts and in the media on the victims rather than on the fake schools is disturbing. While students have been publicly ridiculed, the real criminals get little or no attention and often very light punishment.

Ronald Pellar, operator of the fake Columbia State University, entered a guilty plea to a seven-count indictment. Despite having boasted to a television reporter that he had taken in $72 million selling worthless degrees, he accepted a plea bargain in which he would pay $2 million in restitution and forfeit his $1.5 million yacht, according to a press release. He was sentenced to all of eight months in prison. Think for a moment about the more than twenty thousand people who paid him for degrees, more than a few undoubtedly fooled by his slick materials and his regular ads in *The Economist, Psychology Today, Investors Business Daily*, many airline magazines, and elsewhere.

I am the first to admit that I am not a student of the law, but this example illustrates that the penalties for being convicted of running a degree mill appear too lenient and may actually create an incentive to do it again. The gross profits one can earn and keep, even after being convicted of running a degree mill, far exceeds what any hard-working citizen earns in a lifetime. The light punishment is not a deterrent, especially if you can start up operations again while you are serving out your sentence for the previous conviction.

MASKING THE PROBLEM OR FIXING IT?

Cutting out the degree-mill cancer cannot be done by one person. We need the active participation from people in positions of authority and responsibility to apply critically needed resources to eradicate this menace. We need our elected officials to review the laws and increase the severity of punishments levied upon convicted degree-mill owners and operators. The penalty for running a degree mill should be commensurate with the impact of the crime on its victims. Tip the scales against degree-mill operators. Take away their profits and increase the penalties for their criminal behavior and they think twice about starting a scam.

Encourage state law enforcement agencies to become involved in investigating and prosecuting degree-mill operators. Once a person has been convicted of running a degree mill, take the profits and give the money to the state to cover legal costs. Any remaining funds should go to the state's education fund to benefit students. The potential for financial benefit could encourage the state to be proactive and drive out degree-mill operators.

The federal government, through the Departments of Education and Justice and the Office of Personnel Management, needs to publish a list of known degree mills. The Department of Education has stated in the press it does not have authority to create a degree-mill list, yet it did so in 1960 and promised then it would be a regular event. In any event, the Office of Personnel Management's Adjudications and Suitability Branch apparently *does have* such authority and possesses such a list, but it has never made the information available, either to federal employees or to the general public.

If such a list is being used against employees after the fact, it should be disclosed to employees up front so they too can benefit from the information and avoid questionable schools.

Serious consideration should be given to allocating resources and reactivating the FBI's DipScam taskforce or an equivalent investigative unit. I find it inexcusable for authorities to blame the lack of resources or money needed to find and prosecute degree-mill operators.

Finally, we need the Federal Trade Commission to complete its 1998 task—to publish a definition of the word *accreditation* and to regulate its use.

A structured method of reporting suspected degree mills needs to be developed with a feedback mechanism so that students know the outcome. In addition, if a school has been identified as a degree mill, student records should be seized, and all students should be notified so they become aware the school was fake and can take the appropriate action, depending on whether and how they have used their degrees.

Uniform guidance in the form of action steps should be available for students to follow if they fall prey to a degree mill. Right now, students are left to fend for themselves. It is sad but true that some employers have punished employees (degree-mill students) based on press reports before an investigation had been conducted or all the facts gathered.

The media can play a vital role by transferring the main focus from the victims to the true villains, the degree-mill operators. How did the scams work? What techniques were used? How did students fall prey? What should students do to rectify specific situations? Such information could be genuinely helpful to the victims and genuinely harmful to the villains.

Perhaps most importantly of all, do not assume all students know that they have been involved with a known degree mill. Don't take the easy way out and rush to judgment. Give people the benefit of the doubt unless and until the undeniable facts prove otherwise. Students who *knowingly* engage with a *known* degree mill deserve scrutiny and need to deal with the consequences. The rest of the students need help to manage their way through the situation, and they need support as they heal and learn to trust again.

Appendix J

Ezell, Bear, and US Investigations Services

In 2004, Allen Ezell and John Bear became consultants and advisers to a company called US Investigations Services (USIS), for matters related to unrecognized schools and degrees and fake credentials. With more than seven thousand full-time employees, USIS is one of the nation's largest providers of security investigations and employee-screening services to the federal government and private industry, including advice, counsel, and investigations regarding the use of fake degrees and credentials. Ezell and Bear's involvements may include consulting with USIS researchers, providing new information from the world of degree mills, and putting on workshops and seminars for USIS clients and, on behalf of USIS, for the general public and others. USIS can be found on the Internet at www.usis.com.

Select Bibliography

BOOKS

Association of Commonwealth Universities. *Commonwealth Universities Year-book 2003*, 78th ed. New York: Palgrave Macmillan, 2003. Detailed write-ups on all the recognized universities of Great Britain in one volume and those in the rest of the Commonwealth in another volume.

Bear, Mariah, and John Bear. *Bears' Guide to Earning Degrees by Distance Learning*, 16th ed. Berkeley, CA: Ten Speed Press, 2005. While most of the book focuses on legitimate ways to earn degrees online and by distance learning, there is a long chapter on degree mills, identifying several hundred of the worst, as well as a chapter on schools that apparently operate legally but do not have recognized accreditation.

Berg, Ivan. *Education and Jobs: The Great Training Robbery*. New York: Percheron Press, 2003. Reprint, New York, HarperCollins, 1971. Addresses the issue of whether degree requirements make sense in hiring practices.

Burke, Jeanne M., ed. *Higher Education Directory*. Falls Church, VA: Higher Education Publications, 2004. Until 1983, the US Department of Education published an annual directory of detailed information on every school with recognized accreditation and on the recognized accreditors. When the department stopped, Higher Education Publications (www.hepinc.com) was formed to carry on the work, producing this valuable reference work, which appears annually. Originally it listed California-approved schools but stopped that practice in 1988.

International Association of Universities. *International Handbook of Universities*, 17th ed. New York: Palgrave Macmillan, 2003. More than seven thousand schools described in detail in nearly three thousand pages (which costs more than $300).

Levicoff, Steve. *Name It and Frame It: New Opportunities in Adult Education and How to Avoid Being Ripped off by "Christian" Degree Mills*, 4th ed. Ambler, PA: Institute on Religion and Law, 1995. While the focus is on religious schools, there is much valuable advice on the world of degree mills in general. Out of print.

Reid, Robert H. *American Degree Mills: A Study of Their Operations and of Existing and Potential Ways to Control Them.* Washington, DC: American Council on Education, 1959.

Stewart, David W., and Henry A. Spille. *Diploma Mills: Degrees of Fraud.* New York: American Council on Education/Macmillan, 1988. Originally announced in 1982 as a "hard-hitting" book on the problem, when it finally emerged six years later, the lawyers had marched in, and it turned out a rather soft-hitting look at the problem and a then-useful but now-obsolete look at the relevant laws in each state.

Walston, Rick. *Walston's Guide to Christian Distance Learning.* Longview, WA: Persuasion Press, 1999. The Rev. Dr. Walston covers mostly the legitimate schools, but he pulls no punches in his descriptions of many "Bible" schools with misleading accreditation claims, often following his description with a thundering, "Shame!"

DISSERTATIONS AND A THESIS

Calote, Robin Joyce. "Diploma Mills: What's the Attraction?" Ed.D. diss., University of LaVerne, 2002. Calote looked at the variables in how degree mills present themselves that seemed to be of particular interest to potential customers.

Douglas, Richard. "The Accreditation of Degree-Granting Institutions and Its Role in the Utility of College Degrees in the Workplace." PhD diss., Union Institute and University, 2003. Douglas's research focused on large corporation human resources executives and how they make their decisions on which schools to accept or recognize or pay for. His findings suggest that the majority of HR people do not know nearly as much about accreditation and about bad and fake schools as one might wish.

Reid, Robert H. "Degree Mills in the United States." PhD diss., Columbia University, 1963.

Brown, George. "Are Virtual Universities in Australia a Guise for Degree/Diploma Mills to Thrive?" MEdMgt thesis, Flinders University of South Australia, 2001.

THREE CONGRESSIONAL REPORTS

US Congress, House. A Joint Report by the Chairmen of the Subcommittee on Health and Long-Term Care and the Subcommittee on Housing and Consumer Interests of the Select Committee on Aging. Fraudulent Credentials, 99th Congress, December 11, 1985, Comm. pub. no. 99. Washington, DC: US Government Printing Office, 1986. This is one of the two reports that came from Rep. Claude Pepper's subcommittee and focuses more on health fraud.

US Congress, House. A Joint Report by the Chairmen of the Subcommittee on Health and Long-Term Care and the Subcommittee on Housing and Consumer Interests of the Select Committee on Aging. Fraudulent Credentials, 99th Congress, December 11, 1985, Comm. pub. no. 99-551. Washington, DC: US Government Printing Office, 1986. This is the second report that came from Rep. Claude Pepper's subcommittee and focuses more on federal employees.

US Senate. Hearings before a Subcommittee of the Committee on Education and Labor, United States Senate, Diploma Mills. 68th Congress. January and March 1924. Washington, DC: Government Printing Office, 1924. This was the only time the US Senate looked at the degree-mill problem. The focus was on fake medical degrees.

AACRAO

The American Association of Collegiate Registrars and Admissions Officers (www.aacrao.org) produces many valuable publications on the educational systems of various countries; it also offers two useful publications to help spot fake schools and credentials.

"Fraudulent Academic Credentials: Bogus US Institutions; How to Avoid Fake Schools and Fake Degrees." A somewhat dated (1988) brochure from the National Liaison Committee on Foreign Student Admissions, priced for distribution in larger quantities at thirty cents each.

Misrepresentation in the Marketplace and Beyond: Ethics under Siege, ed. Peggy Askins. A sixty-four-page booklet on how to spot false schools and transcripts.

WEB SITES

www.degreemills.com. This site has been set up by the authors of this book, Allen Ezell and John Bear, to update the information contained in the book, to report on relevant news and developments from the world of higher education, and to offer an opportunity for questions, responses, and the exchange of ideas.

www.degreeinfo.com. This forum is the main Internet location for discussions of bad and fake schools (as well as good and real ones). It has a good search engine linked to the more than a hundred thousand postings covering hundreds of schools—good, bad, and fake. Quite a few experts and competent researchers report their opinions and findings there. The forum is lightly moderated, so the proponents of unrecognized schools—either individual ones or of the concept in general—have their say as long as they are not aggressive or dishonest in what they write.

www.degree.net. The publisher of *Bears' Guide*, Ten Speed Press, maintains this site to provide information on the world of degrees, to offer book excerpts and articles, and, of course, to try to sell books.

Subject Index

The 201 unrecognized accrediting agencies identified alphabetically in appendix G are not listed separately in this index.

Schools Index

Name Index